Reconciling Empirical Knowledge and Clinical Experience

Reconciling Empirical Knowledge and Clinical Experience

The Art and Science of Psychotherapy

Edited by
Stephen Soldz and Leigh McCullough

American Psychological Association
Washington, DC

Published by
American Psychological Association
750 First Street, NE
Washington, DC 20002

Copies may be ordered from
APA Order Department
P.O. Box 92984
Washington, DC 20090-2984

In the U.K., Europe, Africa, and the Middle East, copies may be ordered from
American Psychological Association
3 Henrietta Street
Covent Garden, London
WC2E 8LU England

Typeset in Goudy by EPS Group Inc., Easton, MD

Printer: Data Reproductions Corporation, Auburn Hills, MI
Cover Designer: Design Concepts, San Diego, CA
Technical/Production Editors: Allison L. Risko and Anne T. Woodworth

Library of Congress Cataloging-in-Publication Data
Reconciling empirical knowledge and clinical experience: the art and science of
   psychotherapy / edited by Stephen Soldz, Leigh McCullough.—1st ed.
      p.   cm.
   Includes bibliographical references and index.
   ISBN 1-55798-603-7
   1. Psychotherapy.   2. Evidence-based medicine.   I. Soldz, Stephen.
   II. McCullough, Leigh.
   [DNLM: 1. Psychotherapy.   2. Evidence–Based Medicine.   3. Research.
   WM 420 R311 1999]
   RC480.R395   1999
   616.89′14—dc21   99-168110
   DNLM/DLC   CIP
   for Library of Congress

British Library Cataloguing-in-Publication Data
A CIP record is available from the British Library.

Printed in the United States of America
First Edition

CONTENTS

CONTRIBUTORS

Michael E. Addis, PhD, Department of Psychology, Clark University, Worcester, MA

Timothy Anderson, PhD, Department of Psychology, Ohio University, Athens

Lorna Smith Benjamin, PhD, Department of Psychology, University of Utah, Salt Lake City

Reiner W. Dahlbender, MD, Department of Psychotherapy and Psychosomatic Medicine, Universtität Ulm, Ulm, Germany

Robert Elliott, PhD, Department of Psychology, University of Toledo, Toledo, OH

Marvin R. Goldfried, PhD, Department of Psychology, State University of New York, Stoney Brook

Horst Kaechele, PhD, Department of Psychotherapy and Psychosomatic Medicine, Universtität Ulm, Ulm, Germany

Leigh McCullough, PhD, Professor and Director of the Psychotherapy Research Program, Harvard University, Cambridge, MA

Robert A. Neimeyer, PhD, Department of Psychology, University of Memphis, Memphis, TN

James O. Prochaska, PhD, the Cancer Prevention Center, University of Rhode Island, Kingston

Julia Shiang, EdD, PhD, Pacific Graduate School of Psychology and Stanford University School of Medicine, Palo Alto, CA

Stephen Soldz, PhD, Medical School, Harvard University, Director of Research, Health and Addictions Research Inc., Codirector of Research, Boston Institute for Psychotherapy, Boston, MA

David A. Winter, PhD, Head of Clinical Psychology Services and Coordinator of Research, Barnet Healthcare National Health Service Trust, and Visiting Professor, Division of Psychology, University of Hertfordshire, England, and Department of Clinical Psychology, Edgware Community Hospital, Edgware, Middlesex, England

Reconciling Empirical Knowledge and Clinical Experience

INTRODUCTION

STEPHEN SOLDZ AND LEIGH McCULLOUGH

Imagine sitting across from a man in unremitting despair who insists that he is going to go home, rummage in his attic for his gun, and blow his brains out. He is not kidding. You feel panicked and do a number of things that night and during the coming weeks, hoping to prevent his death. After much concern and some loss of sleep on your part, some months later this man is stable again, and the life-threatening danger has passed. You feel tremendous relief, as well as a deep sense of gratification that you were able to help pull him through. You have some vague hunches about how you did it, but it would be difficult to pinpoint exactly what made the difference. You do know—without a doubt— however, that you saved his life.

Now imagine sitting at a computer analyzing treatment data that have taken years to collect. The data are on the effects of a certain therapeutic intervention that you spent months rigorously defining so that research assistants could reliably pick out its occurrence in transcripts of therapy sessions. Month after month you calmly and steadfastly oversaw the data collection process. Now, with the analysis completed, the numbers come up—only to reveal that the hypothesis you were testing is not supported. The results are virtually the opposite of what you had anticipated. In fact, the data force you to throw out cherished beliefs and to revise your thinking dramatically. You feel vaguely disoriented, and it takes some time to build a new cognitive set as well as to begin generating some new hypotheses. The long tedious effort that you have so carefully constructed still may be a contribution to science—but not the contribution you anticipated.

There are many variations on the above themes with various happy and unhappy endings. Sometimes, tragically, our patients don't pull through, and sometimes our hypotheses are indeed supported. The point, however, is that these two types of pursuits are exceedingly different ones.

Pure clinical knowledge is highly intuitive. Therapists are creative artists, and mavericks as well. They do not want to be confined or restricted in treating their patients. They have very strong convictions about how to go about their healing process. They must act spontaneously and courageously, believing deeply in their felt experience, and trusting that the interventions they use are going to work. Therapists are interacting under rapidly fluctuating circumstances—frequently dealing with life and death issues—and need to be able to resonate to the pain and suffering of the client. Pure clinical knowledge is often metaphorical in nature. It is a process of search and discovery through relationship and feeling. Furthermore, pure clinical knowledge is private and confidential. Therapists are bound by the ethics of their profession not to reveal personal information without express permission of the client. Thus clinical knowledge is often maintained in the realm of ineffable experience often unavailable to others.

Pure research knowledge, however, requires suspension of emotional involvement in the outcome of the hypotheses and the willingness to be led by the results generated by the data. Whereas life and death issues can be pressing for the clinician, they are neither immediate nor salient for the researcher. Clinicians are on the front lines of the mental health field; researchers are behind the scenes. The research process is lengthy and tedious. One must delay gratification. Ideas must be grounded in the precision of operational definitions. Hypotheses must be tested, refined, and retested. Finally, research knowledge must be generalizable and submitted to public scrutiny.

These very disparate modes of responding are both pursuits embraced by the field of mental health. Should we attempt to reconcile them? And if we want to, how on earth should we go about it? These are the questions this book addresses through the personal accounts of psychotherapy researchers–clinicians who struggle with the practice–research relationship on a daily basis.

To provide a background for the contributions of our authors, we briefly describe contemporary societal pressures that have moved the question of the practice–research relationship to the forefront. These include the crisis in the scientist–practitioner model in academic training and pressures on those who provide health services, including psychotherapy, not only to be accountable for the outcomes they achieve but also to use empirically evaluated treatment approaches.

CRISIS OF THE SCIENTIST–PRACTITIONER MODEL

For much of its history, clinical psychology embraced a scientist–practitioner model, also known as the *Boulder model*, in which all clinical students ideally received excellent clinical training along with rigorous research training. The idea was that dual training in these divergent areas would facilitate the development of a critical spirit among students that would contribute to the development of a research-based practice. Many programs in counseling psychology, social work, and related fields have recently developed similar ideologies.

However, the scientist–practitioner model has been quite difficult to implement both in academia and in actual practice. Many academicians treat clinical work with enormous disdain and regard it as a distraction from the research training that constitutes their raison d'être. Nevertheless, every mental health trainee must complete a clinical internship or practicum, and the vast majority of graduate students become practitioners—with little continued involvement in research. Thus, the field of mental health is beset with a contradiction: The scientist–practitioner model is often honored far more in words than in practice. Graduate programs tend to favor either practice or research, with few according equal value to both types of training. Fewer still offer any suggestions about how to integrate the two.

There is thus concern in graduate psychology training as to whether the scientist–practitioner model remains viable. In recent years, with the development of schools of professional psychology, many graduate training programs have abandoned this model. Many students in these schools receive only minimal research training and are not required to conduct a rigorous research study for their dissertation.

Is it reasonable, or even possible, for students to develop expertise in both research and clinical practice? Can the same person wear two hats? Can we be professionally bilingual—or even dual minded—leading with our right brain in providing treatment and analyzing data with our left? And what is the quality of those pursuits if we do? Even if some students do develop such dual expertise, will it influence their postgraduate professional careers?

DRIVE TOWARD ACCOUNTABILITY

Public policy currently is leaning toward mandating what the scientist–practitioner model struggled with implementing: integration of, or at least collaboration between, clinical practice and research. However, because this integration has been rushed and forced, the product falls far short of the standards set out by the Boulder model.

Nonetheless, requirements for data to guide the delivery of services—imposed by the federal and state governments, managed care organizations, and other funding sources—are almost forcing the coexistence (such as it is) of research and practice. Increasingly, funding agencies are considering refusing payment for treatments not proven safe and effective. At a minimum, those providing clinical services are expected to provide data on the outcomes they achieve. Such requirements are influencing the movement toward evaluation and toward the increasing emphasis on "outcomes measurement" (Lambert, Shapiro, & Bergin, 1986; Sperry, Brill, Howard, & Grissom, 1996). Such pressures force practitioners (clinicians and program administrators) to work with researchers and thus to learn how to bridge the researcher–practitioner gap. Presumably, as such pressures increase, so will the extent of collaboration between researchers and practitioners. If such collaboration is going to be required by policymakers, we should strive to have it done well. One should note, of course, that unlike the scientist–practitioner model, this collaboration is not likely to occur within single individuals engaged in both practice and research; it is more likely to involve collaborations between those who are primarily researchers and those who are primarily clinicians. We believe that the experiences of the scientist–practitioners included in this book have much to inform the latter type of collaboration as well as that within single individuals.

EMPIRICALLY SUPPORTED TREATMENTS

A particular form of accountability-invoked integration, for better or worse, is a move by many payers—managed care companies and government agencies—increasingly toward the recommendation (if not mandate) that one must use empirically supported treatments (ESTs) for an evidence-based practice (these approaches were previously referred to as empirically validated treatments; see Chambless, 1996; Elliot, 1998; Task Force, 1991). In psychology in particular, over the past few years there has been increased emphasis on the development of compendia of ESTs that, to the delight of some and the horror of others, could ultimately become practice guidelines delineating what are the boundaries of reimbursable, or even, not actionable (as in malpractice or ethics complaints) professional behavior.

The development of ESTs and the treatment manuals that accompany them hold out the potential of being useful ways of conveying research-based treatment models to a wide clinical audience. Through the dissemination of treatment models that have been shown to work in randomized clinical trials, these manuals and protocols, if successfully implemented, could guarantee that patients are receiving treatments known to be effective. Empirically supported treatments are thus an analog of "best practice" models that increasingly are springing up throughout health care and other social services. However, there are a number of problems and issues that need to be addressed before the potential of ESTs can be appropriately evaluated.

DIFFICULTIES INTEGRATING RESEARCH AND PRACTICE

Our impression upon reading much of the discussion between researchers and practitioners is that they often fail to communicate to each other. They seem, frequently, not to have an inkling of what members of the other camp are talking about.

Researchers, for example, seldom trust the results of a single study. Research publications aim at the gradual accumulation of trustworthy knowledge through the winnowing of useful from less useful conceptualizations. Each study in a field as difficult as psychotherapy research is at best one brick in a much larger edifice. If hundreds of studies involving hundreds of thousands of patients have so far failed to clarify the relationship between dietary cholesterol and heart disease, why should one expect the process of psychotherapy research to be smoother? One implication of this reasoning is that reading research journals, although laudable, is never likely to be a major way in which clinicians become aware of important research findings applicable to clinical work.

In thinking about these issues, we were inspired by our reading of many previous discussions of the relation of practice to research. Some researchers wanted practice to be based directly on research (e.g., Beutler & Davison, 1995; Beutler, Kim, Davison, Karno, & Fisher, 1996; Chambless, 1996; Task Force on Promotion and Dissemination of Psychological Procedures, 1995). However, practitioners often responded that practice was a different endeavor than research and that practitioners had little or nothing to learn from research (Fensterheim & Raw, 1996; Talley, Strupp, & Butler, 1994). We, as people who considered ourselves both practitioners and researchers, found ourselves sympathetic to, yet dissatisfied with, both positions.

Psychotherapy practice, involving as it does a complex interpersonal relationship, cannot be reduced to the application of research findings any more than the construction of a house involves simply knowledge of the materials to be used to construct the house. However, practitioners and their clients cannot afford to ignore the growth of knowledge in psychology in general and psychotherapy research in particular. After all, medicine has taught us that much of clinical wisdom is, in fact, incorrect. One need only think of the enormous number of tonsillectomies that used to be conducted in the not-too-distant past to recognize this fact. Systematic research is, we believe, the best process for winnowing truth from plausible, but ultimately false, belief. This book was undertaken to further the understanding of resistance to fruitful collaboration between researchers and practitioners and to propose paradigms for successful collaboration.

As we reflected on the difficulties in forming a solid relationship between research and practice, we concluded that researchers and therapists seemed to have little appreciation for the concerns, languages, media of communication, and traditions of the other group. Researchers endeavor to speak to other researchers in a precise manner—in peer-reviewed journals—about findings and generalizations derived from careful (usually quantitative) study of groups of patients. Therapists often speak in a more metaphorical manner—in case conferences, training seminars, clinical journals, and conferences—about the generalizations derived from the experience of working with individual patients. Although both groups attempt to form generalizations, what counts as an acceptable generalization is radically different for the two groups.

SELECTION OF AUTHORS

As we thought about the reasons for this lack of productive communication between researchers and practitioners, we decided to explore the experiences of people who could not avoid genuine dialogue between research and practice—namely, those who live in both worlds.

Although it often seems that researchers and practitioners are speaking different languages, we have both spent considerable energy during our respective professional careers scaling the walls separating therapy from research. We considered where we might find like-minded souls and realized that a natural place to look was among those professionals who, like ourselves, kept one foot in both camps, namely psychotherapy researchers who also practiced therapy.

Thus, the idea for this book was born: Gather a group of psychotherapy researchers who also practice psychotherapy to write about how they personally deal with the tension between research and practice in their own lives. We decided to recruit personal accounts from these researcher–practitioners regarding the issues they confront as they attempt to engage in both research and clinical work. We reasoned that these individuals were those in whom the research and practice ways of knowing were most likely to successfully commingle. Surely, if anyone was capable of speaking the languages of both groups, these researcher–practitioners would.

When we began to compile a list of names, however, we had a difficult time finding people who did both functions on a daily basis. When we began recruiting authors, we found that many were excited by the idea, although others were distinctly nervous. The nervous ones tended to be those (often psychodynamic) practitioners who did not perceive a strong relationship between their research and their practice and who were reluctant to admit that fact in public. Some of the reluctant individuals eventually agreed to participate, but others steadfastly declined.

The resultant book is thus somewhat biased toward those participants who perceived a strong research–practice relationship in their work. Virtually on a daily basis, the authors of this book are participant–observers in numerous human dramas, and also calm and patient collectors and analyzers of data. If these scientist–practitioners found the interaction between research and practice to be productive in their own work, perhaps they could also form paradigms for successful interaction between the two groups despite the fact that they are not necessarily embodied in the same individual.

The researcher–practitioners who finally agreed to participate represent a wide range of theoretical and clinical orientations as well as levels of experience in the field. Our contributors include some of the eminent names in psychotherapy research, including several past presidents of the Society for Psychotherapy Research. We also purposefully included several relatively junior colleagues who are nearer the beginning of their careers and can cast light on the researcher–practitioner relationship from the perspective of those who are beginning to chart a path through this minefield. The authors were given broad latitude, and we encouraged them to be as self-revealing as they were willing. A light tone and sense of humor were encouraged, as was respect for those who thought differently.

Implicit in our conceptualization of the relationship of research to practice is that both endeavors will be enriched by a comfortable working relationship. If a successful relationship between the two is to be forged, it is important, as many of the authors in this book indicate, to be aware of the vastly differing natures of therapeutic and research endeavors.

However, some previous authors, especially practitioners, used these differences to argue that research and practice are by their natures such different activities that practice is never likely to be significantly affected by research, at least in terms of traditional psychotherapy research (e.g., as opposed to research on development or psychopathology).

Despite our active recruitment efforts, no one who took the aforementioned position agreed to write a chapter (a process of self-selection, we fear). Therefore, we note points made by Fensterheim and Raw (1996), two of the strongest opponents of integration, whose concerns echo those of many others. These include (a) that research and clinical practice are independent fields, each with its own problems and its own styles of thinking; (b) that there are great differences between actual clinical patients and highly selected research participants; and (c) that there is a great difference between clinical flexibility in real-world treatment versus the rigidity of research manuals.

Although many of the authors we recruited agree with some of these points, none feel that they negate the value of psychotherapy research for improving practice. Thus, this book constitutes, among other things, a respectful yet forceful reply to the strong skepticism expressed by Fensterheim and Raw (1996), among others. The contributors demonstrate through example the multiplicity of ways in which psychotherapy practice can benefit from research endeavors. At the same time, these chapters exhibit a profound respect for psychotherapy practitioners and the clinical wisdom they have developed through laborious, often heroic, effort. They eschew any attempt to reduce practice to a mechanical application of research findings, as is sometimes feared by those for whom conducting therapy is both a living and a calling.

We also failed to recruit any of the foremost proponents of basing psychotherapy practice directly on research, that is, those who view therapy as applied psychological science. Thus, although this was unintentional, most of our authors occupy the middle ground. Perhaps this is fitting, however, as this book is also about the transformation process that can happen when combining two very different entities—the metamorphosis that inevitably transpires when an integration of very different perspectives is attempted. *Bringing two things together into dynamic tension unavoidably changes both. Both are forever altered, just as a marriage of equals changes both.* This book also explores how the process of relating research to practice transforms the people involved. We believe that an understanding of the transformation processes in individual researcher–practitioners illuminates the changes that are rapidly occurring in the relations between research and practice in the field of psychotherapy as a whole.

OVERVIEW OF CHAPTERS

This volume opens with Goldfried's "Reflections of a Scientist–Practitioner," which provides a broad and philosophical overview of the value of integrating research and practice. Goldfried's contribution provides an excellent introduction and overview of the main issues and purposes of this volume, intermingled with touching and humorous accounts of how he struggled with the process. Goldfried points out that clinical work is a process of discovery—in which insights occur during sessions and hunches are followed to develop research hypotheses. His strategy is to have research closely tied to clinical observation, such as listening to tapes or reading transcripts; he reminds us in the following: "Only after having some reason to believe that we are likely to find what we're looking for do we then go through the elaborate and often painstaking process of objectively coding and analyzing what is occurring during the session" (p. 24). Goldfried thus concludes that research that grows out of close examination of the clinical process is more likely to have clinical relevance.

Chapter 2, written by Robert Elliott, describes the process of Elliott's reinvention of himself as a therapist based on his findings from research as well as from clinical discoveries. He relates his struggle to "wean himself away" from his psychodynamic orientation to grow into a richer and fuller understanding of the experiential therapy process. By using a version of Kagan's interpersonal process recall to intensively study client processes, he discovered that therapists often do not know how clients perceive treatment. This led him to be more cautious, more inquiring, and ultimately to change his practice. Other discoveries about what clients were experiencing led him to study significant change events. His research endeavors were sufficiently fruitful, and he was able to develop a book-length treatment manual so that he might "finally do something" for the clinician (p. 43).

In chapter 3, Michael Addis gives thoughtful and excellent suggestions for how to incorporate the Boulder scientist–practitioner model into a graduate training program, as well as how to help students select which path to pursue. He gives a candid account of his own struggle to integrate research into practice in his graduate training and raises our consciousness about the terrible bind imposed on students by demands that they do both without providing proper models or procedures.

In chapter 4, David Winter speaks of the harmonious marriage that is possible between research and practice. He provides a 25-year longitudinal view of his "real-world" provision and simultaneous evaluation of services in the National Health Service in England. Because of his personal experience, his chapter paints a picture of the potential for research and practice living happily ever after. It is not like the reality in some of the other chapters, but it does make us feel optimistic about the possibility of conducting worthwhile research in naturalistic settings.

In chapter 5, Timothy Anderson gives an account of how research humbled his clinical bravado. However, he argues just as strongly that clinicians have been underused by researchers, and he laments how often it seems that the concept of "clinical wisdom" (p. 85) boils the blood of many scientists. Anderson offers a number of thoughtful suggestions for how to incorporate clinical understanding into the research process and how to encourage collaboration between researchers and practitioners.

Leigh McCullough gives a historical account of how her research and clinical work have cross-pollinated, as well as polished and refined each other over the years. In chapter 6, she makes a strong argument for the use of videotapes of therapy sessions as an excellent medium through which the two fields can communicate. She also describes many examples in which her strongly felt convictions about specific clinical change processes were revised and refined again by the research process.

Robert Neimeyer gives us a humorous and impressively articulate account in chapter 7 of the "essential tensions" inherent in combining research and practice. His chapter is an externalization of the internal dialogue between his research and clinical "selves" and describes his dilemmas in maneuvering between "the slippery subtlety required to conduct therapy and the necessary formalization required to investigate it" (p. 123). Neimeyer comes to no firm synthesis, but he will stir the imagination and make the reader chuckle at his creative ways of conceptualizing the "dialectical tension" represented by these two disciplines.

The reader also encounters something quite unique in chapter 8, a pleasantly refreshing alternative to academic discourse in the form of a play. Horst Kachele and Rheiner Dahlbender present an "external dialogue" between two intriguing imaginary characters—Kalle, a German-born American researcher, and Ziffel, a German psychoanalyst. Kalle and Ziffel debate the scientist–practitioner dilemma on scientific, humanistic, and philosophical grounds in ways that are at once stimulating and entertaining.

In chapter 9, Julia Shiang has written about cultural issues and how she wove together many strands of therapeutic interventions within a cultural framework. She tells us how her Asian American background provided her with experiences that later led to her research and the development of treatment approaches. Integrating her research and practice evolved from a heightened consciousness of both perspectives. In other words, she felt she had not been simply "carried downstream" by these two forces but guided by signposts, including cultural concerns, and specific intervention systems. She, like many contributors, remains skeptical about applying research findings "wholesale to the struggles of the individual people" (p. 170).

Lorna Benjamin acknowledges in chapter 10 the difficulty of spanning the gap between the rigidity of research versus the intuitive flexibility of practice. She offers a sage perspective by confessing her gratitude that other professions such as medicine and dentistry persevered with the scientific method. She then goes on to describe her attempt to do the same by developing a "generic theory" that encompasses research and practice. She concludes that it is possible to use scientific principles to greatly improve the sharpness of clinician focus and interventions, and she then describes how it might be done.

In chapter 11, Stephen Soldz provides a model for how research can have a broad impact on service through collaborative research and program evaluation. Soldz strongly advocates a collaborative process between researchers and clinicians, but he feels that treatment is far too complex an undertaking to be based on research alone. Soldz's chapter provides us with several recommendations based on real world experience for facilitating researchers and practitioners working together.

In chapter 12, an appropriate grand finale is supplied by Prochaska's passionate account of his evolution from uncertainty and doubt to thriving, proactive research-based systems that affect tens to hundreds of thousands of clients in the health service world. Prochaska describes his personal journey of discovering stages of change by giving us vivid examples of sex therapy patients who simply did not respond by the book. Readers will be inspired by the way he describes his initial insecurities, his questions, and how these evolved into a story of success and contribution on a grand scale. Prochaska's stages of change model, now widely adopted in a number of clinical domains including the addictions, has profoundly influenced many practitioners who have no personal relationship with its author. This work is being used to develop new interventions in areas somewhat removed from traditional psychotherapy, such as smoking cessation, and is having an impact on the development of major behavioral health treatment approaches.

The concluding chapter reflects the transformation that occurred in us as we edited this volume. This undertaking, and the engagement with the work of our contributors, led to extensive dialogue between us on the challenges facing psychotherapy and the contemporary state of research–practice relations. In keeping with the personal style of the book, we take the liberty of going beyond the individual contributions to make a few recommendations arising out of this dialogue for enhancing the research–practice relationship, both among individuals striving toward an integration of research and practice and, at a social level, through personal and social changes in the ways that researchers and practitioners approach each other. We close with a plea that therapists and researchers recognize and respect the passion that lies at the root of both endeavors and that forms a foundation on which strong bridges can be built.

As we edited this volume, we were extremely pleased that the contributors took up the challenge and provided a range of enlightening, humorous, and often very moving descriptions of their individual struggles as therapists and researchers. We hope these personal accounts will delight and inspire the reader as much as they have us. We further believe that these accounts provide a number of excellent models that may inspire readers, whether researchers or therapists, to try harder to bridge the research–practice gap.

I

CHALLENGES OF PRACTICE
AND RESEARCH

1

REFLECTIONS OF A SCIENTIST–PRACTITIONER

MARVIN R. GOLDFRIED

In thinking about what I wanted to include in this chapter about the relationship between my clinical and research activities, I immediately recalled an experience I had as a graduate student back in the late 1950s. Paul Meehl had visited our program, and I was fortunate enough to be among a small group of students who went out to dinner with him. This indeed was a rare treat, especially as I had read virtually everything Meehl had written and had enormous respect for his insights on research, practice, and the philosophy of science. At one point during the evening, someone asked him the question about the extent to which his clinical work was informed by research. Without any hesitation, he replied, "Not at all."

As someone who was struggling to adopt the identity of scientist–practitioner, I left this memorable dinner disheartened. I don't think I ever fully recovered. The challenge of how we can close the gap between research and practice has stayed with me for all these years, and because I am attracted to challenges—my experiential colleagues would probably say it's more "unfinished business"—I have continued to be intrigued with the integration of practice and research.

CLINICAL–RESEARCH HISTORY

During my graduate years at the State University of New York at Buffalo (known then as the University of Buffalo), projective techniques were all the rage. Indeed, I took three courses on the Rorschach alone. However, there was a great deal of emphasis on learning and experimental psychology. On the one hand, I read books filled with speculation on the meaning of different Rorschach responses (often stated as fact), and on the other, I was schooled in research findings and methodology. Having difficulty living with this dissonance, I began my career conducting research on projective techniques and even ended up writing a book on the research bases for the validity of the Rorschach (Goldfried, Stricker, & Weiner, 1971).

When I joined the department of psychology at the State University of New York at Stony Brook in the 1960s and participated in establishing a graduate training program in clinical psychology that was rooted in learning and experimental psychology, I fully expected that the gap between practice and research would be more readily closed. Moreover, we designed our program so that clinical supervision would be carried by the very same faculty that was involved in research activities. Although it certainly was easier to establish an interface between practice and research—especially because they now both made use of the same language system—discrepancies nonetheless continued to exist. For example, research on behavior therapy in the 1960s and early 1970s tended to eschew cognitive metaphors; at the time, we thought that Skinner and Hull had won out against Tolman. Not being familiar with the literature, our clients didn't know that. They kept interfering with our behavioral interventions by having all sorts of thoughts, expectations, and distorted attitudes. For a while, some behavior therapists resisted this interference, at times maintaining a tenuous defense: "Thoughts have nothing to do with changing or understanding human behavior. I firmly believe that!" Ultimately, however, a therapeutic orientation that was based on the extrapolation of research findings to clinical practice became more cognitive, having been shaped and seasoned by practical attempts at intervention.

Throughout most of my professional career, I have lived in both the world of the researcher and that of the clinician. Much of my teaching, research, and writing has placed me at the academic end of the spectrum. However, my continued involvement in clinical training and supervision, and the limited practice I have maintained in New York City, have kept me in close touch with clinical reality. There have been times when research helped me clinically and times when it limited me. Some years ago, I was treating a woman with a severe bird phobia, whose functioning was seriously impaired by her avoidance of anything remotely associated with birds. Using relaxation and desensitization, she made impressive headway over a period of several months. Toward the end of our work together, we scheduled a session to be held at the Children's Zoo in Central Park. I had visited the zoo some weeks earlier and had concluded she was ready to deal with the duck pond and the newly arrived baby chicks on display. Our in vivo session began without incident, and she was able to approach and even admire the ducks swimming in the pond. As we approached the baby chicks, however, it became feeding time at the zoo—a surprise to me, but not to what seemed like half the pigeon population of New York City. They came noisily flocking overhead, bringing to mind images of Hitchcock's *The Birds*. Fortunately, I was able to cope with my own anxiety by deep breathing and relaxation. However, my client was having more difficulty; in fact, she was starting to panic.

I was clearly at a clinical choice point, and I scanned my memory of what the research literature had to say about this dilemma. What I thought of was the conditioned avoidance paradigm, whereby rats in a shuttlebox learned to jump over a hurdle at a signal that preceded a shock to their feet. Even when the shock was eliminated, and it was safe to remain where they were during the signal, they continued to jump. Exposure to the new state of affairs—that the real danger of shock no longer existed—was what eventually eliminated this unproductive avoidance behavior. So, if we were to leave the zoo, this escape behavior could create a setback, perhaps undoing months of progress. Following the literature, and blending in good clinical sense, I walked my client out of the flight path and under a tree that she could lean against. Her ability to use relaxation to cope with her anxiety needed a little prompting and verbal encouragement, but eventually was successful. Drawing on the modeling research literature, I also disclosed my own initial discomfort in dealing with the unforeseen event. After about 10 minutes of relaxation, she was able to return to where we had been. The pigeons had gone on to their other pursuits, and the session was completed with a successful experience.

There also have been situations in which the research literature has not served me well in my clinical work. One instance that stands out as an example occurred during a time I was demonstrating cognitive–behavior therapy for graduate students behind a one-way mirror. The client was a woman with assertiveness problems, and I believed this would provide me with the opportunity to demonstrate what were fairly straightforward cognitive–behavioral interventions. During the course of working with this client, I encountered choice points during which my clinical experience put me in direct conflict with the research literature. For example, there were times I thought to myself, "She really needs to get in touch with her feelings" and "she is being unassertive in her relationship with me, and it would be good to focus on our in-session interaction." I continued to ignore these clinical musings; after all, I was supposed to be demonstrating cognitive–behavior therapy, and these clinical directions were not consistent with the cognitive–behavioral research literature. What this experience brought home to me was that I no longer was able to do cognitive–behavior therapy "by the book," a realization I reported on one day to the observers during our postsession discussion. They encouraged me to proceed clinically in a way that felt most appropriate and that provided support for my "coming out" from behind the mirror.

THE ART OF THERAPY AND RESEARCH

A certain amount of art is involved in the practice of therapy. This is also the case in many other professions—for example, medicine, music, or athletics—in which the implementation of the practice guidelines are seasoned by the practitioner's experience and creativity. Psychotherapy is probably more of a craft than an art because it has a functional end-product as the result of clinicians' efforts. Thus potters, like therapists, have at their disposal guidelines for the technical aspects of their work and can improve their skills under the apprenticeship of a more experienced tutor. Nonetheless, some individuals possess more of a talent for the craft and can more effectively implement these guidelines. As I have suggested elsewhere,

> the field of psychotherapy will have come of age when it has developed a pool of therapeutic principles and techniques that, in the hands of an experienced, sensitive, and interpersonally skilled clinician, may be used to reach certain therapeutic goals. The extent to which these goals have been achieved, as well as the processes involved in achieving them, comprises the empirical study of the craft. (Goldfried & Padawer, 1982, p. 30)

Although the role of artistry is often acknowledged in the practice of therapy, we all too often mistakenly ignore its place in research activities. Some researchers are better than others, not so much because of their better grasp of methodology and design—although that is certainly crucial —but because of their intuition and creativity. Good research involves knowing what research questions to ask and knowing how they might best be addressed. Aronson and Carlsmith, two particularly successful and creative social psychologists, once summed it up very nicely as follows:

> In any experiment, the investigator chooses a procedure which he *intuitively feels* is an empirical realization of his conceptual variable. All experimental procedures are "contrived" in the sense that they are *invented*. Indeed, it can be said that the *art of experimentation* rests primarily on the *skill* of the investigator *to judge* the procedure which is the most accurate realization of his conceptual variable and has the greatest impact and the most credibility for the subject. (Aronson & Carlsmith, 1968, p. 25, italics added)

Sociologists who have studied the progress of science have made an important distinction between the questions to be studied and the methods of studying them. During the initial phase—the context of *discovery*—we have the "problem finders," who identify the important research questions that are likely to advance the field (Wilkes, 1979). Once these issues are identified, we move to the *confirmation* phase, in which the "problem solvers" investigate the empirical status of those phenomena that have been identified by the frontline observers. In the case of particularly successful researchers, we see both these activities occurring within the same individual. An excellent example is Neal Miller, one of the field's most respected researchers. In a candid commentary on how he approached research problems, he confessed to using his intuition before designing a study with tight or elaborate experimental controls: "During the discovery or exploratory phase . . . I am quite free-wheeling and intuitive—follow hunches, vary procedures, try out wild ideas, and take short-cuts" (Miller, cited in Bergin & Strupp, 1972, p. 348). Thus his goal at first is to convince himself that the phenomenon exists. Having done that, his goal becomes that of convincing his colleagues.

In considering the relationship between psychotherapy practice and research, I have always viewed my clinical work as providing me with the context of discovery. Working with clients directly, or discussing clinical cases with supervisees, provided me not only with the challenge of translating general research findings to the individual case at hand but also with the opportunity to witness firsthand the ever-varying parameters of human behavior and the change process. In my role as a therapist, the problem finder in me has been able to garner clinical hypotheses that I went on to study under better controlled research conditions. In writing about the empirical basis of behavior therapy, Jerry Davison and I have acknowledged the crucial role of ongoing clinical observation:

> While the definition of behavior therapy as deriving its techniques from the well-established body of knowledge in psychology sounds reasonable, it often does not occur that way in clinical practice. We have found instances where "insights" occurred to us in the midst of clinical sessions, prompting us to react in specific ways that paid off handsomely in the therapeutic progress of our clients. These may have entailed personal revelations that we provided to our clients, vaguely articulated hunches that we followed up, or therapeutic moves that we blindly stumbled upon, but which yielded therapeutic benefits well beyond our hard-headed comprehension. (Goldfried & Davison, 1994, p. 16)

I clearly do not pay as much homage to research findings as do some of my academic colleagues, nor do I ascribe to the belief that something necessarily is more "valid" because it has been empirically studied in a research context. This skepticism began in the 1960s, when the research literature came to the conclusion that relaxation training was not an effective clinical procedure. This research grew out of "dismantling" studies of systematic desensitization, which was designed to determine desensitivization's active ingredients. The question being studied was whether the imaginal exposure to anxiety-producing situations and relaxation training used separately, was as effective as the two used together as a clinical procedure. The findings indicated that neither fared as well as the complete package, a result that initially discouraged the use of either exposure or relaxation as therapeutic interventions. At the time, I even came across a study in which relaxation training was used in an outcome study as a placebo control condition. However, these research findings about relaxation training and exposure were contradicted by what I saw clinically. For example, I found that clients who were learning to relax themselves prior to our use of systematic desensitization—what was believed at the time to be the effective intervention—reported that it helped them cope with anxiety in various life situations. Here again, I was fortunate that my clients did not read the literature and consequently were not biased by the current state of our findings. Apparently, these research findings were limited by parametric constraints, whereby the relaxation training that was studied in controlled research designs was too brief. With more extensive training, and particularly when clients viewed the procedure as a skill for coping with anxiety, it appeared to work clinically. As a result of this clinical observation, the researcher in me went on to confirm this observation and to offer guidelines for more effective clinical application (Goldfried, 1971; Goldfried & Trier, 1974).

I can think of no greater justification for the importance of the scientist–practitioner model than that it keeps us honest as clinical researchers. Without an ongoing clinical base, it is all too easy to get caught up in research trends and fads that may have more to do with challenging our methodological acumen than with producing something that is useful to the practicing clinician. This observation was made by Bannister and Fransella (1971), who astutely noted that all too much of our research "could win classification under categories such as exquisitely obsessional or the apotheosis of the platitude, but they could hardly be called acts of imagination. Most of them were born out of the literature and, no doubt, will be buried in it" (p. 193).

TYING RESEARCH TO CLINICAL OBSERVATION

The Bannister and Fransella (1971) observation that research born from the literature is destined to be buried in it has stayed with me as much as Meehl's comment made some years earlier that research findings had no impact on his clinical work. What I have taken from all of this is the importance of having clinical (and basic) research closely tied to clinical observation. This is a general strategy that I have attempted to follow in my psychotherapy process research.

The thinking has been as follows: Something important may be learned about the process of change by going to the clinical literature to see what therapists of different orientations have had to say about why therapy works. By finding commonalities among these varying schools of thought, we might be able to uncover robust change principles, as these have managed to emerge despite the widely varying perspectives inherent in these different orientations. In searching for such commonalities, looking for consistencies at the theoretically abstract level seems fruitless because theoretical differences exist even within each of the general psychodynamic, experiential, and behavioral orientations. Looking for commonalities at the very basic level (e.g., clinical techniques) similarly might reveal little about the change process. Even if similarities were to be found among the widely diverse methods that are used clinically, they might be more in the form than the function of the procedures. Thus role-playing is used by behavior therapists and gestalt therapists, but for very different purposes (i.e., rehearsal of some action to take between sessions vs. completion of unfinished business). However, by looking at a level of abstraction somewhere between theory and technique, it might be possible to uncover common principles, reflecting clinical strategies that have to do with the function of general classes of interventions.

Setting aside theoretical jargon that is associated with different therapeutic orientations, we can derive from the clinical literature a handful of common strategies or principles that cut across different schools of therapy (Goldfried & Padawer, 1982). To begin with, there seems to be agreement that the change process is facilitated initially by clients' *expectations that therapy will help*. Another important common mechanism of change is the presence of *an optimal therapeutic alliance*, providing a significant interpersonal context in which change can take place. Clinicians of different orientations have also written about the therapeutic importance of *providing clients with an alternate way of understanding themselves and their environment*. This new awareness often sets the stage for what many believe to be at the core of therapeutic change, namely the *corrective experience*, whereby clients take the risk of behaving in a therapeutically positive way despite their inhibiting doubts and fears. Much of therapeutic change involves *ongoing reality testing* for clients, consisting of an increased awareness (insight) that facilitates corrective experiences (action) that, in turn, further enhances an ongoing cycle of awareness and corrective experiences.

I have used these common principles as starting points, suggesting potentially fruitful and clinically meaningful arenas in which to conduct our process research. These common principles are clearly too general to be used therapeutically by the practicing clinician, and more detailed guidelines are needed. These more detailed guidelines may be thought of as parameters of these common change principles, and each can be translated into a testable research question, such as the following: How does one facilitate positive expectations in a client who has little motivation for change? What are the potential threats to the therapeutic alliance, and how can they be avoided or remedied? What aspects of a client's functioning (i.e., thoughts, feelings, or action) require increased awareness? Is the corrective experience best accomplished within the session or between sessions? How much ongoing reality testing is required before clients update their views of themselves and others? These are but some of the questions that are born from clinical practice and that may be subjected to controlled research on the process of change.

Following Neal Miller's suggestion that researchers should first convince themselves that the phenomenon exists before conducting controlled studies to convince their colleagues, our process research often begins by listening to tapes and reading transcripts of the therapy sessions we wish to study. The goal here is to decide, on the basis of informal clinical judgment, whether there indeed is merit in more seriously pursuing a particular research question. Only after having some reason to believe that we are likely to find what we are looking for do we go through the elaborate and often painstaking process of objectively coding and analyzing what is occurring during the session. I firmly believe that research that generates and studies these questions in this particular manner is more likely to have direct clinical relevance. It is only reasonable to expect that questions that have their roots in clinical practice will yield answers that can more readily be applied there.

This clinical approach to research is relevant not only in specifying what questions to study but also in interpreting the results once they become available. In studying the more specific parameters of the various common change principles, I have often found it useful to return to the therapy sessions themselves as an aid in making clinical sense of the findings. This procedure can be illustrated by three different studies.

Similarities and Differences in Facilitating Awareness

In the first study, we were interested in looking at the similarities and differences in facilitating awareness in cognitive–behavioral and psychodynamic–interpersonal therapy for depression (Castonguay et al., 1990). One of our particularly intriguing findings was the different impact made by the two orientations when therapists assisted clients in becoming better aware of the difference between how they perceived things and the way things "really" existed. Based on small Ns and therefore only suggestive, a nonetheless near-significant positive correlation of .37 with symptom reduction was obtained for cognitive–behavior therapy, whereas a near-significant negative correlation of $-.51$ was found for psychodynamic–

interpersonal therapy. For cognitive–behavior therapists, this intervention helped, but for psychodynamic–interpersonal therapists, it clearly did not. To better understand these confusing results, we conducted a clinical content analysis to determine what the therapist was saying in each of these instances in which the comparison was being drawn between clients' perceptions and the real nature of things. On the basis of this content analysis, we found that the cognitive–behavioral message being conveyed was that "things are not as bad as you think." Psychodynamic–interpersonal interventions, however, were communicating that "things are not as *good* as you think." Although attempting to have clients view themselves and the world more realistically, each of the two orientations reflected its different conception of "reality," and each had a different immediate impact on symptomatology.

Therapeutic Alliance

A second study addressed the question of the therapeutic alliance, in which we compared the alliance in clinically significant sessions identified by therapists of these same two theoretical orientations (Raue, Castonguay, & Goldfried, 1993). One of the results of this study was the finding that scores for the therapeutic alliance in psychodynamic–interpersonal sessions were both lower and more variable than in the cognitive–behavioral sessions. Here, again, we carried out a clinical content analysis and found that lower alliance scores in psychodynamic–interpersonal therapy reflected a therapeutic focus on clients' dissatisfaction with the therapist and the therapeutic relationship. In higher rated sessions, there was little focus on the therapeutic relationship. A corresponding evaluation of the cognitive–behavioral sessions revealed little focus on relationship issues in lower alliance sessions but, rather, a focus on such issues as the client's reluctance to deal with certain topics. Thus, it is possible that the lower alliance scores found for psychodynamic–interpersonal therapists reflected the very reason they identified these sessions as being clinically significant, namely, that they focused on in-session relationship issues—seen by that orientation as being at the core of therapeutic change.

Therapeutic Change Mechanisms

A final instance in which clinical content analysis proved to be invaluable in interpreting our research findings involved an analysis of the effective change mechanisms in cognitive therapy for depression (Castonguay, Goldfried, Wiser, Raue, & Hayes, 1996). One finding that emerged was that two transtheoretical principles of change—the therapeutic alliance and the client's emotional experiencing—correlated positively with improvement. Quite unexpectedly, however, a specific aspect of cognitive therapy believed to be essential to the change process—the therapist's focus on the impact of thoughts on feelings—correlated negatively with outcome. Our content analysis of sessions revealed that the negative clinical impact was associated with therapists' attempts at times to pursue the cognitive intervention even at the expense of the therapeutic alliance. For example, one client was expressing her great distress upon just having seen her husband driving with another woman with whom he might very well be having an affair. Instead of empathizing with her in her pain and shock, which she apparently needed at the time, the therapist persisted in exploring the cognitions that might be creating the distress. This increased focus on the cognitive intervention, rather than the realistic nature of the situation and the need for interpersonal support, may very well have reflected an adherence to the treatment manual at the expense of clinical judgment.

RESEARCH TOOLS CAN BE CLINICAL MAPS

Those of us involved in psychotherapy process research have at times debated whether the coding systems we use in analyzing therapy sessions have been "invented" or "discovered." I suggest that we have neither invented nor discovered these research tools. Instead, I view these coding systems as having grown out of the interface between our direct experience with the clinical phenomena and our research ability to operationalize and reliably measure it. It is probably more accurate to categorize process researchers as "cartographers," who construct maps that depict the varying aspects of the therapeutic change process. Although the map is not the territory, a knowledge of both can prove to be invaluable in navigating the clinical terrain. Following is the general question addressed by process researchers: "What did the therapist do that was effective?" As a way of answering this question, different types of coding systems have been developed to study the change process. As research is able to produce results that answer this question, these findings can, in turn, provide answers to the question frequently raised by practicing clinicians: "What can I do that can be effective?"

Using as a starting point the common therapeutic principle that change involves helping clients to increase their awareness so that they might develop a better perspective on themselves and their world, we developed the Coding System of Therapeutic Focus (CSTF; Goldfried, Newman, & Hayes, 1989). The CSTF is transtheoretical in nature and was designed as a research tool for coding the extent to which therapists focused on clients' thoughts, feelings, actions, intentions, intrapersonal and interpersonal connections; different time frames; and different people in clients' lives. Although developed as a common metric for studying the change process in cognitive–behavioral and psychodynamic–interpersonal interventions, the clinical use of the measure was brought home to me during the course of my periodic clinical workshops. In preparing material for these workshops, I decided I would allot only about 15 minutes to discussing my process research, as I anticipated that the workshop participants would be more interested in clinical procedures than in research findings. My initial realization of the clinical applicability of the CSTF occurred when I left a workshop feeling frustrated that I was not able to present all the clinical material I had planned to cover. It soon became clear to me that the reason for this was that the participants were more interested in the CSTF than I anticipated, and therefore, I spent far more time describing it than I had planned. This corrective experience helped me to recognize the very practical use of the coding system for formulating clinical problems, clarifying clients' significant intrapersonal and interpersonal dynamics or determinant, monitoring therapeutic focus within the session, and generally tracking change over the course of treatment (Goldfried, 1995).

My experience in applying a psychotherapy process research tool in clinical practice is not unique. For example, Benjamin's Structural Analysis of Social Behavior (SASB; Benjamin, 1993) has proven to be an invaluable method for understanding the nature of interpersonal interactions along the dimensions of affiliation and control, as well as a method for evaluating how individuals deal with themselves along these same dimensions. Safran and Muran (1995) have used their research work on threats to the therapeutic alliance to outline clinical guidelines for dealing with such breaches in the relationship. The research methods Greenberg, Rice, and Elliott (1993) used to study experiential therapy have led to ways of recognizing important in-session choice points ("markers") for intervening therapeutically. Ways of monitoring clients' levels of emotional experiencing, originally devised as a research instrument (Klein, Mathieu-Coughlan, & Kiesler, 1986), provide an important clinical index of the client's emotional involvement in different therapeutic issues. Research methods for categorizing therapists' verbal response style (e.g., Hill, 1986; Stiles, 1992) offer excellent guidelines for training therapists in wording their interventions.

CLINICAL RELEVANCE OF OUTCOME RESEARCH

Before becoming involved in psychotherapy process research, my interest was in studying outcome. Most of the outcome research I conducted in the 1970s dealt with the investigation of cognitive–behavioral methods for reducing anxiety. My work, fortunately, was funded by the National Institute of Mental Health, and the results of these studies were published in respectable journals (see e.g., Goldfried & Trier, 1974). However, I must confess to having been somewhat schizophrenic in this phase of my professional career, in that the treatments I studied in the research context were only tangentially similar to what I did in my clinical practice in which I carefully evaluated what I believed to be the most relevant intervention for any given client. I did not randomly assign them to treatment. Clinically, I worked with clients until therapy was successful; I did not terminate after a predetermined and brief intervention. I made use of nonbehavioral therapy procedures when they seemed to be indicated; I did not administer theoretically pure treatments from a manual. Although the contributions of process research can be readily applied to the clinical setting, the same cannot be said for outcome research.

Some of the findings of my outcome research (and those of my colleagues) are of interest. However, I can see now where I (and they) may have inadvertently contributed to fostering self-doubts among practicing clinicians. It is all too easy to arrive at the conclusion from reading the behavior therapy research literature that the successful implementation of various treatment methods is relatively straightforward. When clinical reality does not conform to the literature, some practicing clinicians—especially those in earlier stages of their careers—may very well ask themselves certain questions, such as, "Am I the only one whose clients don't keep between-session records?" "Why do my clients have difficulty in doing their homework?" "Why don't some of these intervention procedures work for me?" "Am I the only one who is having difficulty in using these methods clinically?"

In more recent years, psychotherapy outcome research has moved to a new level of methodological sophistication by carefully training therapists to adhere to therapy manuals for the treatment of disorders diagnosed in the *Diagnostic and Statistical Manual of Mental Disorders* (4th ed.; *DSM–IV*; American Psychiatric Association, 1994) in the context of large-scale clinical trials. Although internal validity has improved, the research paradigm has continued to be weak on external or clinical validity. Our methodological advances have not cured us of our professional schizophrenia.

Responding to pressures from outside sources to empirically justify the effectiveness of our clinical interventions (e.g., third-party payers, or biological psychiatry), psychotherapy researchers have begun to marshall evidence for empirically validated or supported therapies (Task Force on Promotion and Dissemination of Psychological Procedures, 1995). This has clearly been a natural response to the political and economic challenges that the practice of psychotherapy now faces. The problem, however, is that the list of empirically supported therapies that has been generated is based on our current, clinically limited research paradigm. My good friend and colleague Barry Wolfe and I (Goldfried & Wolfe, 1996, 1998), who share between the two of us more than 50 years of psychotherapy research experience, have recently confessed to having participated in a paradigm that lacks clinical validity, expressing our concern that the methodological constraints associated with our outcome research might result in clinical constraints for the practicing clinician. In discussing the limited conclusions we might draw from our research findings, we depicted our ambivalence as follows:

> Yet, we continue to remain strong advocates of psychotherapy research. In many respects, our dilemma may be thought of as reflecting a conflict between a wish and a fear: Our wish is that therapy interventions be based on psychotherapy research; our fear, however, is that they might. (Goldfried & Wolfe, 1996, p. 1007)

Although the reason for documenting empirically supported therapies was to help make the practice of psychotherapy more accountable in the face of external pressures, it has had the additional impact of causing the clinical and research communities to raise questions about the adequacy of our research paradigm. Indeed, this paradigm has been challenged by researchers and clinicians alike (e.g., Fensterheim & Raw, 1996; Garfield, 1996; Goldfried & Wolfe, 1996, 1998; Sobell, 1996). To close the practice–research gap, we need a closer collaboration between clinician and researcher, the use of replicated clinical case studies, the use of process research findings to improve our therapy manuals, the study of theoretically integrated interventions, the investigation of clinical problems and issues not necessarily tied to *DSM* diagnoses, and a more clinically relevant way of disseminating research findings.[1]

In a way totally unanticipated, we hope that the attempt to certify empirically supported therapies on the basis of our current outcome research paradigm may mobilize collaborative efforts between some researchers and some clinicians to develop more clinically valid research paradigms, demonstrating once again that science progresses in strange and mysterious ways.

CONCLUSION

Being at a critical crossroads, clinicians and researchers need to give careful thought and ongoing dialogue to our future directions. We applaud the recommendations of the Task Force on Promotion and Dissemination of Psychological Procedures (1995) that urge clinician–researcher roundtable discussions of these very important issues. This need to close the unfortunate gap between researcher and practitioner as a way of advanc-

---

[1] I am currently editing *In Session: Psychotherapy in Practice*. The journal has as one of its goals the presentation of research findings for the practicing clinician, together with clinical guidelines and case illustrations.

ing the field hits at the very core of what it means to be a scientist–practitioner. I firmly believe that the advancement of the field requires a blending of both clinical experience and research findings. As I have suggested elsewhere,

> if one views the split between clinicians and researchers from outside the entire system, it becomes more evident that both groups are deluding themselves in thinking that they alone will advance the field. Stated more positively, it is perhaps more productive to conclude that both groups very much need each other. The experience and wisdom of the practicing clinician cannot be overlooked. But because these observations are often not clearly articulated, may be unsystematic or at times idiosyncratic, and are typically kept informal, it is less likely that these insights can add to a reliable body of knowledge. The growing methodological sophistication of the researcher, on the other hand, is in need of significant and ecologically valid subject material. Our knowledge about what works in therapy must be rooted in clinical observations, but it must also have empirical verification. For the researcher and clinician to ignore the contributions that each has to make is to perpetuate a system in which no one wins. (Goldfried & Padawer, 1982, p. 33)

REFERENCES

American Psychiatric Association. (1994). *Diagnostic and statistical manual of mental disorders* (4th ed.). Washington, DC: Author.

Aronson, E., & Carlsmith, J. M. (1968). Experimentation in social psychology. In G. Lindzey & E. Aronson (Eds.), *The handbook of social psychology: Vol. 2. Research methods*. Reading MA: Addison-Wesley.

Bannister, D., & Fransella, F. (1971). *Inquiring man*. Middlesex, England: Penguin Books.

Benjamin, L. S. (1993). *Interpersonal diagnosis and treatment of personality disorders*. New York: Guilford Press.

Bergin, A. E., & Strupp, H. H. (1972). *Changing frontiers in the science of psychotherapy*. Chicago: Aldine-Atherton.

Castonguay, L. G., Goldfried, M. R., Hayes, A. M., Raue, P. J., Wiser, S. L., & Shapiro, D. A. (1990, June). *Quantitative and qualitative analyses of process–outcome data from different therapeutic approaches*. Paper presented at the meeting of the Society for Psychotherapy Research, Wintergreen, VA.

Castonguay, L. G., Goldfried, M. R., Wiser, S. L., Raue, P. J., & Hayes, A. M. (1996). Predicting the effect of cognitive therapy for depression: A study of unique and common factors. *Journal of Consulting and Clinical Psychology, 64,* 497–504.

Fensterheim, H., & Raw, S. D. (1996). Psychotherapy research is not psychotherapy practice. *Clinical Psychology: Science and Practice, 3,* 168–171.

Garfield, S. L. (1996). Some problems associated with "validated" forms of psychotherapy. *Clinical Psychology: Science and Practice, 3,* 218–229.

Goldfried, M. R. (1971). Systematic desensitization as training in self-control. *Journal of Consulting and Clinical Psychology, 37,* 228–234.

Goldfried, M. R. (1995). Toward a common language for case formulation. *Journal of Psychotherapy Integration, 5,* 221–244.

Goldfried, M. R., & Davison, G. C. (1976). *Clinical behavior therapy.* New York: Holt, Rinehart & Winston.

Goldfried, M. R., & Davison, G. C. (1994). *Clinical behavior therapy* (Expanded ed.). New York: Wiley-Interscience.

Goldfried, M. R., Newman, C. F., & Hayes, A. M. (1989). *The coding system of therapeutic focus.* Unpublished manuscript, State University of New York at Stony Brook.

Goldfried, M. R., & Padawer, W. (1982). Current status and future directions in psychotherapy. In M. R. Goldfried (Ed.), *Converging themes in psychotherapy: Trends in psychodynamic, humanistic, and behavioral practice* (pp. 3–49). New York: Springer.

Goldfried, M. R., Stricker, G., & Weiner, I. B. (1971). *Rorschach handbook of clinical and research aplications.* Englewood Cliffs, NJ: Prentice Hall.

Goldfried, M. R., & Trier, C. S. (1974). Effectiveness of relaxation as an active coping skill. *Journal of Abnormal Psychology, 83,* 348–355.

Goldfried, M. R., & Wolfe, B. E. (1996). Psychotherapy practice and research: Repairing a strained alliance. *American Psychologist, 51,* 1007–1016.

Goldfried, M. R., & Wolfe, B. E. (1998). Toward a more clinically valid approach to therapy research. *Journal of Consulting and Clinical Psychology, 66,* 143–150.

Greenberg, L. S., Rice, L. N., & Elliott, R. (1993). *Facilitating emotional change.* New York: Guilford Press.

Hill, C. E. (1986). An overview of the Hill Counselor and Client Verbal Response Modes Category Systems. In L. Greenberg & W. Pinsof (Eds.), *The psychotherapeutic process: A research handbook* (pp. 131–160). New York: Guilford Press.

Klein, M. H., Mathieu-Coughlan, P. L., & Kiesler, D. J. (1986). The Experiencing Scale. In L. Greenberg & W. Pinsof (Eds.), *The psychotherapeutic process: A research handbook* (pp. 21–72). New York: Guilford Press.

Raue, P. J., Castonguay, L. G., & Goldfried, M. R. (1993). The working alliance: A comparison of two therapies. *Psychotherapy Research, 3,* 197–207.

Safran, J. D., & Muran, J. C. (1995). Resolving therapeutic alliance ruptures: Diversity and integration. *In Session: Psychotherapy in Practice, 1,* 81–92.

Sobell, L. (1996). Bridging the gap between science and practice: The challange before us. *Behavior Therapy, 27,* 297–320.

Stiles, W. B. (1992). *Describing talk: A taxonomy of verbal response modes.* Newbury Park, CA: Sage.

Task Force on Promotion and Dissemination of Psychological Procedures. (1995). Training and dissemination of empirically validated psychological treatment: Report and recommendations. *The Clinical Psychologist, 48*, 3–23.

Wilkes, J. M. (1979, September). *Cognitive issues arising from study in the sociology of science*. Paper presented at the 87th Annual Convention of the American Psychological Association, New York.

2

ORIGINS OF PROCESS–EXPERIENTIAL THERAPY: A PERSONAL CASE STUDY IN PRACTICE–RESEARCH INTEGRATION

ROBERT ELLIOTT

Scientific careers sometimes take unexpected turns. For example, an oversight involving a last-minute conference presentation heightened my interest in the relationship between psychotherapy research and practice. In 1980, Al Mahrer asked me to contribute a paper on my ideas about new developments in psychotherapy process research to a symposium at the American Psychological Association (APA) convention in Montreal. Under great time pressure and at the last minute, I wired him an abstract for a presentation describing how my line of research on clients' in-session experiences (e.g., Elliott, 1979; Elliott, Barker, Caskey, & Pistrang, 1982) might eventually lead to useful information for practicing therapists. Unfortunately, in my haste, I had forgotten to provide a title for my presentation. Al Mahrer thoughtfully supplied a title for me: "Fitting Process Research to the Practicing Therapist." When he informed me that he had

The author acknowledges the editorial assistance of Diane Elliott.

done this, I was at first mortified by the grandiosity of this title! However, after further consideration, I decided that I should try to rise to the occasion, and I undertook a thorough review of psychotherapy research methods that held promise for producing clinically useful knowledge. This paper was eventually published (Elliott, 1983a), and led directly to a frequently cited study documenting lack of research utilization by therapists in APA Division 29 (Morrow-Bradley & Elliott, 1986). I have returned to this issue repeatedly over the years (e.g., Elliott, 1995; Elliott & Morrow-Bradley, 1994).

Many different kinds of narratives can be used to characterize a scientific career, including stories of developing knowledge, evolving interests, and recurrent themes. However, in this chapter, I want to unfold a story of substantial current relevance to me because it explains how I came to be associated with the development of the new therapeutic approach, process–experiential (PE) therapy (Elliott & Greenberg, 1994; Greenberg, Rice, & Elliott, 1993), that today characterizes my work as a therapist and a teacher of therapy. I have chosen this "origin tale" because it illustrates most clearly how aspects of my work as a practicing therapist arose out of my work as a therapy researcher.

In addition, this story has the further merits of not having been told previously in print and of being somewhat unusual or at least idiosyncratic. However, to tell this story, I need to provide some background in the form of interwoven "plot threads" involving practice and research.

BACKGROUND

Practice: Eclectic Therapy Orientation

To begin with, I did not start out as an experiential–humanistic therapist. Although my undergraduate training at the University of California, Santa Cruz, was broadly humanistic, at the beginning of my clinical training at the University of California, Los Angeles (UCLA), I considered myself a social behaviorist and was drawn to systematic approaches such as behavioral contracting, single-case experimental design, and behavioral self-control (e.g., Mahoney & Arnkoff, 1978). However, in the course of my clinical training, I developed a broadly psychodynamic perspective, primarily from working with clients for whom psychodynamic processes such as transference and splitting were clearly evident. In this way, I was very similar to the therapists surveyed by Morrow-Bradley and Elliott (1986), who reported having learned more about therapy from their clients or patients than from any other source, including, of course, research (which ranked nearly last).

In addition, early in my graduate studies I was exposed to client-centered therapy from my advisor, Jerry Goodman, from whom I learned to think of therapy in moment-to-moment "process" terms.

Finally, in 1977, at the meeting of the Society for Psychotherapy Research in Madison, Wisconsin, I heard Leslie Greenberg and Laura Rice present their task-analytic-based research on two therapy events, Gestalt two-chair work for conflict splits and systematic unfolding for problematic reactions (the latter is a broadly client-centered intervention). Always eager to try different therapy techniques, I immediately began to add these methods to my work with clients. From that point to the present, Rice and Greenberg's research stands out as the therapy research (e.g., Rice & Greenberg, 1984) that has most influenced my practice as a therapist.

As a result of these multifarious influences, by the time I completed my PhD at UCLA and moved to the University of Toledo to take an academic clinical faculty position, I was a thoroughgoing eclectic–integrative therapist, using a wide variety of therapy techniques conceptualized within a broadly psychodynamic framework.

Research: Phenomenology of Client In-Session Experience

The second thread parallels the first: As I have written elsewhere (Elliott, 1986), when I was in graduate school at UCLA in the mid-1970s, fellow students Chris Barker, Nancy Pistrang, and I developed an application of Kagan's (1975) Interpersonal Process Recall (IPR) procedure for the systematic investigation of client experiences of particular moments in therapy. In a series of studies using this method, I spent many hours reviewing video- and audiotapes of therapy sessions with clients, asking them to describe their ever-shifting experiences within therapy sessions.

We set out to use IPR to test the assumptions of the popular helping skill training approaches (e.g., Ivey & Gluckstern, 1974), which typically favored therapist reflection responses and disfavored the use of questions. However, the first thing that we discovered was that "there is nothing as bad as a bad reflection." Furthermore, we also found that although clients typically found therapist questions to be less helpful than other responses, therapists' open-ended questions that inquire about clients' experiences and meanings (e.g., "What was that like for you?") were often experienced as very helpful (Elliott et al., 1982). In general, I came away from this immersion in the client in-session phenomenology with the humbling knowledge that therapists typically do not know how their clients perceive the therapy process. This research-based insight forced me to change my practice, as I evolved into a more cautious, inquiring therapist (Elliott, 1986; cf. Rennie, 1994).

In addition to learning about client covert processes and therapist questions (and reflections!), I learned a number of other things that would later turn out to figure prominently in PE therapy. These included the discovery that clients are at least partially conscious of many processes that psychodynamic approaches generally attribute to the unconscious. For example, clients were able to report fleeting, often preverbal, experiences that they did not generally acknowledge to themselves and that they immediately set aside. Clients also described their defensive processes, at times giving accounts of how they deliberately led therapists off course to avoid dealing with painful experiences or themes. Finally, I repeatedly found that in spite of the operation of these defensive processes, most clients do not reflexively avoid painful or difficult therapeutic topics but instead willingly approach them, believing this process to be necessary for them to resolve their difficulties. Altogether, these experiences led me to an understanding of clients (even severely disturbed clients) as active, aware "processors" of their therapy experiences.

Even more important, the phenomenological data I was collecting led me to develop an interest in significant change events in therapy: It was clear from talking to clients in IPR interviews that some therapy events were more important or helpful than others. I decided to collect significant therapy events, without really knowing how to study them. I experimented with various quantitative rating methods (e.g., Elliott, Cline, & Shulman, 1983); however, none of these seemed to really capture the important aspects of the significant events or what brought these events about.

As a result, I began to read the literature on qualitative research methods (e.g., Bogdan & Taylor, 1975; Glaser & Strauss, 1967; Wertz, 1983). Thus, in spite of my primarily positivist research training in graduate school, I felt compelled by my data to develop increasingly qualitative procedures for analyzing significant therapy events, including clients' descriptions of their experiences. I began with methods that used qualitative data (clients' verbal accounts of significant events) but converted these into quantitative data by way of content analysis systems (e.g., Elliott, James, Reimschuessel, Cislo, & Sack, 1985) or numerical cluster analysis (Elliott, 1985). I also experimented with a hybrid data analytic approach that was primarily quantitative but that included some qualitative data (Elliott, 1983b, 1984); I referred to this approach as comprehensive process analysis (CPA). Between 1980 and 1984, this approach gradually evolved into a more complex, largely qualitative method for analyzing the processes, effects, and contexts of significant therapy events (Elliott, 1989; Elliott et al., 1994; Labott, Elliott, & Eason, 1992).

ORIGINS OF PROCESS–EXPERIENTIAL THERAPY

Dissatisfaction With Eclecticism

In 1985, while I was on sabbatical in England, I was asked to give a workshop on CPA at the yearly meeting of the United Kingdom chapter of the Society for Psychotherapy Research. To provide a concrete example, I decided to present a significant event from a case in which I was the therapist. As noted above, my orientation at this time was an eclectic mix of primarily dynamic and experiential interventions, understood within a broadly psychodynamic theoretical frame. The significant event I presented to the workshop involved psychodynamic dream interpretation. I presented the transcript of the significant event along with the client's account of her moment-by-moment experiences during the event, gathered through the use of IPR.

As I presented these data to the audience of primarily psychodynamically oriented therapists, one of them offered a psychodynamic interpretation of something the client had reported to the researcher in the IPR interview. In response, I told the audience that one should not make such high-level inferences about phenomenological data. The analyst who had made the interpretation then pointed out that I had obviously felt no such compunction against interpreting my client's dream in the therapy session. Wasn't I being inconsistent, he asked, if I refused to do in my research what I did in my practice as a therapist? I agreed that it was inconsistent but argued that research and therapy were very different enterprises. In qualitative research, I answered, it is very important to stay close to the research informant's meanings and not to impose the researcher's meanings. This argument did not impress the analyst, but we were forced to leave the issue there.

However, I was deeply troubled by this conversation. Although I greatly enjoy doing therapy, my primary identity since graduate school has been that of a psychotherapy researcher; at the time, I had already spent 10 years thinking about how to study therapy and trying different methods for doing so. My commitment to understanding the client's internal experience of therapy had, by that time, evolved into a deeply held value. It was clear to me that my phenomenological orientation as a researcher was more important to me than my eclectic, mixed orientation as a therapist. If something had to give, it was going to have to be my therapeutic orientation!

Furthermore, I had just spent a year working with David Shapiro and his team in Sheffield, England, as they completed work on the First Sheffield Psychotherapy Project, a complex process–outcome study comparing cognitive–behavioral and interpersonal–dynamic treatments of depression (Shapiro & Firth, 1987). I was inspired by what I had seen to try something similar on my return to the United States. However, I realized that if I was going to attempt a substantial psychotherapy process–outcome study, I would have to focus on a particular population and treatment. The population was easy: Following the examples of the National Institute of Mental Health Treatment of Depression Collaborative Research Program (Elkin, 1994) and the First Sheffield Psychotherapy Project, I decided to study clients with major depressive disorder. However, regarding the treatment, I realized that I no longer felt comfortable with either cognitive–behavioral or psychodynamic–interpersonal approaches. The client-centered and Gestalt tasks that Leslie Greenberg and Laura Rice were studying were closest to what I did and were also consistent with the phenomenological orientation of my research. Having already shed my behavioral influences (another story, too long to tell here), I decided that I would give up the dynamic elements in my approach to working with clients, in a way "reinventing" myself as a therapist.

Developing the Process–Experiential Approach

One drawback to this strategy was that Greenberg and Rice's work at that time involved two very different therapy tasks: two-chair work for conflict splits (currently experienced internal conflicts; Greenberg, 1984), taken from Gestalt therapy, and systematic unfolding for problematic reactions (i.e., puzzling overreactions in specific situations; Rice & Sapiera, 1984), an adaptation of client-centered therapy. These two therapeutic tasks did not yet add up to one complete therapy. For one thing, it was not yet clear that the two tasks could be combined within an internally coherent treatment. An overall frame for such a treatment had not yet been developed; there was no specific, unifying theory of function and dysfunction. In addition, a fully articulated, comprehensive theory of treatment and the change process had not been developed, although a number of promising elements were in place. Finally, no research had been carried out on the application of these tasks with a clinically distressed population, and most of the existing research used very brief treatments of only a few sessions (e.g., Greenberg & Webster, 1982; Rice & Sapiera, 1984).

Fortunately, Greenberg and Rice were just beginning to move in this direction, and because I was undertaking a research study and had other relevant background (expertise on therapist response modes and Gendlin's focusing technique), they invited me to join them in this project. In 1985, I began a series of regular visits to Toronto, which culminated in a year's sabbatical there in 1991–1992. Eventually, we decided to name the emerging approach process–experiential (PE) therapy to distinguish it from other experiential treatments (e.g., Gendlin, 1996; Mahrer, 1989).

Personally, the first thing I had to do in developing this approach was to wean myself away from making psychodynamic interpretations. I had always prided myself on my ability to make sense out of complex phenomena, and I quite enjoyed developing and offering interpretations to clients. At the same time, it was not at all clear to me that my interpretations actually helped my clients.

It was not easy, however, for me to give up interpreting my clients.

Laura Rice helped me with this: She pointed out that clinical observation reveals that the self-understandings that clients develop always differ from the interpretations originally held by their therapists. Thus, clients' self-interpretations possess their own idiosyncratic character, grounded in their own personal histories and ways of looking at the world; it is impossible to predict in advance the exact nature of these emergent systems of self-understanding. I had to agree with her, in part because my own research on the negotiated nature of therapist interpretations (Elliott, 1984; Elliott et al., 1994) supports this conclusion.

With some trepidation, my students and I began our process–outcome study of PE therapy with major depressive disorder. We used the pressure of the study and our work as therapists in the study to drive the development of the general treatment model and of the specific application to depression (Elliott et al., 1990; Greenberg, Elliott, & Foerster, 1990).

Greenberg, Rice, and I then began to articulate a new humanistic–experiential treatment that would integrate what we saw as the best elements of client-centered and Gestalt therapy. This therapy offers clients a primarily client-centered relationship based on empathic exploration of important experiences in a context of therapist empathy, prizing, and genuineness. It was, however, more process directive, meaning that the therapist suggests "experiments" at appropriate moments, in the tradition of Gestalt therapy. These process-directive interventions offer clients encouragement to work in quite different ways ("microprocesses") at different times, according to the therapeutic tasks that the client raises in the form of *markers*, that is, behavioral signs of the desire to work on a particular kind of difficulty.

For example, if the client describes an internal conflict, defined by being pulled in two contradictory directions or acting on oneself (i.e., criticizing or attempting to make oneself do something), this "split" marker signals that the client is ready (in the presence of an adequate therapeutic alliance) to imagine and enact a dialogue between the conflicted parts of the self. This active expression of partial aspects of self is very different from the inward-turned self-exploration favored in other PE tasks (e.g., the careful reexperiencing or "unfolding" of puzzling personal overreactions to specific situations). Furthermore, on the basis of extensive research by Greenberg (reviewed in Greenberg, 1984; Greenberg, Elliott, & Lietaer, 1994), within the two-chair dialogue task, the client is offered the opportunity to work in very different ways at different times: At first, role-playing and exaggerating is used to heighten the client's experience of the conflict; next, the therapist helps the client to specify and deepen each partial aspect of self while maintaining psychological contact between these parts; after this, the client negotiates between the partial self-aspects; and, finally, the client reflects on and symbolizes any changes that have occurred.

These therapeutic tasks occur within a larger therapeutic framework of six treatment principles, which succinctly summarize the PE therapist's stance:

1. Try to develop and maintain *empathic attunement* to the client's moment-to-moment experiencing.
2. Develop a *therapeutic bond* with the client, characterized by the expression of empathy, caring, and emotional presence.
3. Facilitate *task collaboration* with the client, in the form of mutual involvement in goals and tasks of therapy.
4. Foster different forms of client *experiential processing* as appropriate to different therapeutic tasks within sessions.
5. Help clients *identify and complete* important therapeutic *tasks* within therapy.
6. Foster client *growth* and *self-determination* within therapy.

This means that the PE therapist begins each session by trying to understand vividly the client's immediate emotional state and concerns. The therapist then tries to express this understanding to the client and to develop a shared sense of what the client feels is important to work on in the session (e.g., unresolved resentment of a neglectful parent). Having identified what needs their shared attention, the therapist helps the client to work on this task in ways that are likely to lead to progress with the particular task (e.g., helping the client to actively express anger toward the important other). If the client seems to wander off track, the therapist offers the client the opportunity to return to the original task, but does not impose strict adherence to the original task, and may even at times offer the client the explicit choice of whether to continue with or to drop the task.

Specific Research Influences on PE Therapy

My primary contributions to the development of this treatment approach reflected the influence of my previous research on classifying therapy processes: To begin with, based on my background of previous research on therapist response modes (Elliott, 1979, 1985; Elliott et al., 1987), I developed a description of the therapist "experiential response modes" used in the therapy (subsequently revised by Davis, 1994). These include measurable therapist interventions, such as empathic conjecture (tentative guesses about what the client may be feeling), action suggestion (instructions to try something in the therapy session), and process disclosure (revealing appropriate immediate therapist experiences).

In addition, Leslie Greenberg and I built on my research on the experiential therapy of depression to develop a description illustrated with treatment cases of practical treatment issues such as treatment length, client selection, therapeutic difficulties, and therapist training. Finally, we reviewed the existing research on the different tasks and proposed a general model of how clients moved through the different experiential tasks.

Thus, the resulting book-length treatment manual (Greenberg et al., 1993) reflects the influence of research on practice at a number of levels: First, the specific therapeutic tasks (e.g., empty-chair work for unfinished emotional business with significant others) were developed through a series of studies with the task-analytic research approach (Greenberg et al., 1994; Rice & Greenberg, 1984). Second, a number of treatment components are based on more general descriptive research on therapy process. This includes the presentation of experiential response modes, already described, plus material on client in-session reactions, which was based on earlier research on immediate therapeutic "impacts" (Elliott et al., 1985; Elliott & Wexler, 1994). Third, the PE approach is now supported by outcome data, in the form of (a) a meta-analysis of outcome research on various experientially oriented treatments (Elliott, 1996; Greenberg et al., 1994); and (b) a recent study (Greenberg & Watson, 1998), which suggests that PE therapy brings about change more quickly than client-centered therapy. For these reasons, Grawe (1996) recently cited PE therapy as an example of research-informed psychotherapy.

Current Directions for PE Therapy

Working in the PE approach to therapy has given me a greater sense of groundedness as a therapist, as I have developed a clearer sense of direction and consistency. Promising outcome data from our initial studies with clinical depression (Elliott et al., 1990; Greenberg & Watson, 1998) and with "unfinished business" (i.e., unresolved relationships; Paivio & Greenberg, 1995) have encouraged us to extend the treatment to post-traumatic stress disorder (Elliott et al., 1996; Elliott, Davis, & Slatick, 1998). In the process, we have added further research-based treatment tasks, such as the creation of meaning (Clarke, 1989, 1996), marked by "meaning protest," in which the client struggles against the unfairness or senselessness of the trauma. This is often the most important task for trauma survivors. Another important research-based task we have added to the treatment model is relationship dialogue for alliance problems, derived from research by Agnew, Harper, Shapiro, and Barkham (1994) and Safran and colleagues (Safran, Crocker, McMain, & Murray, 1990). Thus, the PE approach continues to build on relevant research to provide a humanistic research-informed psychotherapy.

DISCUSSION

Types of Research-to-Practice Influence

Given this narrative of research-based treatment development, it may be useful to reflect on the possible general meanings that can be taken from the experiences described. Research can influence practice in a variety of ways (cf. Patton, 1997). Thus, one strategy would be to analyze the story that I recounted here for evidence of these possible influences:

1. *Research values* can act as a general influence on therapy practice, in that one can transfer values that guide one's research to one's therapeutic practice. Thus, the central value I put on the direct representation of participant or client experience led me to change my therapeutic orientation.

2. *Research-based knowledge* emerging from the systematic investigation of psychotherapy may provide useful guidance or orientation for practice. In other words, one may learn things from research that help one become more effective as a therapist. Thus, the articulated PE theory of function, dysfunction, tasks, and change processes, developed in the process of constructing the treatment manual, has in turn lent greater clarity and focus to my work with clients.

3. *Specific research procedures* can be extended directly into therapeutic practice. For example, as a direct result of my research, I now generally favor the use of three research-based procedures in my clinical work: (a) thorough diagnostic workups, especially on the *Diagnostic and Statistical Manual of Mental Disorders* (4th ed., DSM–IV; American Psychiatric Association, 1994; DSM–IV Axes 1, 2, and 5); (b) the use of therapeutic treatment adherence self-ratings as a productive form of training and self-supervision; and (c) the regular use of the Personal Questionnaire (an individualized change measure; Phillips, 1986), to allow each client to develop a rank-ordered list of treatment-relevant personal goals.

4. *Research-derived constructs* can act to sensitize therapist perceptions of therapy process. In other words, researching therapy forces one to think more clearly and precisely about it, and encourages one to apply new constructs to therapy process and outcome; these new or newly refined constructs then help one think differently or more clearly about what is going on in session with clients. Thus, my students and I have found that adhering to a treatment model is substantially a function of being able to perceive key aspects of the thera-

peutic process, including client markers signalling readiness for specific therapeutic tasks, therapist response modes, and immediate client reactions.

From this it is clear that research can have a variety of different effects on the practice of therapy, some of which have not been adequately addressed in the literature.

Treatment Manuals as Research-to-Practice Influence?

In the controversy over empirically supported treatments (Chambless et al., 1996; Elliott, 1998b), one hotly contested issue regarding the potential influence of research on practice has been whether research-based treatment manuals should guide clinical practice (e.g., Bohart, O'Hara, & Leitner, 1998). In fact, the development and dissemination of treatment manuals may be the clearest example of therapy research influencing (or trying to influence) practice. In this respect, my own story exemplifies a common contemporary "career track" for psychotherapy researchers: using one's research to develop a treatment, typically presented in the form of a book-length treatment manual. By this time, a substantial number of therapy researchers have taken this tack. In addition to Greenberg et al. (1993), a selective list of others includes Beck, Rush, Shaw, and Emery (1979; which started the whole thing), Hill (1996), Klerman, Rounsaville, Chevron, Neu, and Weissman (1984), Luborsky (1984), Strupp and Binder (1984), and Vaillant (1997).

The reasons for this development are numerous: First, treatment manuals are required by research grants and can be readily expanded to book length. Second, systematic psychotherapy research provides tools and material that facilitate treatment development; one can easily argue that these resources allow researcher–therapists to develop better (i.e., more specific, realistic, and research-informed) treatment manuals than nonresearcher–therapists.

Most important, working on treatment manuals enables researcher–therapists to engage simultaneously in research and clinical work, thus achieving—at least temporarily—the state of research–practice integration that approximates nirvana for applied social scientists. Extrapolating from my own experience, writing a book-length psychotherapy treatment manual gives a researcher the sense that he or she is "finally doing something" of use to the practice community. This allows some relief from the common feeling that one's research publications are permanently buried in archival journals, where they are read only by anxious graduate students, jealous rivals, people with too much time on their hands, and the occasional odd meta-analyst ferreting about for effect sizes. (Worries about how many practicing therapists read one's manual and actually change their approach to therapy is partly compensated for by the reassuring specificity of biannual royalty statements and the accompanying checks.)

CONCLUSION: NAGGING DOUBTS

As can be seen, my research on PE therapy has, to a large extent, assuaged worries about my research not being relevant to clinical practice, worries that bothered me during much of my early career as a psychotherapy researcher. I can now experience directly, in my work as a therapist and in that of my students, how my therapy research can benefit practice. Nevertheless, some important, nagging doubts remain: In particular, how generalizable are the results of "research therapy" to ordinary, "real-world therapy" (cf. Weisz, Donenberg, Han, & Weiss, 1995)? In my research program, my students and I have typically seen carefully selected and thoroughly screened and prepared clients, under ideal conditions (i.e., carefully trained and supervised therapists). In my local community, however, my former students work full time (or more), seeing unselected, unprepared clients under difficult conditions, with minimal or no supervision, and with the regular interference of managed care companies.

On the one hand, my current students and I find value in our current work under relatively controlled circumstances. We, at least, are experiencing the integration of research and practice because we are both practicing in our research and researching our practice. On the other hand, my former students don't have time for such things, at least until managed care or other political–economic pressures force some narrowly delimited form of research (i.e., "outcomes assessment") on them. Of what value to them is my research? To even begin to answer this question, several new types of research are needed: (a) process and outcome research with an expanded range of clients (including those with Axis II disorders; cf. Elliott, 1998a); (b) investigations of the therapeutic effects of taking part in research (Slatick, 1997); and (c) mental health services research on the therapeutic activities and outcomes of frontline therapists (e.g., Lambert & Brown, 1996).

For these reasons, I feel the need to do more research in real-world practice settings and under conditions that more closely resemble typical therapy practice—that is, in settings in which research has not already had such a strong influence. Until therapist researchers pay more attention to actual field conditions and client populations, it is not clear to me how far "real-world" practicing therapists should embrace results and treatment manuals derived from carefully controlled therapy research, including my own.

REFERENCES

Agnew, R. M., Harper, H., Shapiro, D. A., & Barkham, M. (1994). Resolving a challenge to the therapeutic relationship: A single-case study. *British Journal of Medical Psychology, 67,* 155–170.

American Psychiatric Association. (1994). *Diagnostic and statistical manual of mental disorders* (4th ed.). Washington, DC: Author.

Beck, A. T., Rush, A. J., Shaw, B. F., & Emery, G. (1979). *Cognitive therapy of depression.* New York: Guilford Press.

Bogdan, R., & Taylor, S. J. (1975). *Introduction to qualitative research methods.* New York: Wiley.

Bohart, A. C., O'Hara, M., & Leitner, L. M. (1998). Empirically violated treatments: Disenfranchisement of humanistic and other psychotherapies. *Psychotherapy Research, 8,* 141–157.

Chambless, D. L., Sanderson, W. C., Shoham, V., Johnson, S. B., Pope, K. S., Crits-Christoph, P., Baker, M., Johnson, B., Woody, S. R., Sue, S., Beutler, L., Williams, D. A., & McCurry, S. (1996). An update on empirically validated therapies. *The Clinical Psychologist, 49,* 5–18.

Clarke, K. M. (1989). Creation of meaning: An emotional processing task in psychotherapy. *Psychotherapy, 26,* 139–148.

Clarke, K. M. (1996). Change processes in a creation of meaning event. *Journal of Consulting and Clinical Psychology, 64,* 465–470.

Davis, K. L. (1994). *The role of therapist actions in process–experiential therapy* (Doctoral dissertation, University of Toledo, 1994). *Dissertation Abstracts International, 56,* 519B.

Elkin, I. (1994). The NIMH Treatment of Depression Collaborative Research Program: Where we began and where we are. In A. E. Bergin & S. L. Garfield (Eds.), *Handbook of psychotherapy and behavior change* (pp. 114–139). New York: Wiley.

Elliott, R. (1979). How clients perceive helper behaviors. *Journal of Counseling Psychology, 26,* 285–294.

Elliott, R. (1983a). Fitting process research to the practicing psychotherapist. *Psychotherapy: Theory, Research & Practice, 20,* 47–55.

Elliott, R. (1983b). "That in your hands . . .": A comprehensive process analysis of a significant event in psychotherapy. *Psychiatry, 46,* 113–129.

Elliott, R. (1984). A discovery-oriented approach to significant events in psychotherapy: Interpersonal Process Recall and Comprehensive Process Analysis. In L. Rice & L. Greenberg (Eds.), *Patterns of change* (pp. 249–286). New York: Guilford Press.

Elliott, R. (1985). Helpful and nonhelpful events in brief counseling interviews: An empirical taxonomy. *Journal of Counseling Psychology, 32,* 307–322.

Elliott, R. (1986). Interpersonal Process Recall (IPR) as a psychotherapy process research method. In L. Greenberg & W. Pinsof (Eds.), *The psychotherapeutic process* (pp. 503–527). New York: Guilford Press.

Elliott, R. (1989). Comprehensive Process Analysis: Understanding the change process in significant therapy events. In M. Packer & R. B. Addison (Eds.), *Entering the circle: Hermeneutic investigation in psychology* (pp. 165–184). Albany, NY: State University of New York Press.

Elliott, R. (1995). Therapy process research and clinical practice: Practical strategies. In M. Aveline & D. A. Shapiro (Eds.), *Research foundations for psychotherapy practice* (pp. 49–72). Chichester, England: Wiley.

Elliott, R. (1996). Are client-centered/experiential therapies effective? A meta-analysis of outcome research. In U. Esser, H. Pabst, & G.-W. Speierer (Eds.), *The power of the person-centered-approach: New challenges–perspectives–answers* (pp. 125–138). Köln, Germany: GwG Verlag.

Elliott, R. (1998a). *Center for the Study of Experiential Psychotherapy research protocol.* Unpublished manuscript, Department of Psychology, University of Toledo, Toledo, OH.

Elliott, R. (1998b). Editor's introduction: A guide to the empirically-supported treatments controversy. *Psychotherapy Research, 8,* 115–125.

Elliott, R., Barker, C. B., Caskey, N., & Pistrang, N. (1982). Differential helpfulness of counselor verbal response modes. *Journal of Counseling Psychology, 29,* 354–361.

Elliott, R., Clark, C., Wexler, M., Kemeny, V., Brinkerhoff, J., & Mack, C. (1990). The impact of experiential therapy of depression: Initial results. In G. Lietaer, J. Rombauts, & R. Van Balen (Eds.), *Client-centered and experiential psychotherapy towards the nineties* (pp. 549–577). Leuven, Belgium: Leuven University Press.

Elliott, R., Cline, J., & Shulman, R. (1983, July). *Effective processes in psychotherapy: A single case study using four evaluative paradigms.* Paper presented at the annual meeting of the Society for Psychotherapy Research, Sheffield, England.

Elliott, R., Davis, K., & Slatick, E. (1998). Process–experiential therapy for post-traumatic stress difficulties. In L. Greenberg, G. Lietaer, & J. Watson (Eds.), *Handbook of experiential psychotherapy* (pp. 249–271). New York: Guilford Press.

Elliott, R., & Greenberg, L. S. (1994). Experiential therapy in practice: The process-experiential approach. In B. Bongar & L. Beutler (Eds.), *Foundations of psychotherapy: Theory, research, and practice* (pp. 123–139). Stanford, CA: Oxford University Press.

Elliott, R., Hill, C. E., Stiles, W. B., Friedlander, M. L., Mahrer, A., & Margison, F. (1987). Primary therapist response modes: A comparison of six rating systems. *Journal of Consulting and Clinical Psychology, 55,* 218–223.

Elliott, R., James, E., Reimschuessel, C., Cislo, D., & Sack, N. (1985). Significant events and the analysis of immediate therapeutic impacts. *Psychotherapy, 22,* 620–630.

Elliott, R., & Morrow-Bradley, C. (1994). Developing a working marriage between psychotherapists and psychotherapy researchers: Identifying shared purposes. In P. F. Talley, H. H. Strupp, & S. F. Butler (Eds.), *Research findings and clinical practice: Bridging the chasm* (pp. 124–142). New York: Basic Books.

Elliott, R., Shapiro, D. A., Firth-Cozens, J., Stiles, W. B., Hardy, G., Llewelyn, S. P., & Margison, F. (1994). Comprehensive process analysis of insight events in cognitive–behavioral and psychodynamic–interpersonal therapies. *Journal of Counseling Psychology, 41*, 449–463.

Elliott, R., Suter, P., Manford, J., Radpour-Markert, L., Siegel-Hinson, R., Layman, C., & Davis, K. (1996). A process–experiential approach to post-traumatic stress disorder. In R. Hutterer, G. Pawlowsky, P. F. Schmid, & R. Stipsits (Eds.), *Client-centered and experiential psychotherapy: A paradigm in motion* (pp. 235–254). Frankfurt am Main, Germany: Lang.

Elliott, R., & Wexler, M. M. (1994). Measuring the impact of treatment sessions: The Session Impacts Scale. *Journal of Counseling Psychology, 41*, 166–174.

Gendlin, G. T. (1996). *Focusing-oriented psychotherapy: A manual of the experiential method.* New York: Guilford Press.

Glaser, B. G., & Strauss, A. (1967). *The discovery of grounded theory: Strategies for qualitative research.* Chicago: Aldine.

Grawe, K. (1996). Research-informed psychotherapy. *Psychotherapy Research, 7*, 1–20.

Greenberg, L. S. (1984). A task analysis of intrapersonal conflict resolution. In L. Rice & L. Greenberg (Eds.), *Patterns of change* (pp. 67–123). New York: Guilford Press.

Greenberg, L. S., Elliott, R., & Foerster, F. (1990). Experiential processes in the psychotherapeutic treatment of depression. In N. Endler & D. C. McCann (Eds.), *Contemporary perspectives on emotion* (pp. 157–185). Toronto, Ontario, Canada: Wall & Emerson.

Greenberg, L. S., Elliott, R., & Lietaer, G. (1994). Research on humanistic and experiential psychotherapies. In A. E. Bergin & S. L. Garfield (Eds.), *Handbook of psychotherapy and behavior change* (4th ed., pp. 509–539). New York: Wiley.

Greenberg, L. S., Rice, L. N., & Elliott, R. (1993). *Facilitating emotional change: The moment-by-moment process.* New York: Guilford Press.

Greenberg, L. S., & Watson, J. (1998). Experiential therapy of depression: Differential effects of client-centered relationship conditions and active experiential interventions. *Psychotherapy Research, 8*, 210–224.

Greenberg, L. S., & Webster, M. (1982). Resolving decisional conflict by means of two-chair dialogue: Relating process to outcome. *Journal of Counseling Psychology, 29*, 468–477.

Hill, C. E. (1996). *Working with dreams in psychotherapy.* New York: Guilford Press.

Ivey, A. E., & Gluckstern, N. B. (1974). *Basic attending skills: Participant manual.* North Amherst, MA: Microtraining Associates.

Kagan, N. (1975). *Interpersonal process recall: A method of influencing human interaction.* Unpublished manuscript, University of Houston, Educational Psychology Department.

Klerman, G., Rounsaville, B., Chevron, E., Neu, C., & Weissman, M. (1984).

Manual for short-term interpersonal therapy for depression. New York: Basic Books.

Labott, S., Elliott, R., & Eason, P. (1992). "If you love someone, you don't hurt them": A comprehensive process analysis of a weeping event in psychotherapy. *Psychiatry, 55,* 49–62.

Lambert, M. J., & Brown, G. S. (1996). Data-based management for tracking outcome in private practice. *Clinical Psychology: Science & Practice, 3,* 172–178.

Luborsky, L. (1984). *Principles of psychoanalytic psychotherapy: A manual for supportive-expressive treatment.* New York: Basic Books.

Mahoney, M. J., & Arnkoff, D. B. (1978). Cognitive and self-control therapies. In S. L. Garfield & A. E. Bergin (Eds.), *Handbook of psychotherapy and behavior change* (2nd ed., pp. 689–722). New York: Wiley.

Mahrer, A. R. (1989). *How to do experiential psychotherapy: A manual for practitioners.* Ottawa, Ontario, Canada: University of Ottawa Press.

Morrow-Bradley, C., & Elliott, R. (1986). The utilization of psychotherapy research by practicing psychotherapists. *American Psychologist, 41,* 188–197.

Paivio, S. C., & Greenberg, L. S. (1995). Resolving "unfinished business": Efficacy of experiential therapy using empty chair dialogue. *Journal of Consulting and Clinical Psychology, 63,* 419–425.

Patton, M. Q. (1997). *Utilization-focused evaluation* (3rd ed.). Thousand Oaks, CA: Sage.

Phillips, J. P. N. (1986). Shapiro personal questionnaire and generalized personal questionnaire techniques: A repeated measures individualized outcome measurement. In L. S. Greenberg & W. M. Pinsof (Eds.), *The psychotherapeutic process: A research handbook* (pp. 557–590). New York: Guilford Press.

Rennie, D. L. (1994). Clients' deference in psychotherapy. *Journal of Counseling Psychology, 41,* 427–437.

Rice, L. N., & Greenberg, L. (Eds.). (1984). *Patterns of change.* New York: Guilford Press.

Rice, L. N., & Sapiera, E. P. (1984). Task analysis and the resolution of problematic reactions. In L. N. Rice & L. S. Greenberg (Eds.), *Patterns of change* (pp. 29–66). New York: Guilford Press.

Safran, J. D., Crocker, P., McMain, S., & Murray, P. (1990). Therapeutic alliance rupture as a therapy event for empirical investigation. *Psychotherapy, 27,* 154–165.

Shapiro, D. A., & Firth, J. (1987). Prescriptive vs. exploratory psychotherapy: Outcomes of the Sheffield Psychotherapy Project. *British Journal of Psychiatry, 151,* 790–799.

Slatick, E. (1997). *The effects of research participation on psychology training clinic clients.* Unpublished master's thesis, University of Toledo, Toledo, OH.

Strupp, H. H., & Binder, J. L. (1984). *Psychotherapy in a new key: A guide to time-limited dynamic psychotherapy.* New York: Basic Books.

Vaillant, L. M. (1997). *Changing character: Short-term anxiety-regulating psychotherapy for restructuring defenses, affects, and attachment.* New York: Basic Books.

Weisz, J. R., Donenberg, G. R., Han, S. S., & Weiss, B. (1995). Bridging the gap between laboratory and clinic in child and adolescent psychotherapy. *Journal of Consulting and Clinical Psychology, 63,* 688–701.

Wertz, F. J. (1983). From everyday to psychological description: Analyzing the moments of a qualitative data analysis. *Journal of Phenomenological Psychology, 14,* 197–241.

3

GRADUATE TRAINING IN BOULDER MODEL CLINICAL PSYCHOLOGY PROGRAMS: THE EVOLVING TENSION BETWEEN SCIENCE AND ART

MICHAEL E. ADDIS

This chapter is about wrestling with inevitable tensions between research and clinical work in the context of clinical training. I choose the terms *wrestling* and *tensions* consciously. They convey what I see as a central part of my experience both as a former graduate student and as someone now working to train clinical graduate students. My goal is not to critique or reformulate the basis of graduate training in clinical psychology because many others have done so, and have done it well (e.g., Goldfried, 1984; Peterson, 1995). Instead, I want to describe the types of psychological experiences that affect graduate students as they struggle to integrate research and clinical work. I hope that by viewing the process from the trainee's perspective, psychologists can develop better strategies to help our students and ourselves keep the Boulder model from crumbling.

I should start by defining the type of graduate training context I am referring to. At its heart, the Boulder model is about the attempt to integrate science and clinical intervention. This integration can take many different forms. For example, should psychologists (a) do both research and clinical work, (b) read research to support clinical practice, (c) take a scientific approach to clinical cases, or (d) do research that is clinically relevant? Ultimately, the different ways in which research and clinical work diffuse and coalesce during training create the types of tensions I intend to explore. The essence of the Boulder model is in the experiences of those trained within it.

The issues I describe are not limited to PhD students in clinical psychology programs. Students in social work, psychiatry, or counseling programs may experience similar tensions. I have chosen to focus on clinical psychology graduate students because I have the most personal experience in this area and because the tensions are probably more acute. I should also make clear that because my own research focuses on treatment, struggles between research and clinical work are particularly relevant. There are many clinical researchers who do not study treatment yet continue to treat psychotherapy clients in a variety of different contexts.

As a relatively recent graduate of a Boulder model doctoral program, certain experiences are still fresh in my mind. I remember feeling caught in a tug-of-war with various incarnations of the scientific and the clinical enterprise on either side. This was not a tension solely between alternative career choices, although many students feel torn between clinical practice and academia. The struggle was broader and more far-reaching. How am I to view the process of psychotherapy? Is it an art or a science? What is the role of accountability in clinical training and practice? Can research ever meaningfully capture the complexities of the therapeutic process? Do we treat disorders or people? How can I know for sure that I am actually helping people? Is it unethical to use treatments without demonstrated efficacy? These are just a handful of the questions that I asked (and continue to ask) myself.

It may be presumptuous to assume that my personal struggles with these dialectical tensions are representative of the experiences of current trainees. Programs vary widely in their emphasis on research versus clinical training. At the same time, I have reasons to think that my experiences are not unique. First, I spent a considerable amount of time discussing these issues with fellow graduate students and faculty at the University of Washington. At the end of my first year of graduate school, two fellow students and I formed a group called Research and Private Practice Rapprochement. Although we failed to achieve ultimate rapprochement (two of us are academics, one is doing full-time clinical work!), we shared many of our experiences of trying to balance research and clinical work. Currently, I spend a good deal of time supervising the research and clinical work of graduate students in a Boulder model clinical PhD program. Within the context of research design, theory development, testing, case formulation, and clinical skills, we spend much time discussing the relationship between research and clinical practice. The issues are also strikingly transparent in informal conversations regarding career options and future plans. Thus, my own experience, and the feelings and thoughts of two cohorts of doctoral students from Boulder model clinical programs, form the basis of what is to follow.

THE EVOLVING RELATIONSHIP BETWEEN RESEARCH AND CLINICAL WORK

I assume that education plays a central role in determining whether and how a psychologist integrates research and clinical work. For example, although survey studies indicate that most practicing psychologists are not directly influenced by research (Barlow, 1981; Sargent & Cohen, 1983), many are (Beutler, Williams, Wakefield, & Entwhistle, 1995). Like any individual difference variable, we can explain this either as a result of experience or of some internal and stable disposition. Because I am doubtful that scientists will find a research or practice gene in the near future, I emphasize experience in accounting for these differences. For example, by the time I completed my PhD, I had received a steady diet of education in psychology for over 12 years. My own attitudes toward research and clinical work quickly began to crystallize in my undergraduate years. If my experience is at all representative, it is worthwhile to consider existing attitudes toward research and clinical work before a student even enters graduate training.

Undergraduate Years

Psychology undergraduate majors typically sort into two groups: those interested in basic research questions and those who "want to help people." I was clearly in the latter camp. In fact, I had no doubt that psychotherapy could both change a person's life and provide a rich context for exploring the intricacies of the human psyche. If one starts with this assumption, then systematic research with all its rigor and skepticism looks either irrelevant or like much rain on an otherwise fascinating parade. Thus, I am not surprised that in my own advising of undergraduate psychology majors, the majority who express interest in a psychology career want to be practicing therapists. There are many reasons why this is the case. Students differ in their degree of inquisitiveness or their ability to think critically, and professors also vary in their ability to bring research to life. But for most students, research is simply not as interesting as personally relevant insights, interpretations, and explanations for why people are the way they are. If a student's interest already leans toward the clinical, then it typically takes only one negative experience with research (e.g., a dry course, a bad grade in statistics) to solidify an "antiresearch" stance. Research courses are then seen as necessary hurdles on the way to a BA, but rarely as intrinsically interesting. Interestingly, many students equate research with reading summaries of studies in textbooks. Thus, I am often surprised by students who express a disinterest in research without ever having conducted it.

Transition to Graduate School

If I am correct that undergraduate education is influential in shaping a student's attitudes toward research and clinical practice, then it follows that many students will have well-formed attitudes by the time they apply to graduate school. It also follows that many students will have a much stronger interest in clinical work than in research, and herein lies the beginnings of an ongoing tension for many clinical graduate students. To be accepted to a Boulder model program, a student must express a strong interest in and commitment to research. Personal statements suggesting that an applicant's raison d'être is a commitment to helping people are often treated by reviewers as serious red flags. Thus, intelligent students interested primarily in clinical work typically learn to lie about or bend their interests. For example, when I applied to graduate school, I was somewhat interested in research, and really interested in becoming a practicing clinician. However, my statement of purpose contained phrases such as the following: "I have come to believe that reliable and valid idiographic research can be conducted and will yield a more holistic understanding of both normal development and psychopathology. A graduate education in clinical psychology will teach me the intervention and research skills necessary for academic pursuit in these areas."

Now, over 10 years later, the statement is quite relevant. During graduate school, I developed a much stronger interest in research than in clinical practice. But *at the time* it was not an accurate description of my interests but, rather, what I needed to write to get a PhD. Although I seriously doubt that I'm the first person to have creatively adapted my interests in service of gaining admission to a PhD program, the value system favoring research over clinical work is so strong in Boulder model programs that part of me hesitates, even now, to share this information publicly, despite the fact that I'm primarily a researcher and not a practicing clinician! This is a problem for many students because the system teaches them to deemphasize their interest in clinical work and publicly amplify their commitment to research. As I describe later, this personal tension within many students can actually lower the likelihood that they will evolve into a Boulder model psychologist.

Personal Experiences in Psychotherapy

Students' personal experiences with psychotherapy can have a profound effect on their attitudes toward research and clinical work. For example, a student who has successfully worked through an episode of major depression in psychotherapy may take for granted that talking therapies are effective. Such a student may have difficulty taking seriously data that question the strength or stability of outcomes in psychosocial interventions (e.g., Dawes, 1994; Lambert & Bergin, 1994), or the necessity of training to achieve effectiveness as a therapist (Christensen & Jacobson, 1993). In contrast, some students may have a strong intellectual interest in clinical research but no personal experience with psychotherapy. Such students may naturally gravitate toward research but have more difficulty putting themselves fully into the process of clinical training.

I'm not suggesting here that students' attitudes are fixed in stone by their personal experiences with psychotherapy. What I want to emphasize is that for most psychologists, the marriage between science and clinical work is far from harmonious. Tensions within the relationship (like all relationships) are partly formed by past experiences with similar relationships. A strong personal relationship with a therapist can't help but shape one's attitudes toward clinical practice and research. As a personal example, I had a very positive relationship with a therapist toward the end of graduate school. This experience made me more optimistic about the effectiveness of psychotherapy. However, it also created a tension within me because my therapist was eclectic, not particularly research oriented, and not practicing within any of the structured protocols I had been studying. Moreover, what I experienced as meaningful (e.g., particular stories or metaphors) were not the techniques I was attempting to measure for my dissertation research. Thus, I experienced a direct and personal confrontation with the fact that psychotherapy research often bears little relationship to clinical practice.[1] This experience was very influential in shaping my research interests in the effectiveness of psychotherapy as it is practiced in the "real world."

EXPERIENCING THE TENSION BETWEEN RESEARCH AND CLINICAL WORK

The tension between research and clinical work is intensified when a student begins clinical training per se. Exactly how a student reacts to it

---

[1]I'm still not convinced that it should. The trade-off between internal validity (control) and external validity (generalizability) is a fundamental dialectic in any science. The decision to favor one or the other is complicated and inexorably linked to the questions one is asking. Persons (1991) and Persons and Silberschatz (1998) provide excellent analyses of the pros and cons of making psychotherapy research more representative of clinical practice.

depends partly on his or her attitudes and partly on the types of clinical–research experiences he or she encounters. The relationship is multidimensional, involving time, professional identity, values, and the psychological compatibility or conflict between research and clinical intervention. In what follows, I describe some of the psychological tensions as well as the tangible conflicts students experience between research and clinical work.

Research as a Support in the Face of Clinical Uncertainty and Despair

As often as it is gratifying and intellectually challenging to help another person, psychotherapy can be complicated, unpredictable, contradictory, vague, and emotionally challenging. Knowing that what one is doing as a therapist is based on empirical data can be a source of great support and confidence in the face of inevitable uncertainty. I remember the first depressed client I ever worked with. She was 34 years old, socially isolated, profoundly depressed, and had regular suicidal ideation with intent. The week before our first meeting she had sat up one night with a rope tying various nooses and contemplating where she could suspend the rope. I had been assigned to my supervisor in order to gain experience with the cognitive–behavioral treatment (CBT) of depression—a treatment that I knew to have a strong empirical base but one with which I had only a theoretical grasp and no practical experience.

In the face of my client's despair, my natural inclination was either to lamely reassure her that life was worth living, to agree with her that life was hopeless, or to run from the room to escape the aversiveness of her despair. My supervisor gently encouraged me to elicit and discuss the client's thoughts, and I did so with little success. My client was barely able to describe her own thought process and when she did, was unable to challenge her view of life as meaningless, unfair, and hopeless. My own thoughts were something like the following: "How can I possibly help this person, this isn't the right treatment because she's still depressed, there's probably something more helpful for her and I just don't know about it." Following our third session, my supervisor encouraged me to not become discouraged and to remember that the treatment I was using was empirically supported. This meant that, whether or not the client ultimately improved, I was doing what I was doing as a therapist for a reason. I knew that not all clients would benefit from CBT. But I also realized that, on average, I had a better chance of helping this client by sticking with CBT. In effect, the research base became a solid support for me psychologically and helped me to tolerate my client's pain without immediate signs of her improvement. I was also able to communicate to the client that the treatment had a high likelihood of helping her to become less depressed.[2]

There were other challenging situations in which basic empirical principles provided strong psychological support in my clinical work. I was fortunate in my training to receive intensive supervision in CBT for borderline personality disorder. Dialectical behavior therapy (DBT; Linehan, 1993) rests on an integration of behaviorism, biological emotion regulation theory, and Zen meditation. The approach is active, with the clinician often using the therapeutic relationship as a means of contingency management to extinguish suicidal behavior. Basically, this involved phone contact with clients, crisis management, and a great deal of "distress tolerance" on my part as a therapist. My own distress was significant at times but was greatly eased by the knowledge that (a) DBT had been shown to be effective in reducing suicidal behavior (Linehan, Armstrong, Suarez, Allmon, & Heard, 1991; Linehan, Heard, & Armstrong, 1993); (b) no other treatment had been shown to be effective; and (c) a number of the interventions were based on empirically derived principles of change. For example, I can remember clearly the first time a client threatened suicide in a session. Then she did it twice in the following session. Feeling bewildered, anxious, and more than a little guilty, I arrived at supervision wondering how I could explain that I was failing to help this client; in fact, I appeared to be harming her as evidenced by the rise in suicidal behavior. What I had failed to realize (but my supervisor hadn't) was that the client was showing an extinction burst. Following the treatment, I had consciously removed the contingent relationship between validation, attention, concern, and suicidal behavior. The client, like all people, was showing a natural increase in a behavior following removal of the reinforcer. Psychologically, this said to me: "What is happening is predictable, it's part of the change process, *and we know this from a large body of research on human and nonhuman organisms.*" The last point was especially powerful. I had had plenty of supervisors reassure me that a setback in therapy was part of the change process. But any new behavior can be labeled *progress* with the right interpretation. Admittedly, an extinction burst is an interpretation as well, but it is one rooted in scientific evidence and verifiable in the individual case (i.e., the behavior should decrease once the burst has peaked). Empirical ground was a welcome comfort when treating a person who herself was afloat in a sea of chaos and uncertainty.

---

[2]I also told her that the treatment was much more likely to work if she and I agreed on the treatment rationale, and if she completed the homework assignments between sessions, two processes also supported by empirical data.

Research Creating Anxiety, Guilt, and Paralysis

I recall a discussion with a second-year doctoral student following a seminar in which, as a professor and supervisor, I argued strongly for the superiority of some CBTs for anxiety disorders. The student approached me tentatively and said, "Wow, I just realized that we are ethically obligated to use certain treatments if we know they work. It would be wrong not to. I can't believe I never realized this before." I agreed and, after a short pause, the student continued, "What if we don't know what works?" The fact is that we don't know what works, nor do we have data available for a large proportion of the problems that people bring to therapy. Most trainees see clients with a variety of adjustment disorders and V codes long before they see a client with a pure major depression. Where are the treatment manuals and empirically based interventions for adjustment disorders, life stress, family conflicts, and personal growth? They simply don't exist.

To a student who adopts the scientist–practitioner value system, the dilemma is this: I know that what I do in my clinical work should be based on solid empirical research, but there is no solid empirical research for the majority of clinical situations I face. The effects of this lack of empirical guidance depend, of course, on the individual trainee. Some trainees may have an unshakable faith in psychotherapy, if only for the emotional support it offers clients. Ironically, one could argue that such a trainee is the most empirically supported in his or her clinical work because we know that various nonspecific factors, such as the presence of a strong supportive relationship between the therapist and the client, are associated with positive outcomes (e.g., Horvath & Symonds, 1991; Ilardi & Craighead, 1994). But in my experience as a trainee and clinical supervisor, such students are not particularly concerned with research data; their belief in psychotherapy is implicit. For such students, a hard look at the data may actually be necessary to help critically question some of the beliefs supporting various interventions.

For other, more empirically minded students, lack of data can be very unsettling. To the degree that empirically based practice has become inculcated in the training context, lack of data can be paralyzing. If a student is able to confront and truly wrestle with the tension between research and direct intervention, there is no shortage of large questions. For example, it is possible to interpret convincingly the history of psychotherapy research as a "house of cards" providing little evidence that training and expertise make any difference in psychotherapy outcomes (Christensen & Jacobson, 1993; Dawes, 1994). At a process level, a student might start to wonder the following: "How do I know this is at all helpful? Why are we discussing this client's childhood? Why am I trying to be empathic?"

The danger for trainees is that a lack of empirical support can lead to an unwillingness or inability to take necessary risks and to choose a course of action in ambiguous situations. I remember a story an internship supervisor told me about an eminent cardiac surgeon called in to consult on an emergency case. The surgeon delivered a brilliant review and synthesis of the research literature on similar cases to an awed group of residents and interns. At the end, a resident tentatively raised a hand and said, "Doctor, with all due respect, it seems to me that the research offers no clear course of action in this situation." The surgeon promptly left the room and, as he did, replied, "That is correct, and now we must take action."[3] When I first heard this story, I wondered why the famous surgeon had spent the time reviewing all the literature knowing that it provided no useful information. It has since occurred to me that this is precisely the point. The surgeon was modeling appropriate scientist–practitioner behavior: Know the research literature, use it when it provides guidance, and *use your best judgment when it doesn't*. What would have happened to the patient if this eminent surgeon was unable to take action because the research offered no clear direction? To the degree that we inculcate empirically based practice as an ethical imperative for out trainees, we can expect periodic skepticism, fear, anxiety, and unwillingness to take risks when the stakes are high and research offers little or no guidance. To the degree that students can tolerate ambiguity and lack of information, many clinical situations provide opportunities for growth as therapists (i.e., learning to think through the possible consequences of various courses of action). I suspect that these are the skills we try and teach budding clinicians: to consult available empirical data, to reason through various options, and to decide on a course of action. But my concern is much more with the psychological experience of the trainee than with the idealized synthesis between research and clinical action.

Perhaps skepticism and doubt are well founded because the scientific basis of psychotherapy is not nearly as comforting as we'd like it to be. But what happens when healthy skepticism translates into anxiety and an unwillingness to take calculated risks in a therapeutic situation? Jerome Frank (1973) and others have repeatedly suggested that a clinician's confidence in the interventions he or she is itself a change mechanism in psychotherapy. If anxiety and fear replace confidence and belief, change is less likely to occur. Let me be very clear. I am not saying that empirical data should be abandoned in favor of blind faith. I am suggesting that the *psychological effect* of the *absence of empirical data* within the therapy session can be harmful in some contexts. I am also arguing that pervasive doubt is a rational reaction to a moral value placed on research-based practice and to a concomitant lack of data to support action in most clinical situations.

---

[3]Thanks to Hans Doerr for this and other well-timed anecdotes.

How will an empirically minded trainee react to a client or problem for whom no research exists to support a particular course of action? Ideally, a student would view such a situation as an opportunity for scientific study —perhaps a case study, or better yet a single subject repeated-measures design (Barlow, Hayes, & Nelson, 1984). Some students do exactly this, but many don't; below, I explore some of the reasons. For now, let us assume that a student believes strongly in the need for empirical guidance but finds little available. I don't think it's overly dramatic to assume that such a student might feel afraid, skeptical, or even paralyzed and that these reactions may have a negative effect on the therapeutic process. For example, in my own training, I think that my skepticism regarding the scientific basis of psychotherapy benefited my clients only because it kept me from practicing bizarre "fringe" therapies with little or no empirical basis.[4] I don't think it helped my clients feel enhanced confidence in me or the therapy we were engaged in. It was helpful in my research to ponder questions such as the following: "What is a successful outcome? How can we know when a client is improved? Is psychotherapy anything more than purchased support?" Such existential–empirical dilemmas were, however, generally an unnecessary distraction in the therapy room. As researchers, we encourage practitioners to contemplate these issues and accuse them of ignorance if they don't. However, we rarely stop to consider their psychological power for trainees trying to develop a balance between healthy skepticism and the confidence and security necessary to develop solid clinical skills.

OBSTACLES TO INTEGRATION

There are numerous examples of successful Boulder model clinicians and researchers. Many of them have written compelling and articulate treatises on the integration of research and practice from clinical, theoretical, and methodological perspectives (Barlow et al., 1984; Goldfried, 1984; Persons, 1991). Their examples suggest to me that the tension I have been describing in this chapter ultimately can be accepted and perhaps even integrated at a personal level. But why aren't more of our students able to do similarly?

A Tension in Time Between Research and Clinical Work

For many students, the tension between research and clinical practice is stressful in very concrete and immediate ways. Between teaching assis-

---

[4]Of course, if I had been 100% consistent in my practices, I would have refrained from all activities without empirically demonstrated clinical use (e.g., seeing clients once a week for 50 minutes, assigning a diagnosis, and paraphrasing). Obviously, not all therapeutic behaviors can be empirically based, and I'm exaggerating to make a point.

tantships, course work, research, clinical work, and having a life, most clinical graduate students are chronically pressed for time and feel like impostors in one or more of these roles. This conflict is not conducive to creating a healthy synthesis between research and clinical work. First, it is not good modeling for clients. Because many clients suffer from multiple role demands, feelings of inferiority, and stress, a graduate student may be able to empathize but should also have within his or her repertoire ways of coping effectively with such stress. Second, a hectic and competing schedule does not help students to develop important nonspecific clinical skills such as relaxing, focusing one's attention, and emotionally preparing for difficult sessions. I remember as a graduate student sprinting from a research meeting to drop off some copying before seeing a client at our clinic. I arrived at the session on time, out of breath, and not at all ready to connect with a difficult client who was making steady but extremely slow progress in therapy. Experiences like these are common for practicing clinicians working in multiple roles. Graduate school is a time when these experiences should be dealt with as important aspects of clinical training. In my own training, one faculty member offered a weekly meditation group for graduate students and faculty. Practicing mindfulness (Nhat Hanh, 1987), we learned to meditate on the phrase "breathing in I am a flower, breathing out I am fresh." After our second meeting, a fellow student dropped by my office and exclaimed, "breathing in I am a flower, breathing out . . . what time is it? I'm late!"

Time pressures also make it difficult for students to commit psychological and intellectual resources to research. High-quality research is difficult to conduct. It requires great intellectual rigor and an ability to sort through and come to terms with all kinds of conceptual and methodological ambiguities. We are all familiar with the "wonder student" who has boundless energy as she devours bodies of literature, publishes at (or beyond) the rate of her professors, and still manages to read all of her course materials. But such students are far from the norm. I assume that the majority of clinical psychology graduate students do not have, or are unable to make, the time necessary to really get into their research. Instead, they manage to insert isolated chunks of "reading articles" in between therapy sessions, supervision, course work, and teaching or research assistantships. As a result, many students move through their research with a chronic sense of insecurity and of being an impostor because they have not spent the time necessary to integrate and come to terms with the many loose ends and contradictions common to clinical research. Of course, the tension between research and clinical demands is not the only reason graduate students are stressed. Financial strains, relationship problems, and the constant ambiguity of being a student and a semiprofessional at the same time contribute as well. But these problems are more often discussed, perhaps because they are common to nonclinical students as well as to medical residents and interns. The specific tensions between research and clinical work are more rarely discussed.

A Tension in Identity and Career Choice Between Research and Clinical Practice

First-year Boulder model graduate students quickly figure out what kinds of self-presentations and career goals are rewarded by faculty. Put simply, academic careers are at the top of the ladder, and full-time clinical work is typically discouraged. The value system may be explicit in discussions between faculty and graduate students, or it may be more of an unspoken assumption. For example, if you were to ask a large sample of PhD students in scientist–practitioner programs, "which would likely bring you more praise from your faculty, publishing a paper in a midlevel journal, or completing a year-long training in empirically based treatment for personality disorders?" I suspect the results would favor the former. In my own training, faculty were often concerned about students who spent too much time in clinical training at the expense of their research. Although it may well have occurred, I never heard of a student who was negatively evaluated for spending too much time on research.

Of course, the differential value placed on science versus practice in training is not some kind of secret bylaw. Programs are quite direct in labeling themselves as scientist (first) and practitioner (second) in orientation, and the majority of them are very serious about offering high-quality clinical training. I believe my own clinical training was of a very high quality. My concern is with the trickle-down effects on students of the subtle devaluation of clinical work. My sense is that despite the best efforts of many programs, trainees quickly feel a pressure to choose between an academic career and a purely clinical one. Why is this a problem? First, students often feel pressured to choose between alternatives that don't accurately reflect the diversity of careers involving both clinical work and research. At one extreme are academic faculty members who seem overworked and under immense pressure to "publish or perish." At the other extreme are clinicians working in private practice or in the public sector, most of whom neither produce nor consume any clinical research. We can all think of people who fall somewhere between these two extremes. But in my own training, and in subsequent conversations with graduate students I supervise, these gray areas appear mysteriously lost. Instead, research becomes synonymous with tenure-track academia, and clinical work with full-time private, HMO, or public sector practice. Those who have successfully integrated research, clinical work, and their personal lives may know that it is indeed possible, but students still operate from perceptions and future expectations based largely in an academia–clinical practice dichotomy.

The second danger is that students will prematurely disregard a career involving research because of a perceived inability or unwillingness to manage the associated personal and professional demands. I have often heard students say things like, "I look at Dr. X and I know I don't want a life like that." It is already difficult enough for trainees to feel passionate about and competent in clinical research. When research then becomes associated with a future of stress, cardiac problems, and failed relationships, many students develop a strong fear of such careers. These same students must then continue research for their master's and doctoral degrees. What follows is a stressful period of "faking" an interest in research and doing the minimum necessary to mollify advisors and committee members. There are obviously all kinds of reasons why a student ends up going down this path. My argument here is that early pressure to choose between research and clinical practice does not make the situation better, and probably makes it worse. How many students who ran from research careers early in graduate training may ultimately have developed a natural curiosity and desire to integrate science and practice?

RECOMMENDATIONS

It may seem like I have a rather bleak outlook on the possibility of successfully managing the tensions between research and clinical work in graduate training. This is certainly not my belief. Rather, I've tried to get some important issues out on the table for consideration. As psychologists, we need to take a hard and honest look at the actual experience of our trainees vis-à-vis clinical work and research. Integrating research and clinical work is something a person does. Like all actions, its form and effectiveness evolve differently depending on each individual and his or her unique history. Graduate school is a crucial part of that history because the very behaviors we are interested in begin to take shape in that context. Thus, we need to examine the process closely from the student's perspective. As that has been my goal, I'd like to end by offering a few suggestions for places to start.

1. *Discuss directly the tension between research and clinical work in all its manifestations.* There is nothing like direct open discussion to ease conflict around inevitable tensions. It would be a great service to our students to initiate and maintain such discussions about the relationship between research and practice. Case presentations, for example, could allow those faculty engaged in clinical work to discuss those aspects of their work that are guided by research data *and those that are not.* Students should similarly be encouraged to identify dilemmas in their own clinical work that may or may not be helped by available empirical data. Faculty also need to recognize and explicitly discuss the difficulties in being an empirically ori-

ented clinician. How do we cope with the inevitable lack of information, the need to make clinical decisions in the absence of data, and the need to consider the power of actuarial data versus the apparent uniqueness of individual cases? Numerous political and economic factors also make the research–practice integration difficult. These include increasingly rigid licensing requirements, managed care settings requiring excessive patient contact quotas, and the increased difficulty of obtaining research funds. Without discussing such difficulties, students end up measuring their own uncertainty and confusion against a nonexistent idealized empirically based clinician whose every intervention and decision is rooted in firm scientific ground.

2. *Describe and provide models of a wider variety of successful integrations of research and practice.* Ironically, many students enter PhD programs expressing a future goal of integrating research and practice but somehow this gets lost over the course of their education. Too many Boulder model students view their career options dichotomously: They will either work in academia or in clinical practice. I suspect that the narrowing of career options has mostly to do with the limited available role models in graduate education. The most powerful figures are full-time academics who typically want their students to follow in their footsteps. If a student is ambivalent about academia, he or she may look to clinical supervisors in the community who are not typically involved in research. With only two models, many students eventually become worried when they hear that "clinical practice is dying" and wish neither to publish nor to perish in the halls of academia.

Despite the many problems of managed care and health care reform, the field is changing in ways that offer many more possible integrations of research and clinical practice than existed previously. Doctoral-level psychologists in clinical settings are increasingly being called on to supervise and treat difficult cases, to train clinicians, and to conduct evaluation research. Although these changes are unsettling, they provide new opportunities to integrate research and practice. Because most of us in academia are not out in the real world navigating these changes, we cannot provide role models for students. In my own department, we provide monthly clinical workshops in which we bring in people from the community engaged in both research and clinical work, whether it be in managed care, medical schools, or other professional settings. One hopes that students are seeing that although they may not choose a traditional academic job, they can still conduct research in applied settings.

3. *Emphasize the empirical basis of nonspecific factors in psychotherapy during training.* There is ample evidence that a range of nonspecific factors are associated with positive outcomes in psychotherapy (Horvath & Symonds, 1991; Ilardi & Craighead, 1994; Lambert & Bergin, 1994). These factors include the therapeutic relationship, expectations for change, client

success experiences in psychotherapy, and provision of a treatment rationale. In my experience, although it has often been discussed, research supporting the importance of these variables has been underused in graduate training. Most students are aware of the research supporting the so-called dodo bird verdict in psychotherapy and its implication that specific techniques or schools are not responsible for therapeutic change. But such research is typically presented as a reason to question the scientific basis of psychotherapy rather than as a support for certain interventions. In reality, it is both, and my view is that we should emphasize the latter. For example, there is a difference between a student thinking "all I'm doing is providing a supportive relationship to this client" and "I'm trying to create the kind of relationship with this client that I know, on the basis of empirical data, is associated with successful treatment outcomes." The former type of thinking will probably be associated with skepticism. The latter provides confidence and support for the trainee's intervention, even if it is "only" providing a supportive relationship to the client.

CONCLUSION

I have tried in this chapter to outline some of the psychological experiences that shape Boulder model graduate students toward integrating or segregating research and clinical work. Empirical research can be a comfort and a source of guidance to a student during clinical training. It can also be a source of frustration, anxiety, and paralysis when empirical values are strongly entrenched and no data are available to support a course of action. Such conflicts and tensions need to be addressed openly and directly in graduate training. A trainee's experiences of research and clinical intervention are enormously different. Students, like all people, will gravitate toward one or the other, depending on their degree of interest and success in either. Faculty need to approach the students' process not from an idealized construction of the ultimate scientist–practitioner but from a realistic appraisal of the psychological and practical difficulty of integrating research and practice. This recognition and acceptance will help to model attainable integrations and to deter unnecessary and premature dichotomizing of clinical and empirical pursuits.

REFERENCES

Barlow, D. H. (1981). On the relation of clinical research to clinical practice: Current issues, new directions. *Journal of Consulting and Clinical Psychology, 49*, 147–155.

Barlow, D. H., Hayes, S. C., & Nelson, R. O. (1984). *The scientist practitioner:*

research and accountability in clinical and educational settings. New York: Pergamon Press.

Beutler, L. E., Williams, R. E., Wakefield, P. J., & Entwhistle, S. R. (1995). Bridging scientist and practitioner perspectives in clinical psychology. *American Psychologist, 50*, 984–994.

Christensen, A., & Jacobson, N. S. (1993). Who (or what) can do psychotherapy: The status and challenge of nonprofessional therapies. *Psychological Science, 5*, 8–14.

Dawes, R. M. (1994). *House of cards: Psychology and psychotherapy built on myth.* New York: Free Press.

Frank, J. D. (1973). *Persuasion and healing: A comparative study of psychotherapy,* (2nd ed.). Baltimore: Johns Hopkins University Press.

Goldfried, M. R. (1984). Training the clinician as scientist–professional. *Professional Psychology: Research and Practice, 15*, 477–481.

Horvath, A. O., & Symonds, B. D. (1991). Relation between working alliance and outcome in psychotherapy: A meta-analysis. *Journal of Counseling Psychology, 38*, 139–149.

Ilardi, S. S., & Craighead, W. E. (1994). The role of nonspecific factors in cognitive-behavior therapy for depression. *Clinical Psychology Science and Practice, 1*, 138–156.

Lambert, M. J., & Bergin, A. E. (1994). The effectiveness of psychotherapy. In A. E. Bergin & S. L. Garfield, (Eds.), *Handbook of psychotherapy and behavior change* (4th ed., pp. 143–189). New York: Wiley.

Linehan, M. M. (1993). *Cognitive behavioral treatment of borderline personality disorder.* New York: Guilford Press.

Linehan, M. M., Armstrong, H. E., Suarez, A., Allmon, D., & Heard, H. L. (1991). Cognitive–behavioral treatment of parasuicidal borderline patients. *Archives of General Psychiatry, 48*, 1060–1064.

Linehan, M. M., Heard, H. L., & Armstrong, H. E. (1993). Naturalistic follow-up of a behavioral treatment for chronically parasuicidal borderline patients. *Archives of General Psychiatry, 50*, 971–974.

Nhat Hanh, T. (1987). *The miracle of mindfulness: A manual on meditation.* Boston: Beacon Press.

Persons, J. B. (1991). Psychotherapy outcome studies do not accurately represent current models of psychotherapy: A proposed remedy. *American Psychologist, 46*, 99–106.

Persons, J. B., & Silberschatz, G. (1998). Are results of randomized controlled trials useful to psychotherapists? *Journal of Consulting and Clinical Psychology, 66*, 126–135.

Peterson, D. R. (1995). The reflective educator. *American Psychologist, 50*, 975–983.

Sargent, M., & Cohen, L. (1983). Influence of psychotherapy research on clinical practice: An experimental survey. *Journal of Consulting and Clinical Psychology, 51*, 718–720.

4

A HARMONIOUS MARRIAGE: PERSONAL REFLECTIONS ON 25 YEARS OF RESEARCH AND THERAPEUTIC PRACTICE IN A NATIONAL HEALTH SERVICE SETTING

DAVID A. WINTER

John had increasingly presented himself in therapy as a man not to be meddled with. This culminated in a session in which he opened his jacket to reveal a holster containing a pistol.

* * *

Mandy consistently ignored my telling her that her therapy session had come to an end. My opening the office door made little impression on her, and even if, exasperated, I left the office she would generally not leave for some considerable time.

* * *

Julie attended therapy religiously, but in her sessions, she sat gazing at the floor and saying barely a word. When given homework tasks, she never completed them.

* * *

Philip attributed his depression to a belief that his tragic history had
left him with life circumstances that allowed little prospect of fulfilling
his potential. His degree of social and financial deprivation was such
that it was difficult not to share this belief, and his pessimism regarding
the likely benefits of psychotherapy.

* * *

Albert sought help for his fears of hell. However, in therapy sessions,
he would talk about little other than Bing Crosby!

These are just some of the problems with which my clients have
presented me. Every psychotherapist will be able to produce a similar list
of situations, many of which appear to demand an intervention but in
which he or she feels at a loss as to exactly how to intervene. Would that
a catalogue of research findings were available to help us select our approach in such cases! That this is not so is in part because such findings,
even when of some relevance to the specific problems that our clients pose,
are inevitably generalizations that may be difficult to apply in the immediacy of the therapy relationship in a particular case. However, this is not
to say that I find research to be irrelevant to my clinical practice; indeed,
my entire career has involved a generally harmonious marriage of these
two activities. A particularly formative influence was the fact that when,
in the early 1970s, I obtained my first job as a clinical psychologist, I was
fortunate that this was in a psychology department that was attached to a
psychotherapy clinic and that also had a long research tradition. My wish
to register for a PhD was fully supported by the head of department, Tom
Caine, and his successor, Brian Wijesinghe; I found myself with a satisfying
blend of work, spending about half of my time practicing therapy and the
other half contributing to a research program on selection criteria for alternative therapeutic approaches. I felt that both of these areas of work
raised interesting questions about the other, and this experience of cross-
fertilization of research and clinical practice was influential in shaping my
future approach to the two activities.

Equally influential has been my allegiance, also dating back to the
early 1970s, to personal construct theory. George Kelly (1955) viewed people as operating much like scientists in that they constantly formulate, test,
and if necessary revise, hypotheses. Because therapists are no exception to
this, personal construct psychotherapists might be expected to make no
major distinction between therapeutic practice and research. This is certainly so in my case. For me every therapy session involves experimentation, the results of which may have implications for my approach not only
to the client in question but also for that to subsequent clients.

EXAMPLES OF RESEARCH WITH RELEVANCE TO CLINICAL PRACTICE

In an attempt to illustrate the relevance of research to clinical practice, I shall now consider a few of the projects in which I have been involved.

Personal Styles and Therapeutic Outcome

The psychology department in which I obtained that first job was situated in a psychiatric hospital that, in the early 1960s, had opened one of the first therapeutic community units in the British National Health Service. This development aroused strong feelings among the hospital staff, who divided into two camps: those who championed the new approach and those who, with equal conviction, resisted it with such intensity that it was eventually virtually abandoned. To explore this conflict, Caine and Smail (1969) constructed a questionnaire that assessed staff attitudes to treatment on a medical–psychosocial dimension and that differentiated between staff working in different treatment settings. Staff favoring a traditional, medical treatment approach were found to be conservative in their social attitudes and outer directed, as opposed to those favoring a psychosocial approach, who tended to hold radical social attitudes and to be predominantly concerned with their inner worlds. In other words, the preferences of these staff for different types of psychiatric treatment appeared to be based not on scientific considerations but on these individuals' "personal styles": core beliefs, values, and strategies (Caine, Wijesinghe, & Winter, 1981). Hence, some staff members experienced threat when confronted with a new treatment approach that was inconsistent with their personal styles.

The adoption of this perspective, and its associated research methodology, enabled me in the clinical setting where I now work to understand a similar conflict between proponents of a 24-hour crisis intervention service, which views problems in terms of family systems rather than of individual pathology, and staff working in a more traditional manner. These two sets of staff were found to differ in terms of personal styles, which were again found to be related to attitudes to treatment (Winter et al., 1987).

However, in terms of implications for clinical practice, the most significant findings of this research program emerged when clients' expectancies of, and responses to, treatment were investigated. Here, as with staff, clients' preferences for different types of treatment were found to reflect their personal styles. In addition, clients' personal styles appeared to be expressed in the types of symptoms that they presented. Specifically, outer-directed, conservative clients tended to present symptoms—such as phobias, obsessions, and somatic complaints—with a circumscribed external locus, whereas inner-directed, more radical clients tended to present more diffuse symptoms, such as interpersonal difficulties or free-floating anxiety.

A central aspect of individuals' personal styles in all of these investigations appeared to be the extent to which they were predominantly concerned with internal or external aspects of their world (Caine et al., 1981). Therapies may also be differentiated in terms of this internal–external dimension, as in Rychlak's (1968) distinction between *introspective* and *extraspective* approaches, the former tending to focus more on the client's personal constructs and to be less structured and directive than the latter. Therefore, a service was examined in which most clients were allocated either to an introspective approach, group analysis, or to an extraspective approach, behavior therapy. It was found that inner-directed, radical clients were more likely to be allocated to, and to respond to, the former approach and outer-directed, conservative clients to the latter. In one study, which must count as the peak of my psychotherapy research career, our measures of personal style were able to predict with 100% accuracy the classification of clients as *improvers* or *nonimprovers* in group analytic psychotherapy. Improvers in group analytic and behavior therapy were also found to be differentiated by responses to a repertory grid, a method of assessing the system of constructs used by an individual to anticipate his or her world. Specifically, those who improved in behavior therapy had significantly tighter (i.e., more rigid), more logically consistent construct systems, in which their symptoms carried more implications, than did improvers in group psychotherapy (Winter, 1983).

A limitation of these early studies of clients was that the treatments we examined differed not only on the introspective–extraspective dimension, but also on the group–individual dimension. Accordingly, in subsequent research, we have examined an individual introspective form of treatment, personal construct psychotherapy, and a group extraspective approach, social skills training. Sue Watson's study of personal construct psychotherapy has indicated that in inner-directed clients, the therapeutic process is more facilitative, as reflected in measures of the therapeutic relationship and of clients' perceptual processing (Winter & Watson, 1995). Although these results were as predicted, those of the study of social skills training were not, in that inner-directedness was highly predictive of a positive treatment outcome (Winter, 1988a). In an attempt to explain this finding, I examined clients' responses to interviews concerning their perceptions of the principal therapeutic ingredients of their groups and was intrigued to discover that not one client mentioned training in social skills as such an ingredient! For the vast majority, the most beneficial aspect of the groups was the opportunity to find that they were not unique, or to use Yalom's (1970) term, the experience of universality. If universality is an active ingredient of group therapies whatever their theoretical basis, it may be that inner directedness predicts response to such approaches because, as research has shown, it is associated with the ability to share the perspectives of other group members (Smail, 1972; Wood, 1977). However, perhaps a more important message from this study, also reflected in the findings of other therapy process investigations (Lambert & Hill, 1994), is that the clients' perceptions of their therapy may be very different from those of the therapist or researcher.

Therapy outcome research generally, including my own comparative outcome studies of personal construct and alternative forms of therapy, tends to suggest that although the Dodo bird may be long extinct, its verdict in *Alice in Wonderland*, famously quoted by Luborsky, Singer, and Luborsky (1975, p. 995), is alive and well in that it still seems that "everybody has won and all must have prizes." However, studies such as those in the research program described here indicate that overall similarities in the outcomes of different types of therapy mask differences in outcomes with particular types of clients. Research that delineates these differences can have a significant impact on the clinician's selection of treatment approaches for his or her clients.

Specifically, the so-called personal styles research program, which has been extended in several further studies (Caine & Winter, 1993; Winter, 1990), has provided a framework for the matching of clients, therapists, and therapeutic approaches. Its implication for my own clinical practice is that if I consider (perhaps on the basis of assessment with the measures used in this research) that my client is outer-directed, conservative, and a tight construer, I shall be likely to adopt a structured, directive approach, at least in the initial stages of therapy. I shall assume that if I do not do so, the client is likely either to drop out of therapy or to show little response to it. Conversely, with an inner-directed, more radically oriented client, who construes more loosely, I shall in most cases initially adopt an introspective, less structured approach and might consider allocation of the client to a therapy group. In the broader context of a treatment service using a number of therapists, clients might be allocated to therapists on the basis of congruence in their personal styles (Winter, 1985).

A Personal Construct Theory Perspective on Agoraphobia and Its Treatment

One of the most common presenting problems of clients referred to my department is agoraphobia. When I joined the department, behavior therapy involving graduated exposure was regarded as the treatment of choice for this condition and was the subject of research investigation by Kevin Gournay. He was open to the incorporation of the repertory grid technique in this research in an attempt to identify features of construing characteristic of agoraphobia, as well as changes in these areas over the course of therapy.

From the perspective of personal construct theory, agoraphobia may be considered a strategy in which a person constricts his or her world to avoid events that are anxiety provoking by virtue of their unpredictability. Our research gave an indication of the nature of these anxiety-provoking events in that it provided evidence that clients suffering from agoraphobias and their spouses tend not to perceive others in such terms as angry, selfish, jealous, and uncaring (Winter, 1989; Winter & Gournay, 1987). This suggested that constructs concerning interpersonal conflict were at a low level of cognitive awareness in such clients and that situations involving conflict with others might therefore be particularly anxiety-provoking for them.

However, marital infidelity was found to be a very salient construct in these clients and their spouses, particularly when the phobic symptoms were very severe. There was also some indication that the ability to go out was associated by the clients with agoraphobia with the risk of infidelity. Apart from this implication, both agoraphobic clients and their spouses held a very idealistic view of the ability to go out, anticipating that they would each become more similar to their ideal selves than they had ever been if only the client could go out. It was apparent in this study that the agoraphobics and their spouses viewed the world in a very similar way, and, indeed, the greater this similarity the less likely was the agoraphobic to go out of the house. Agoraphobics symptoms essentially allowed clients' interpersonal worlds to be delimited to spouses with very similar construct systems, who would therefore be a constant source of validation. The spouses in these studies, who were not agoraphobic themselves, appeared able to maintain a construction of their own strength by contrasting this with their partners' perceived weakness.

Several of the grid measures that we used were predictive of the response of individuals with agoraphobia to behavior therapy. For example, a good outcome was less likely if infidelity was a salient issue for the agoraphobic or for his or her spouse, and more likely if anger was salient for the agoraphobic client. There was also evidence that improvement during therapy was associated with changes in the construing of both the agoraphobic client and the spouse.

The results of Gournay's (1989) research indicated that behavior therapy may not be, as once thought, the treatment of choice for agoraphobia, at least if used as the sole treatment method. In fact, 44% of clients in this study were classified as treatment failures. This raised the question of whether a more effective treatment approach might combine exposure with a focus on the above-mentioned aspects of construing that we had associated with agoraphobia. The method that was devised used the interpersonal transaction group (Landfield & Rivers, 1975), in which clients engage in brief interactions with each member of the group on themes supplied by the therapist, followed by a plenary discussion of these inter-actions. The themes chosen were issues that the repertory grid study had found to be relevant, namely situations involving interpersonal conflict (with the aim of elaborating clients' construing of conflict); advantages and disadvantages of the ability to go out and independence (with the aim of addressing some of the perceived disadvantages); and the self without agoraphobia (with the aim of developing a viable construction of a non-phobic self). Because our research had indicated the possible role of the agoraphobic client's spouse in the maintenance of the phobic symptoms, the treatment approach also involved the inclusion of spouses in some sessions.

In our present research, this treatment method, coupled with expo-sure, is being compared with a combination of exposure and a supportive interpersonal transaction group method in which the themes (e.g., "situ-ations in which I do, and those in which I do not, experience phobic anxieties") do not focus on the aspects of construing considered pertinent to the maintenance of agoraphobia. Clients' experiences of these two types of group have been found to differ, with the personal construct groups being characterized by a climate of less avoidance of problems and greater smoothness. Events involving self-understanding were more often seen by clients as important in these groups (Winter, 1997). Preliminary results have also indicated that clients attending personal construct groups show greater reduction in panic frequency and in trait anxiety than do those attending supportive groups.

The results of our initial study not only have allowed a new group treatment method to be developed for agoraphobics but also have influ-enced my approach to individual therapy with agoraphobic clients. In par-ticular, I now tend to focus more on the agoraphobic's approach to situa-tions of interpersonal conflict and to involve the spouse in therapy whenever possible.

Construing and Rehabilitation in Clients Diagnosed With Schizophrenia

My first venture into clinical research was as an undergraduate in-spired by Don Bannister's (1960, 1962) repertory grid investigations of thought-disordered schizophrenic clients. Bannister had found the con-struct systems of such clients to be loosely organized and, therefore, not to provide them with a firm basis for predicting their worlds. In my study, although this was so when chronic schizophrenic clients were asked to use the constructs with which Bannister had supplied his participants, when they used their own constructs, their construing was no less tightly struc-tured than that of control participants (Winter, 1971). Their personal con-structs, although often idiosyncratic and in some cases expressed in neologisms, did allow them to make predictions about the world. This finding was replicated in a study in which I also found the construct systems of the parents of individuals with schizophrenia showed similar characteristics to those of their schizophrenic offspring (Winter, 1975).

Some 15 years later, I again explored the construing of schizophrenic clients; in this case the population was the long-stay residents of a psychiatric hospital who had been referred to a rehabilitation and resettlement program (Winter, Baker, & Goggins, 1992; Winter, Goggins, Baker, & Metcalfe, 1996). These studies demonstrated that clients were less likely to feel able to leave the hospital, and to survive in the community once discharged, if their construing of the world outside the hospital was relatively poorly structured, as compared with their construing of the world within it, and if they used few constructs concerning people's psychological characteristics. For such clients, the social world beyond the hospital gates would most likely be very unpredictable, and thus anxiety-provoking, as Kelly (1955) defined this concept. Consistent with this view was the finding that an interview measure of Kellyan anxiety was also predictive of failure to be succesfully resettled in the community.

For me, a major implication of these studies and their relevance to psychotherapy was that they demonstrated the importance of exploring, and taking seriously, the view of the world of the person diagnosed with schizophrenia. Rehabilitation programs for long-stay psychiatric inpatients traditionally focus on areas deemed essential by mental health workers—such as domestic and self-care skills—but these skills had no value in predicting the success of resettlement in our study. Indeed, it was apparent that these programs are viewed as demeaning, or at best irrelevant, by many clients; for example, one said that the staff are "telling you stupid things like how to cook, how much to spend on cooking for a 30-year-old and a 50-year-old . . . how to clean" (Winter et al., 1996, p. 263). What they might prefer was eloquently expressed by another client, who said that

> I would like to have discussions with someone where I could talk about my reality, where it would not be denied, where there would not be any talk of madness, where my reality would be appreciated and understood. It is a terrific burden keeping this reality to myself. (Winter et al., 1996, p. 263)

Psychotherapy of the type described by this client may well be more appropriate than current rehabilitation regimes, as may approaches that focus on developing a system of constructs that will enable clients to anticipate life in the community. My colleagues and I are, therefore, hoping to develop and to evaluate the effectiveness of such approaches.

Psychotherapy as Research With the Individual Client

Rodney's presenting problem was that he had never been able to ejaculate, except in nocturnal emissions. As we discussed his past, it became increasingly apparent that his childhood relationship with his mother may have been relevant to this problem. He described her as hypochondriacal and as consequently making numerous demands on him, many of which he now saw as thinly veiled sexual advances. She also exhorted him to "do everything for others but do not love yourself" and, not insignificantly in view of his presenting problem, that "you yourself must always come last." The hypothesis that he might experience particular difficulties in relationships in which he construed the women concerned as similar to his mother received some support when we completed a repertory grid. Included in this grid were two women with whom he had had a sexual relationship and another two with whom, despite his sexual attraction to them, the relationship had, inexplicably to him, remained platonic. Results of the repertory grid indicated that the latter two women were perceived as very much more similar to his mother than were the former two. Both this grid and a further type, an implications grid, revealed that sexual responsiveness carried several negative implications for Rodney, for example, that it involved "playing games based on sexuality" and "having a deceptive method of getting others to do things," both characteristics that he attributed to his mother. These findings provided support for the use in therapy of Kelly's (1955) time-binding technique, in which constructs that had served a purpose in anticipating his mother's behavior, and in particular her sexuality, were "bound" to those early experiences of his relationship with her, thereby freeing him to develop new constructs to apply to his adult sexual relationships.

Rodney and I also completed another repertory grid in which he was asked to consider a series of sexual situations. Its results indicated that he viewed sexual situations that he "desired to achieve" as associated with fear, uneasiness, unreality, and as something he shies away from. As we have seen in the two previous examples, from a personal construct theory perspective, anxiety is experienced when one's construct system is ill equipped to enable one to predict one's world. It therefore seemed that Rodney might have a poorly elaborated system of constructs concerning sexual situations, and, consequently, he would experience anxiety in such situations. He had been asked to rate on a daily basis the frequency of his sexual urges, and I hypothesized that this would be inversely correlated with his anxiety, as defined in personal construct theory terms. Such anxiety was measured by a scale devised by Viney and Westbrook (1976), which was applied to audiotapes of his treatment sessions. Contrary to predictions, there was no relationship between the anxiety expressed in treatment sessions and the number of sexual urges in the weeks prior to sessions. However, on examining the data further, it was apparent that the level of anxiety in sessions was significantly negatively correlated with the number of sexual urges in the weeks following sessions. In other words, when he expressed difficulty in anticipating experiences in therapy, he was less likely to feel sexually aroused the following week. This suggested that he was using a strategy of constriction, delimiting his world to exclude situations of sexual arousal at times when he might have difficulty in construing such situations, which would thus have provoked anxiety. One of the treatment approaches adopted, therefore, was to attempt to elaborate his subsystem of sexual constructs by, for example, homework assignments involving exploring his bodily sensations, which were then discussed in therapy sessions.

The results of Rodney's therapeutic experiment proved successful in that after 16 sessions, he reported that he had masturbated to orgasm for the first time in the 35 years of his life. Corresponding changes in his construing were reflected in his repertory grid scores (Winter, 1988b).

THE VALIDATIONS AND INVALIDATIONS OF PSYCHOTHERAPY RESEARCH

That early finding from the "personal styles" research of 100% success in the prediction of clients' response to group analytic psychotherapy led me to anticipate a future rich with significant findings. However, the subsequent 20 or so years of my research career have occasionally been a vain quest for p values that even remotely approached .05. Such statistical wizardry as analysis of covariance and exclusion of outliers has scarcely enhanced these significance levels. This has particularly been the case when the studies concerned have involved the comparison of alternative therapeutic approaches, perhaps because there is now much greater commonality between different forms of therapy than at the time of commencement of the personal styles research program.

In therapy, the constant validation of the client's view of the world, although making him or her feel supported, will be unlikely to produce any fundamental change in the client's construing. Rather, successful therapy, in my view, involves a delicate balance of experiences of validation and invalidation. This is also the case in research, in which, although every researcher's dream is that results will support their hypotheses, as they so strikingly did in the personal styles research, it is from the rejection of these hypotheses that developments in the researcher's theory are most likely to ensue. For me, the experience of carrying out research on therapy has provided enough validation that I have persevered despite the occasional invalidation. The invalidations have in most cases provided the basis for developing new hypotheses and, in some instances, new research projects.

All of the studies and the various other research projects in which I have been involved, have been conducted in a national health service setting. This has led to numerous frustrations and imperfections, at least from the perspective of conventional standards of research design. Thus, samples have often been very heterogeneous, it has not been possible in most cases for therapies to be conducted in terms of neatly packaged contracts, and it has generally been difficult to control other relevant variables (e.g., clients' medication). Therapists have sometimes required considerable persuasion to allow their treatments to be investigated, and if I were a psychoanalyst, the numerous cases of audio- or videorecorder malfunction or of forgetting to carry out research procedures would provide abundant material for interpretation. The length of waiting lists has often reduced clients' motivation to participate in research, although it has, of course, facilitated the use of waiting-list control groups!

Despite such frustrations, I believe that the experience of carrying out investigations in the "real world" of the National Health Service, rather than on highly selected samples in a setting specifically designed for research, has reinforced my view of the relevance of research to therapeutic practice. Also significant in reinforcing this view has been the use in my research, and increasingly in psychotherapy research in general, of measures that are not far removed from the client's and the therapist's experience of their worlds and of therapy. Such methods include those that examine the personal meaning of events for client or therapist and those that allow intensive analysis of the therapeutic process.

A further valuable opportunity provided by the setting in which I work has been the sheer range of clients and therapies that are available for research investigation. Although occasionally I have been able to follow through programs of research, as in the studies of personal styles and agoraphobia, more usually my research activity has involved investigating on a shorter term basis whichever client groups were being treated in the settings concerned. As well as those in the projects described above, these client groups have included clients with depression in group therapy; police officers in therapy for posttraumatic stress disorder; brain-injured people undergoing rehabilitation; clients with schizophrenia in family therapy; those referred to a pain relief clinic; and those who deliberately harm themselves, who are being treated by personal construct psychotherapy. Although such research may appear to have a somewhat opportunistic flavor, rather than involving the systematic and dogged pursuit of some particular research question, the projects concerned have, in fact, shared the common thread of exploring the clinical use of personal construct theory. Not only have they provided me with considerable evidence of the applicability of this theory to the understanding of a very diverse range of clinical problems but, more generally, they have also invariably shown me the value of conducting research on the problems and therapies concerned. In not one of these studies has the research investigation failed to provide at least some results with implications for therapeutic practice.

This does not necessarily mean, however, that clinical practice has in every case been modified to take into account the research findings concerned. In some instances, this has been due to the constraints of the health service setting. For example, while in the department of which I am head, I would ideally wish to allocate clients to therapists on the basis of their personal styles; however, when a client has been waiting approximately a year before reaching the top of the list, there is little option but to allocate him or her to whichever therapist has a vacancy. In other instances, the primary factor hindering the implementation of changes in practice suggested by research findings has been the resistance of therapists to such change. The extent of this resistance is indicated by the fact that it is even present when the therapist is also the researcher! For example, although the personal styles research indicates that it may be useful to incorporate the treatment selection battery developed in this research in every therapy assessment interview, I rarely do so. My interpretation of my own paradoxical behavior is that, having completed clinical psychology training at a time and in a setting in which routine psychometric assessment of clients was the norm, seemingly regardless of whether this had any clinical use, I am reluctant to engage in any procedure that smacks of such a mechanistic approach to clients.

The English National Health Service Executive (1996) now advises purchasers of health care that they "need to take account of the strength of scientific evidence . . . about clinical practices and cost effectiveness when making investments in new and existing services" (p. 5). Just as in the United States (Barlow, 1996), psychotherapy in the United Kingdom has not been exempt from the requirement for the development of "evidence-based practice." Indeed, with a view to facilitating such practice, the National Health Service Executive commissioned a review of research on the efficacy and effectiveness of psychotherapy. This review (Roth & Fonagy, 1996) has identified some therapeutic approaches for which there is clear evidence of efficacy with particular diagnostic groups. However, the resulting report cautions against an overprescriptive, cookbook approach to planning and purchasing based on such findings because this might stifle innovations and developments in therapy and because "the absence of evidence for efficacy is not evidence for ineffectiveness" (p. 44) in the case of relatively underresearched treatments. The report also provides an indictment of much psychotherapy research in that it has sacrificed external validity in its attempt to maximize internal validity. As Roth and Fonagy concluded, "most of the trials are unrepresentative of clinical practice, and they cannot be considered to guarantee the effectiveness of the same treatments in the framework of everyday service provision" (p. 372). In view of such considerations, the National Health Service Executive has decided that "it would be premature and unjustified to imagine that certain treatments have been 'validated'" and "will not therefore publish a list of 'effective' therapies on which funding decisions should be based" (Parry & Richardson, 1996, p. 42). Instead, it points out that there is an "urgent need" for further research, particularly on the clinical effectiveness of psychodynamic and eclectic therapies, and indeed that "it is unacceptable for the NHS to continue to provide any therapy or service which declines to subject itself to research evaluation" (p. 43).

As a practitioner of a form of therapy that has not as yet figured prominently in meta-analyses of the psychotherapy research literature, it was with some trepidation that I began to read the recommendations of the National Health Service Executive. My considered reaction to the recommendations is "Phew!" They support not only the continued provision in the National Health Service of a range of psychological therapies, unless these are clearly shown to be ineffective but also an increase in research in naturalistic settings on therapies such as that which I practice.

At about the same time as the National Health Service review of psychotherapy services landed on my desk (when this chapter was half written), so did an invitation to a party to commemorating the closure and impending demolition of the building housing the psychotherapy clinic in which I obtained that first clinical post. I will be very sad to see the arrival of bulldozers in this tranquil, wooded setting that over the years has witnessed so much innovative cross-fertilization between research and psychotherapeutic practice. However, National Health Service policies of community care for mental health problems, requiring the closure of psychiatric hospitals, are no respecters of old buildings and sentimentalities. Thankfully, a similarly bulldozing approach has not been applied by this same health service in reviewing its psychotherapy services. With luck the review might even give me the leeway to see out the remainder of my working life, researching and practicing personal construct psychotherapy in the National Health Service!

REFERENCES

Bannister, D. (1960). Conceptual structure in thought-disordered schizophrenics. *Journal of Mental Science, 106,* 1230–1249.

Bannister, D. (1962). The nature and measurement of schizophrenic thought disorder. *Journal of Mental Science, 108,* 825–842.

Barlow, D. H. (1996). Health care policy, psychotherapy research, and the future of psychotherapy. *American Psychologist, 51,* 1050–1058.

Caine, T. M., & Smail, D. J. (1969). *The treatment of mental illness: Science, faith and the therapeutic personality.* London: University of London Press.

Caine, T. M., Wijesinghe, O. B. A., & Winter, D. A. (1981). *Personal styles in neurosis: Implications for small group psychotherapy and behaviour therapy.* London: Routledge & Kegan Paul.

Caine, T. M., & Winter, D. A. (1993). Personal styles and universal polarities. *International Journal of Therapeutic Communities, 14,* 91–102.

Gournay, K. (1989). Failures in the behavioural treatment of agoraphobia. In K. Gournay (Ed.), *Agoraphobia: Current perspectives on theory and treatment* (pp. 120–139). London: Routledge.

Kelly, G. A. (1955). *The psychology of personal constructs.* New York: Norton.

Lambert, M. J., & Hill, C. E. (1994). Assessing psychotherapy outcomes and processes. In A. E. Bergin & S. L. Garfield (Eds.), *Handbook of psychotherapy and behavior change* (pp. 72–113). New York: Wiley.

Landfield, A. W., & Rivers, P.C. (1975). An introduction to interpersonal transaction and rotating dyads. *Psychotherapy: Theory, Research and Practice, 12,* 366–374.

Luborsky, L., Singer, B., & Luborsky, L. (1975). Comparative studies of psychotherapies: Is it true that "everybody has won and all must have prizes"? *Archives of General Psychiatry, 32,* 995–1008.

National Health Service Executive. (1996). *Promoting clinical effectiveness: A framework for action in and through the NHS.* London: Author.

Parry, G., & Richardon, A. (1996). *NHS psychotherapy services in England: Review of strategic policy.* London: National Health Service Executive.

Roth, A., & Fonagy, P. (1996). *What works for whom? A critical review of psychotherapy research.* New York: Guilford Press.

Rychlak, J. F. (1968). *A philosophy of science for personality theory.* Boston: Houghton Mifflin.

Smail, D. J. (1972). A grid measure of empathy in a therapeutic group. *British Journal of Medical Psychology, 45,* 165–169.

Viney, L. L., & Westbrook, M. T. (1976). Cognitive anxiety: A method of content analysis of verbal samples. *Journal of Personality Assessment, 40,* 140–150.

Winter, D. A. (1971). *The meaningfulness of personal and supplied constructs to chronic schizophrenics and normals.* Unpublished BSc dissertation, University of Durham, Durham, England.

Winter, D. A. (1975). Some characteristics of schizophrenics and their parents. *British Journal of Social and Clinical Psychology, 14,* 279–290.

Winter, D. A. (1983). Logical inconsistency in construct relationships: Conflict or complexity? *British Journal of Medical Psychology, 56,* 79–88.

Winter, D. A. (1985). Personal styles, constructive alternativism and the provision of a therapeutic service. *British Journal of Medical Psychology, 58,* 129–136.

Winter, D. A. (1988a). Constructions in social skills training. In F. Fransella & L.

Thomas (Eds.), *Experimenting with personal construct psychology* (pp. 342–356). London: Routledge and Kegan Paul.

Winter, D. A. (1988b). Reconstructing an erection and elaborating ejaculation: Personal construct theory perspectives on sex therapy. *International Journal of Personal Construct Psychology, 1,* 81–99.

Winter, D. A. (1989). An alternative construction of agoraphobia. In K. Gournay (Ed.), *Agoraphobia: Current perspectives on theory and treatment* (pp. 93–119). London: Routledge.

Winter, D. A. (1990). Therapeutic alternatives for psychological disorder: Personal construct psychology investigations in a health service setting. In G. J. Neimeyer & R. A. Neimeyer (Eds.), *Advances in personal construct psychology* (Vol. 1, pp. 89–116). Greenwich, CT: JAI Press.

Winter, D. A. (1997). Personal construct perspectives on group psychotherapy. In P. Denicolo & M. Pope (Eds.), *Sharing understanding and practice* (pp. 210–221). Farmborough, United Kingdom: EPCA Publications.

Winter, D., Baker, M., & Goggins, S. (1992). Into the unknown: Transitions in psychiatric services as construed by clients and staff. *International Journal of Personal Construct Psychology, 5,* 23–40.

Winter, D., Goggins, S., Baker, M., & Metcalfe, C. (1996). Into the community or back to the ward? Clients' construing as a predictor of the outcome of rehabilitation. In B. M. Walker, J. Costigan, L. L. Viney, & B. Warren (Eds.), *Personal construct theory: A psychology for the future* (pp. 253–270). Carlton South, Victoria, Australia: Australian Psychological Society.

Winter, D., & Gournay, K. (1987). Constriction and construction in agoraphobia. *British Journal of Medical Psychology, 60,* 233–244.

Winter, D. A., Shivakumar, H., Brown, R. J., Roitt, M., Drysdale, W. J., & Jones, S. (1987). Explorations of a crisis intervention service. *British Journal of Psychiatry, 151,* 341–348.

Winter, D., & Watson, S. (1995). *Personal construct psychotherapy and the cognitive therapies: Different in theory but can they be differentiated in practice?* Paper presented at the 11th International Congress on Personal Construct Psychology, Barcelona, Spain.

Wood, R. R. (1977). *Empathy and similarity of perception in a married couples' psychotherapy group: A repertory grid study.* Unpublished diplomate in clinical psychology dissertation, British Psychological Society, Leicester, England.

Yalom, I. D. (1970). *The theory and practice of group psychotherapy.* New York: Basic Books.

5

INTEGRATING RESEARCH AND PRACTICE IN PSYCHOTHERAPY

TIMOTHY ANDERSON

The gulf between research and practice has, in many respects, widened in recent years, as seen in the movement away from Boulder model graduate training, and is accompanied by an increasing belief that one must be exclusively devoted to either clinical practice or research. Although the dilemma between science and practice may also exist in other fields (Beutler, Williams, Wakefield, & Entwistle, 1995), familiar questions continue to be asked for which answers are not immediately forthcoming. Why do researchers continue to fill the professional journals with empirical research that seems to have little relevance for the practitioner? How can practitioners offer their services to the public without concern for applying the most current research of their profession (or worse, making "scientific" claims that are not based on empirical research)? Unfortunately, accusations and polemics have frequently replaced attempts to create open dialogue, contributing even further to the separation between research and practice.

In this chapter, I refer to a number of personal experiences as both a researcher and a practitioner to illustrate the extent of the gap between research and practice and to suggest some possible new directions for addressing this problem. My professional career has been largely devoted to understanding what skills are needed for the successful practice of psychotherapy, what requisite therapist attributes underlie competent performance, how to train others to attain these abilities, and how to detect individual variability in performance. These activities have demanded participation in both the research and practice ends of our profession, and have forced me to give serious consideration to how these activities might be better integrated. I begin this chapter by focusing on how the activities of research and practice, as they currently exist in our field, create and perpetuate isolation. I then consider how each activity has the potential to contribute to the advancement of the other. Finally, I discuss some promising avenues for the synthesis of research and practice.

INTEGRATING CLINICAL PRACTICE:
THE RESEARCHER'S DILEMMA

Assumptions about the separation of research and practice are common and often create the perception that it is not possible to dwell in both worlds. For example, when applying for my psychology internship, I had stated my long-term plan of being active both as a practitioner of psychotherapy and as a researcher in a department of psychology. During the internship, however, I directed all of my attention to clinical practice, and discussions with supervisors focused on the professional practice of psychotherapy. I once again became aware of the isolation within the worlds of research and practice when, a month into the internship, one of my primary supervisors seemed to question my devotion to the world of practice. He noted, "I think it's a good idea to take a year to do some practice." I was somewhat taken aback by this comment because I hadn't previously mentioned to this supervisor that I had serious research interests, nor had I said anything indicating that I viewed my internship year as a hiatus from research activities. Had I been branded as the sole "researcher" of my internship class? Had I shown myself to be even more of a neophyte practitioner than I had previously thought? Had I accidently brought in research data and left it behind in the lunchroom or some other conspicuous location?

My supervisor's comment had been a friendly invitation to discuss the shaping of career goals, but the comment also illustrates that research and practice are commonly perceived as separate domains, with radically different career paths. This was also an eye-opening and realistic portrayal of one of the unwritten rules of clinical psychology. That is, my supervisor had been correct to note that remaining on a research–academic career path would require not indulging in full-time clinical practice beyond the internship year. It is exceedingly rare to devote a year to full-time clinical practice, beyond rudimentary training, and then enter the research–academic world (I can't think of anyone who has done this). I had not previously realized that devoting more than the required amount of time to clinical practice would be viewed by some as equivalent to a "gap in the vita"—or worse!

The gulf between research and practice has also widened because of various marketplace forces that have drastically altered the nature of clinical practice. Researchers, who have a smaller portion of time to devote to practice, are less likely to invest more time to procure placement on managed care provider lists. In addition, many beginning researchers are effectively shut out of clinical practice by increasingly stringent and adversarial state licensing laws that require 1 to 2 years of postdoctoral clinical practice. Some states also place strict limits on the amount of time that can be taken to accumulate these clinical hours and do not make exceptions for researchers. To receive the privileges of licensure, the researcher must not only work 70+ hours per week doing research and teaching (with the accompanying worries of promotion and tenure) but must also "moonlight" in clinical practice to be recognized as a legitimate practitioner. Curiously, many of these unlicensed researchers are developing new treatments and are instructing the next generation of clinical practitioners.

The researcher may also become frustrated by the inclusion of metatheoretical postulations that predominate the practice of some clinicians. Many of these clinicians practice from a psychoanalytic theoretical perspective and have little interest in empirical findings. I also rely on a psychodynamic theoretical orientation in my practice and have personally experienced how metatheory may transform clinical data. Although I have, at times, previously engaged in this sort of "wild analysis" (Anderson, 1986), I have become convinced of the dangers of theory that is not informed by more critical observational checks and formal empirical efforts. Equally frustrating for the researcher is the "lone ranger" mentality of some clinicians, who rely exclusively on their clinical wisdom, an entirely intuitive approach that is not informed by either research or theory.

Part of the problem, as I see it, is that the assumptions of many psychoanalytic theories are not easily testable, and most theorists are not interested in using research to modify theory (e.g., Grunbaum, 1984). As theory increasingly replaces systematic procedures for observation, its perceived explanatory powers grow exponentially. For example, one of my colleagues described a patient who had been slowly picking the fuzz from his sweater and carefully collecting it in his hand throughout the course of a session. The therapist conceptualized this incident as evidence for the patient's oral-phase issues and his desire for enmeshment with the therapist because he had been symbolically "making a nest" from his sweater. I heard the audiotape recording of this session but believed that the patient sounded disengaged from the therapist and, if anything, his picking was self-punitive. "But then why did he carefully place the fuzz in his curled hand?" asked the therapist. This was a good question for which I have no answer. The therapist may have been "right" and may have been in a better position than I to understand the patient. From the lens of a scientist, however, I see this incident as an example of what may happen when global, untested theoretical postulates are used, unabated, to explain micro-observations of behavior.

Clearly, the researcher is at a loss for how to assist the practitioner in understanding highly specific incidents and may feel unfairly alienated when asked to explain behavior that is currently well beyond the reach of our science. However, clinicians must frequently make sense of powerful interpersonal transactions, with theory commonly as the only conceptual guide available. Although there are clearly limits to what research can do, I also believe that contemporary research—especially in the past 15 years —has been accumulating findings that could be of great use to the practitioner.

RESEARCHER'S CONTRIBUTION TO PRACTICE

Although a number of barriers have been established that discourage the researcher from venturing into the world of practice, the findings from contemporary applied research have the potential to greatly benefit practitioners. This increased applicability of research for clinical practice may be largely due to the move away from "horse race" comparison studies between treatments of competing theoretical orientations and toward an increased attention by some researchers to identifying effective processes within psychotherapy (Strupp, 1989).

One of the more valuable lessons that research has to offer the practitioner is the broad and pervasive influence of the therapeutic relationship. For example, research on the therapeutic alliance has repeatedly shown that a positive alliance between therapist and patient is related to good outcomes in psychotherapy (Horvath & Symonds, 1991). Although a positive therapeutic alliance has been found to be significantly related to outcome across therapeutic modalities (Gaston, Marmar, Gallagher, & Thompson, 1991), this relationship may be slightly higher when outcome is measured with interpersonal measures and somewhat lower when outcome is measured with symptomatic measures (Horvath & Greenberg, 1994). Research also shows that these relational qualities may be especially crucial in the early stages of treatment (e.g., O'Malley, Suh, & Strupp, 1983). The success of the therapeutic alliance construct is also evidence of how our profession may profit from the collaboration of practice, theory, and research. The construct arose out of observations from clinical work and was quickly incorporated into theory and later entered into the researcher's vocabulary (Horvath & Greenberg, 1994).

It is partly the cooperation of these practice and research communities that led me increasingly to focus more on basic relational qualities and less on pure technical considerations in my own clinical work. I believe that there have been a number of healthy by-products, increasing my therapeutic focus on the relational atmosphere and the transference. Perhaps the greatest change has been an increased interest in listening to my patient's communications at face value and without translation into abstract, metatheoretical conceptualizations. This point was never lost with my post-doctoral mentor, Hans Strupp, who repeatedly emphasized to me, with only some humor, the essential principles of psychotherapy: "There are three essential ingredients to successful psychotherapy that you should carefully note: First, there is the relationship. Second, there is the relationship. And third, there is the relationship." Could there be a better integration of clinical wisdom and scientific parsimony? I think not!

Research on the alliance also might provide a useful lesson about some of the issues involved in the successful collaboration of research and practice. The definition of the alliance is quite broad, which may allow it the flexibility needed to be useful for both researchers and clinicians. While practical and effective, the alliance construct remains somewhat vaguely defined, and it is unclear, for example, whether the alliance is made up of multiple underlying components or of a single general factor. This allows some flexibility in interpretation, both for the researcher and the practitioner, but may influence researchers (myself included) who wish to understand the nature and underlying causes of the alliance's positive effect.

Another research area that has arisen out of the work of practitioners concerns the effects of affective experiencing in psychotherapy. Exploratory therapies, particularly Rogerian ones, have observed that encouraging clients to deepen their awareness and expression of emotion in therapy was related to positive outcomes. These clinical observations were then tested with a number of empirical studies that used Klein's Experiencing Scales and similar measures, resulting in findings that linked experiencing to outcome (Klein, Mathieu-Coughlan, & Kiesler, 1986). The successes of the experiencing construct are limited by the same difficulties surrounding the alliance construct. Both phenomena are broadly defined, allowing for mutual understanding by researchers and practitioners. However, this also makes it more difficult for researchers to specify the nature and underlying causes of experiencing and equally difficult for the clinician to know how to differentially apply the findings from this research.

Recent research has elaborated the experiencing construct so as to make it somewhat more precise and clinically useful. Stiles et al. (1990), for example, developed a stage model that incorporated components of affective experiencing as well as more recent developments in experiential theory (e.g., Greenberg, Rice, & Elliott, 1993). The Assimilation of Problematic Experiences Scale is a developmental–stage model for therapy process and outcome that progresses from a client's increasing awareness of problematic experiences toward cognitive insight and mastery.

As a graduate student, I became involved in attempts to apply Stiles' scale to clinical cases (e.g., Stiles, Meshot, Anderson, & Sloan, 1992). As a member of Stiles' research group, I presented one of my therapy cases for consideration in an initial attempt to apply the assimilation model to clinical material. This was a client whom I had been seeing in the department's psychology clinic and whom I had boldly proclaimed as a remarkable clinical success (dare I say "cure"!). Week after week, this client had demonstrated a willingness to explore her problems and had seemed to make numerous personal "discoveries." As we examined the case with the scale, however, it was difficult to identify the events in which change occurred. Indeed, our group had great difficulty in identifying any of the client's problematic experiences, and it became increasingly clear that she had spent most of her time reciting a series of neatly packaged "insights." Furthermore, there had been little affective experiencing in her weekly reports, and her insights seemed canned and intellectual. We speculated that she had been attempting to ward off unwanted thoughts about other issues that were more personally meaningful (the first level of this scale). Examining this case with a research-informed focus (Soldz, 1990) was instrumental in altering my approach, and this marked a turning point in my work with this client toward greater focus on current and substantive issues.

It is important to note that the lessons from research will not only benefit the neophyte therapist but also the more experienced and savvy one. Perhaps one of the more valuable applications of a research orientation consists in the heuristic value of applying process methods and scales to one's own clinical cases. As Strupp (1986) noted, many experienced therapists believe that some of the most basic and essential lessons from research are not applicable to themselves. For example, practitioners often readily agree that pejorative interpersonal communications by the therapist are harmful but that half also tend to believe that they are immune from such events. Research indicates, however, that the therapist who can withhold pejorative responses to a hostile patient is exceedingly rare!

Other aspects of the patient's affective experiencing in therapy have been informed by my own research into the lexical use of affect in psychotherapy sessions. For example, I found that the total frequency of the affective language used by patients was not predictive of outcome, but the nature of the affect was (Anderson, 1995). Early in treatment, patients who spoke with a greater proportion of negative affect words were more likely to have *good* outcomes. In another study, I found that the strength of a person's use of affect constructs to influence evaluative and behavioral constructs was indicative of mental health (Anderson & Leitner, 1996). What has made these types of studies personally useful in practice is my thorough knowledge of the data, including a working knowledge of the affect lexicon and how these words are classified. The usefulness of this research is not so much in the creation of carefully planned interventions or in consciously counting words but, rather, in developing a larger knowledge base and well-rehearsed strategies for intervening.

Much of clinical research is also likely to be most usefully applied to the clinical work of those directly involved in the research process, and these practitioners who later read a research report of the findings will be hard pressed to apply the findings in clinical work. Practitioners may find it difficult to gain more than a cursory understanding of group-difference findings found in research journals. Therapists may also have difficulty finding and implementing measures from research into practice, even though some have made great strides toward making these measures more "user-friendly" (e.g., Greenberg & Pinsof, 1986; Ogles, Lambert, & Masters, 1996). Practitioners may also have problems in generalizing research into more tangible clinical applications. Although the increased number of newsletters and practitioner journals should continue to assist practitioners to make use of empirical findings, it might be useful to expand these avenues of communication to provide greater detail and to better link the data to clinical phenomena. Extensive clinical examples, perhaps videotapes of clinical phenomena that illustrate empirical principles, may make our research findings even more useful. However, creating this link may mean additional work for the researcher. Most researchers consider their work to be complete after publication of their findings in a professional journal. Practitioners may have difficulty making use of the lessons of research because the format of research journals tends to be more congenial to the production of future research than to the direct application of clinical work. However, researchers may be instrumental in developing new media for communicating data that is relevant to the types of problems that the therapist encounters.

INTEGRATING RESEARCH: THE PRACTITIONER'S DILEMMA

The practitioner's underinvolvement in the research process does not appear to stem from a disinterest in research but is more likely related to negative attitudes of some researchers about clinical practice. The vast majority of practitioners are respectful of science and regularly read scientific journals but hold to a different scientific criteria of evidence than the researcher (e.g., Beutler et al., 1995, reported that 80% of clinicians regularly read scientific articles and journals). Beutler et al. also noted that researchers do not reciprocate this interest and generally fail to acknowledge the value of clinical practice. Thus, the practicing clinician is faced with the dilemma of finding a way to integrate research into his or her practice, while gleaning this information from researchers who are often disinterested in the practitioner's work.

Practitioners know that the environment in which most research takes place, the academic department of psychology, is often disdainful of clinical practice. Clinical faculty in many psychology departments may feel that their active interest in clinical work, clinical training, and the concerns of "service providers" are on the order of an ignominious secret. This fact alone illustrates the extent to which the concerns of practitioners are perceived by many as alien and disruptive to the activities of clinical science. For example, the research–practitioner faculty member often must take any practice-related activities to nonuniversity facilities. Although there are many reasons for this, other faculty who have no interest in practice are reluctant to acknowledge that the experience of practice informs research in vital ways (especially with psychotherapy process research) and is not simply a salary supplement. This attitude contributes to preventing departmental psychology clinics, if they exist at all, from developing truly applied laboratories for the intensive study of individual cases. Instead, these facilities often become a distant outpost in departments, serving only to meet minimal training requirements or perhaps as a site for a few larger studies.

Graduate students, the vast majority of whom become practitioners (even in clinical science programs), observe the intense disdain for practice by their mentors and are compelled to hide any genuine interest in a career as a service provider. For example, a colleague told me about his graduate training in such a department. When he asked a faculty member about career options, he was bluntly told, "Students who graduate from this program have two clear career paths. You can go into research or you can go to hell." He also noted that those graduates of his program who went into clinical practice were simply erased from the faculty's memory!

Practitioners may also be wary of researchers because they may perceive the conclusions drawn by some researchers as actively undermining the professional existence of practitioners. For example, Dawes (1994) concluded that because research shows no effects on patient outcomes for doctoral-level training in psychotherapy, there is no need to continue to train clinicians to be service providers. It is understandable that many practitioners would be defensive in the face of such an interpretation of the data. It is also arguable that practitioners may not be in the best position to render a fair and balanced interpretation of the research on training (and similar professional issues) because the practitioners' livelihood will be influenced by the verdict. Clinical scientists who do not engage in the activities of practice are also potentially biased. Those who engage solely in practice or research belong to separate guilds with differing, and often conflicting, interests to promote in regard to training and maintenance of their group's power. Research guilds, in academia, and applied clinical guilds, in licensed practice, often battle over control of the same knowledge domain. As Krause (1996) noted, guilds exist through monopolies of their domain and protection of their skills:

> The skill and the group possessing the skill were thus equated. Without solidarity in the guild system, the skill would no longer be a mystery. Without sole possession of the skill and the tools to use it (which often meant fighting closely related crafts over turf) the guild had no power. (p. 5)

It may be that the "turf battles" between researchers and practitioners have grown in recent years because there is greater pressure from outside forces to compromise the integrity of both research and practitioner guild systems (i.e., compromises in the tenure system and in managed care). These turf battles often emerge over issues of state licensing, professional associations, and the curriculum in clinical programs. Arguably, those who are engaged in both research and practice may be able to be the most objective in interpreting the meaning of controversial data (e.g., studies showing no treatment outcome differences between trained practitioners and paraprofessionals) because they have both the understanding of the scientific issues of inference and, perhaps, the least conflict of interest. Scientists who engage in practice may also have a deeper understanding of the intricacies involved in psychotherapy and training, allowing them to be more attentive to the potential confounds that might exist in past studies and thus less likely to accept some studies at face value.

PRACTITIONER'S CONTRIBUTION TO RESEARCH

A 20-year-old college student who was exceptionally bright and driven came for several sessions of psychotherapy. He was depressed and somewhat anxious, which he attributed to having little personal sense of his identity and what he valued. He complained of having simply coopted his parent's goals and values without having struggled to find his own answers. Throughout the therapy, which lasted a little over a year, he came to realize that much of his need to achieve related to the hope that others would approve of him. My sense was that he had realized that he wanted others to accept him as a "whole" person and not simply perform for the approval of others. He ultimately decided to leave school for a year or two and move to another state to become a ski instructor. It was not his belief, nor mine, that this decision was reactive or impulsive, and we spent the final 2 months of therapy considering the implications of this decision.

Can such an ending to therapy be considered a "good" outcome? He clearly improved in regard to symptom reduction, and I considered him to have made some structural change as well. However, he was at an impasse, and it seemed that we had progressed as far as possible without further maturing on his part, which would require him to have experiences that would help shape his identity. His parents, however, had a completely different view of the outcome, which I became thoroughly aware of when he told them of his decision to leave school. They were convinced that their son was "throwing away" his life by leaving school, and their view was likely representative of society's view of this outcome. Yet the parent's assessment of his outcome was also valid in that there could be some serious consequences to his decision, and I was also sympathetic to their point of view.

Although the above case would likely be considered successful in most research settings, the practitioner must often consider a wide variety of competing values that are intertwined within the context of a person's life. The fact that clients may change in numerous ways highlights the importance of contextual factors for both researcher and clinician. In the above case, the client had improved in some regards but had not changed in other ways—the evaluation of the outcome depends, to a large extent, on whose perspective and values are considered. Unfortunately, research to date has often neglected this multidimensional view of outcome, and the few complex outcome models that exist (e.g., Strupp, Hadley, & Gomez-Schwartz, 1977) have not received sufficient empirical attention (Lunnen & Ogles, 1998).

The goal of the treatment researcher is, by and large, to remove the contextual aspects of treatment to isolate the effects of specific techniques and outcomes. The practitioner, however, tends to be more cognizant of the fact that techniques are always applied within a wide variety of contexts.

The practitioner is typically faced with a highly diverse patient population and often must negotiate the problems of external validity on his or her own. The practicing clinician will frequently treat patients who would have been excluded from many studies because the selection criteria from large-scale efficacy studies often exclude the majority of patients who apply for treatment. Those patients who are the least disturbed (e.g., who do not have dual diagnoses), and who are especially suited for the planned intervention, tend to be the patients who are selected. Treatments are of circumscribed duration and highly controlled, often through the use of a treatment manual (Seligman, 1995).

Given these limitations, researchers can do little to assist clinicians in negotiating how to make these interventions within a complicated clinical context. Research has only been moving incrementally toward answering the following basic question: "What treatment, by whom, is most effective for this individual with that specific problem, under which set of circumstances, and how does it come about?" (Paul, 1969, p. 44). This attention to contextual complexity is often viewed as a nuisance variable by the researcher. However, as Leitner (1995) noted, "clinicians are likely to demand that assessment devices be more relevant to complex clinical realities" (p. 57). Because practitioners spend an inordinately larger amount of their time negotiating numerous contextual factors (i.e., what intervention may be most beneficial to this individual, at this particular moment, within the specific history of this unique patient–therapist relationship?), the researcher may learn directly from the practitioner about the numerous contextual factors of clinical practice, if only to understand the sources of such nuisance variables. Ironically, the direct knowledge about delivery of psychotherapy and interpersonal processes, acquired through *extensive* training, may be one of the most valuable, yet underused, observational tools available to treatment researchers.

As Stricker and Trierweiler (1995) have aptly noted, research data that are collected in clinical practice are exceedingly complex because both the participant (or "subject") and the scientist contribute to the phenomenon being studied. Thus, the relationships among psychotherapy researcher, therapist, and patient may also have "generative" qualities, because of both demand characteristics and experimenter effects. These influences are not readily recognized in psychotherapy research, even though they have been repeatedly demonstrated in social psychological research (e.g., Orne, 1962; Silverman, 1977). Gergen (1973) and Rychlak (1985) have even suggested that these effects are not simply confounds but are analogous to Heisenberg's uncertainty principle in physics because the observation of interpersonal phenomena, by definition, cannot be unobtrusive and necessarily influences the nature of the phenomenon being studied.

Extensive experience with clinical practice may be one of the best means for developing methods and measures that are sensitive to the complexity of most therapeutic settings. Contextual influences were the focus of a study that examined the potential influence of demand characteristics in the Vanderbilt II Psychotherapy Study, a study on the effects of manualized training. The main findings of the study were that therapists applied more of the interventions from the manual after training but that patient outcomes were not significantly altered. Anderson and Strupp (1996) examined how the results were influenced by the research setting and role demands of patients and therapists. Using interviews that were specifically designed to measure demand characteristics, we found that those patients who were especially aware of their role as a "subject" in the experiment had outcomes that were dramatically different from those patients who did not report such demands. Patients who experienced high demand characteristics had outcomes that were consistent with the researchers' hypotheses, even though these hypotheses were not directly communicated to patients by the researchers. These effects existed for patient and therapist assessments of outcome but did not exist for the outcome assessment of independent clinicians. Furthermore, therapists altered their approach to treatment with those patients who were acutely aware of their role as a "subject" and did not use the manualized interventions that had been taught by the researchers. That is, therapists seemed to withhold the research-based interventions when they sensed that their patients were sensitive to being in a research project.

When patients play the role of a "subject," they generally do so at the expense of deepening their understanding of core issues and of their ability to make use of therapy. Leitner (1985) has highlighted the distinction between "roles," as in the many social roles that most people use (e.g., "subject," "patient"), and the more difficult *roles*, which refers to the unique capacity that another can play in more vulnerable aspects of intimate relationships. As Leitner noted, roles often protect or prevent one from taking the risks to develop *role* relationships. If some research methods create greater demand characteristics and increase the patient's awareness of their role as "subject," then it may be more difficult to develop a *role* relationship. Regardless, attention to the research context is required by the therapist. We found that some therapists were reluctant to explore the patient's role as a "subject" even though these therapists readily explored a variety of other limiting roles and maladaptive patterns. The issue of demand characteristics, then, has the potential to dramatically distort the nature of treatments that occur in a research setting and to likewise distort the validity of research findings. One solution to this methodological problem would be to increase the involvement of the participants in the research process, which would also help narrow the gap between research and practice. The use of a participant–observer research paradigm would imply a reconsideration of our view of scientific control. For example, the researcher who also engages in clinical practice would be a participant–observer, as would his or her clients. Such a model would also imply that patients and therapists in research studies would no longer be treated as "subjects," but as true collaborators in the research process.

Practitioners can play an important role in research because they are intimately involved in these and other contextual factors that exist in the therapeutic relationship. Without working with practitioners, researchers may not be able to discover the intricacies of outcome and process measurement. However, because practitioners are also participants, they may not always be aware of how or why the context influences their clinical work. Psychotherapy researchers may benefit from a strategy of collecting as many unique reports, or lenses, as possible to fully "expose" the phenomena being studied (e.g., Packer & Addison, 1989). Clearly, the practitioner's perspective is one lens that has been underused in psychotherapy research.

CONCLUSION

Although the relationship between research and practice may often appear to be analogous to a stormy marriage (Elliott & Morrow-Bradley, 1994), a working relationship is necessary for the sustenance of any applied science. I have come to see the separate activities of research and practice as necessarily interrelated and complementary, but not naturally well suited for one another.

The mix of cognitive and interpersonal skills used to perform research and practice is often quite different and not easily interchanged. For example, as both a psychotherapy researcher and a practitioner, I have found that the processes involved in each activity are sufficiently different to require time to transition when changing from one sphere to the other.

On the one hand, research skills place an optimal weight on critical and logical thinking. Research involves a cognitive style that involves procedural knowledge and a focus on control and exclusion of variables to achieve the most parsimonious explanation. Context is typically important only to the extent that it alerts the researcher to confounds that interfere with external validity or, at best, the existence of moderating variables that have a "fixed" position in the researcher's nomenological net.

On the other hand, the practitioner's skills are more interpersonal, less critical, and often involve being open to a range of explanations (regardless of their formal logical integrity) that are taken at face value and from the perspective of another person. The practitioner is less narrowly attuned to the issue of parsimony and may be more prone toward the contextual nature of clinical data. Because of the complex and vast amount of meaningful data in the clinical setting, the clinician may best rely on implicit or tacit strategies. That is, the practitioner uses numerous clinical skills with little or no forethought, and often the clinician cannot immediately explain the complex processes used in reaching a solution. These processes of complex ways of knowing may be difficult for the practitioner to verbally articulate and are sometimes referred to as "clinical wisdom," a phrase that is poorly understood but is certain to quickly boil the blood of some clinical scientists (e.g., Dawes, 1994). Researchers, for example, are often more interested in the clinician's formal cognitive decision-making strategies (e.g., diagnostic decision making) than in the interpersonal skills that occupy most of the therapist's time. Another way to understand the practitioner's abilities is that they involve interpersonal intelligence or knowing (Gardner, 1983), whereas the researcher's talents may draw more heavily from traditional quantitative and verbal intelligences. These different problem-solving strategies may account for some of the disparagement between researchers and practitioners.

Perhaps the most important lesson to learn about the division between research and practice in our field is that there are no simple solutions for better integration of research and practice. The answers to how the gap can be narrowed are probably as apparent as are the answers to questions that both researchers and practitioners regularly ponder: What treatments are superior? What processes lead to good outcomes? How can therapists be optimally trained?

Creating better collaboration between researchers and practitioners will likely require a realization by both parties that answers are hard to come by in this field and will depend on cooperation. As Beutler et al. (1995) noted, the researcher may be more dependent on the practitioner in this regard. The advancement of our field will likely take place through open-minded inquiry and acceptance of alternative scientific paradigms. This goal may best be achieved through a more modest attitude and an appreciation for generating the right questions.

In conclusion, a number of changes in research and clinical activities may facilitate better cooperation in our profession. These changes might include *greater concern for clarifying the goals and activities of clinical work.* This does not necessarily imply specifying techniques in as narrow a manner as has been articulated through treatment manuals (Strupp & Anderson, 1997). However, researchers would be better able to collaborate with clinicians if there were more attention given to defining clinical activities. Another useful change might be for *researchers and clinicians to find some common ground* through greater use of naturalistic observation and qualitative research so long as there is structured use of the clinician's skills.

Researchers may find clearer and less cumbersome avenues to communicate their research to clinician and make the tools for self-evaluation more accessible. Perhaps most important, *both researchers and clinicians could better cooperate if each were considerably more humble.* Although easier said than done, researchers could be less condescending about clinical work, and practitioners could be more amenable to the suggestion that the basic lessons of research are likely to apply to their own efforts.

REFERENCES

Anderson, T. (1986). The specimen dream as a childhood trauma. *American Imago*, *43*, 171–190.

Anderson, T. (1995). *The lexical analysis of verbalized affect in time-limited dynamic psychotherapy.* Paper presented at the 26th annual meeting of the Society for Psychotherapy Research, Vancouver, British Columbia, Canada.

Anderson, T., & Leitner, L. M. (1996). Symptomatology and the use of affect constructs to influence value and behavior constructs. *Journal of Counseling Psychology, 43*, 77–83.

Anderson, T., & Strupp, H. H. (1996). The ecology of psychotherapy research. *Journal of Consulting and Clinical Psychology, 64*, 776–782.

Beutler, L. E., Williams, R. E., Wakefield, P. J., & Entwistle, S. R. (1995). Bridging scientist and practitioner perspectives in clinical psychology. *American Psychologist, 50,* 984–994.

Dawes, R. M. (1994). *House of cards: Psychology and psychotherapy built on myth.* New York: Free Press.

Elliott, R. E., & Morrow-Bradley, C. (1994). Developing a working marriage between psychotherapists and psychotherapy researchers: Identifying shared purposes. In P. F. Talley & H. H. Strupp (Eds.), *Psychotherapy research and practice: Bridging the gap* (pp. 124–142). New York: Basic Books.

Gardner, H. (1983). *Frames of mind: The theory of multiple intelligences.* New York: Basic Books.

Gaston, L., Marmar, C. R., Gallagher, D., & Thompson, L. W. (1991). Alliance prediction of outcome beyond in-treatment symptomatic change as psychotherapy process. *Psychotherapy Research, 1,* 104–113.

Gergen, K. J. (1973). Social psychology as history. *Journal of Personality and Social Psychology, 26,* 309–320.

Greenberg, L. S., & Pinsof, W. M. (Eds.). (1986). *The psychotherapeutic process: A research handbook.* New York: Guilford Press.

Greenberg, L. S., Rice, L. N., & Elliott, R. (1993). *Facilitating emotional change: The moment-by-moment process.* New York: Guilford Press.

Grunbaum, A. (1984). *The foundations of psychoanalysis.* Berkeley, CA: University of California Press.

Horvath, A. O., & Greenberg, L. S. (1994). *The working alliance: Theory, research, and practice.* New York: Wiley.

Horvath, A. O., & Symonds, D. B. (1991). Relationships between working alliance and outcome in psychotherapy: A meta-analysis. *Journal of Counseling Psychology, 38,* 139–149.

Klein, M. H., Mathieu-Coughlan, P., & Kiesler, D. J. (1986). The experiencing scales. In L. S. Greenberg & W. M. Pinsof (Eds.), *The psychotherapeutic process: A research handbook* (pp. 21–71). New York: Guilford Press.

Krause, E. A. (1996). *Death of the guilds: Professions, states, and the advance of capitalism, 1930 to the present.* New Haven, CT: Yale University Press.

Leitner, L. M. (1985). The terrors of cognition: On the experiential validity of personal construct theory. In D. Bannister (Ed.), *Issues and approaches in personal construct theory* (pp. 83–103). London: Academic Press.

Leitner, L. M. (1995). Dispositional assessment techniques in experiential personal construct psychotherapy. *Journal of Constructivist Psychology, 8,* 53–74.

Lunnen, K. M., & Ogles, B. M. (1998). A multiperspective, multivariable evaluation of reliable change. *Journal of Consulting and Clinical Psychology, 66,* 400–410.

Ogles, B. M., Lambert, M., & Masters, K. S. (1996). *Assessing outcome in clinical practice.* Needham Heights, MA: Allyn & Bacon.

O'Malley, S. S., Suh, C. S., & Strupp, H. H. (1983). The Vanderbilt Psychotherapy

Process Scale: A report on scale development and a process–outcome study. *Journal of Consulting and Clinical Psychology, 51,* 581–586.

Orne, M. T. (1962). On the social psychology of the psychological experiment: With particular reference to demand characteristics and their implications. *American Psychologist, 17,* 776–783.

Packer, M. J., & Addison, R. B. (1989). *Entering the circle: Hermeneutic investigation in psychology.* Albany: State University of New York Press.

Paul, G. L. (1969). Behavior modification research: Design and tactics. In C. M. Franks (Ed.), *Behavior therapy: Appraisal and status* (pp. 29–62). New York: McGraw-Hill.

Rychlak, J. F. (1985). *A philosophy of science of personality theory.* Malabar, FL: Krieger.

Seligman, M. P. (1995). The effectiveness of psychotherapy: The *Consumer Reports* study. *American Psychologist, 50,* 965–974.

Silverman, I. (1977). *The human subject in the psychological laboratory.* New York: Pergamon Press.

Soldz, S. (1990). The therapeutic interaction: Research perspectives. In R. A. Wells & V. J. Giannetti (Eds.), *Handbook of the brief psychotherapies* (pp. 27–53). New York: Plenum Press.

Stiles, W. B., Elliott, R., Llewelyn, S. P., Firth-Cozens, J. A., Margison, F. R., Shapiro, D. A., & Hardy, G. (1990). Assimilation of problematic experiences by clients in psychotherapy. *Psychotherapy, 27,* 411–420.

Stiles, W. B., Meshot, C. M., Anderson, T. M., & Sloan, W. W. (1992). Assimilation of problematic experiences: The case of John Jones. *Psychotherapy Research, 2,* 81–101.

Stricker, G., & Trierweiler, S. J. (1995). The local clinical scientist: A bridge between science and practice. *American Psychologist, 50,* 995–1002.

Strupp, H. H. (1986). Psychotherapy: Research, practice, and public policy—How to avoid dead ends [Special issue]. *American Psychologist, 41,* 120–130.

Strupp, H. H. (1989). Psychotherapy: Can the practitioner learn from the researcher? *American Psychologist, 44,* 717–724.

Strupp, H. H., & Anderson, T. (1997). On the limitations of therapy manuals. *Clinical Psychology: Science and Practice, 4,* 76–82.

Strupp, H. H., Hadley, S. W., & Gomez-Schwartz, B. (1977). *Psychotherapy for better or worse: An analysis of the problem of negative effects.* New York: Jason Aronson.

II

DIALOGUE AND
CROSS-POLLINATION

6

CROSS-POLLINATION OF RESEARCH AND PRACTICE: THE HONEYBEE, THE UNICORN, AND THE SEARCH FOR MEANING

LEIGH McCULLOUGH

As I wrote this chapter two images came to me: a honeybee and, later, a unicorn. At first I didn't understand them. But with consideration I realized the former is methodical, whereas the latter is more mystical—and both play crucial parts the research and practice of psychotherapy.

The first image arose while I was sitting in my garden watching the methodical honeybees alighting first on one flower, and then on another, each time leaving some pollen behind and lifting off laden with more. The comforting and systematic moving back and forth reminded me of a similar cross-pollination between my psychotherapy research and practice. My colleagues and I examine our videotaped sessions for things well done—or poorly done. In the next therapy session, we try to implement what we learned, and then review these adjustments on the tapes. Eventually some of this data makes its way back to the computer—our hive—where we go to work, putting the data into cells, then analyzing and writing it up. How sweet it is.

Yet this honeybee metaphor carries us only so far. We are not insects making honey, but sentient beings trying to make sense of things. We are not endowed with instincts that direct our actions; how are we to navigate these uncharted pathways? What shall guide us?

In the back of my mind—I did not know it was there until the chapter was almost finished—was the powerful, although less comforting, and somewhat challenging message I had learned in a small book about the philosophy of our science, written by an English psychological scientist, Liam Hudson. The book, entitled *The Cult of the Fact: A Psychologist's Autobiographical Critique of His Discipline* (Hudson, 1972), puts forth the thesis that scientists are not mindless drones buzzing from data set to data set, and back to the computer. We are, rather, willful and biased creatures who are pulled and pushed—passionately at times—by forces that we do not fully understand, but that are all the more powerful for being so.

The data are there to inform and test our constructs, and to keep us honest. However, we construct meaning not only from data but also from all manner of hopes, dreams, and experience. Staying open to these possibilities of discovery is a daunting process in comparison to that of the bee—one that requires trust and risk taking.

To this end, Hudson quoted Rilke's poem about the mythical unicorn, "the creature there has never been," that bears repeating here:

> Not there, because they loved it, it behaved
> As though it were. They always left some space.
> ... They fed it, not with corn,
> But only with the possibility of being. And that was able to confer
> Such strength, its brow put forth a horn. (Hudson, 1972, p. 19)

As researchers, we must be as methodical and systematic as the honeybees. As searchers, we need the courage to open ourselves to what we love and to what gives us passion—fed at times with only the "possibility of being." Much of what guides us in research as well as in clinical practice is what Hudson described as "precisely our tendency to mythologize, to construct elaborate systems of ideas around a core of simple values" (Hudson, 1972, p. 177).

Therefore, one level of the cross-pollination I address is that of practicalities between research and practice. But at a deeper level, cross-pollination must also occur between method and passion: between the methodical honeybee and the mythical unicorn.

DISCOVERING VIDEOTAPES FOR INTEGRATING RESEARCH AND PRACTICE

What is more "true," our biases, or feelings, or the "facts" that we know? Both are subject to falsehood, and both are potentially valid. How can we know the difference? When I discovered the use of videotapes for the study of psychotherapy, I realized that the tapes provided a record—forever captured—to study again and again. These tapes, and this method I felt, would ground me and keep me close to the data.

I learned about videotaping from a visit to David Malan in England. Because I could not continue ongoing supervision on another continent, Malan encouraged me to look up Habib Davanloo, who, some years later, was able to supervise a group of us in Manhattan, by use of videotaped therapy sessions.

It was not long after I began watching tapes of therapy that I knew that there needed to be some mechanism to systematically analyze the information the tapes contained. David Malan (1979; Malan & Marziali, 1984) inspired me with his research studies that counted the frequency of a "patient's marked response to transference interpretations" as reported by therapists in their session notes. Malan had demonstrated that these patients' responses to therapists' interventions were correlated with improvement—one of the pioneering steps toward demonstrating the efficacy of brief psychotherapy interventions. It seemed that the research efforts could be even more grounded if the actual behaviors in the videotapes were coded and counted. This led me to develop systems to code videotapes.

I began by reviewing the coding of mother–infant interactions. These investigators took weeks, if not months, to analyze a few minutes of tape. Considering the hundreds of psychotherapy patients to study, each with 20–40 hours of therapy, it would take centuries to collect enough data. It therefore became crucial to learn how to code videotaped sessions as efficiently as possible.

Originally, the existing coding systems for psychotherapy focused on therapist interventions, but not on patient responses because patients were much less predictable in their reactions than were therapists. Therapists quite reliably do certain catagories of things: questioning, interpreting, clarifying, confronting, giving support, and so forth. Patients, on the other hand, respond so idiosyncratically that initially their behavior seemed impossible to categorize or rate. If patients never seemed to do the same thing twice, how could we ever analyze patient–therapist interactions? It seemed impossibly complex. However, I have learned that with patience, it is just a matter of time before the fog clears and figure emerges from ground.

In this case, it took almost 3 years of close scrutiny of patients' behavior on videotape before three main categories of patient behavior relevant to our psychodynamic orientation emerged: (a) defensive responding, (b) affective responding, and (c) cognitive elaboration. Combining these patient categories with standard therapist intervention categories, we now could code patient–therapist interaction throughout the session. In each speaking turn, we could rate the therapist intervention and the patient response that followed it. As a result of many years of pondering videotapes,

I developed a coding system named the Psychotherapy Interaction Coding System (McCullough, 1991).

Although this discovery process was intended as a research endeavor, the clinical benefits were remarkable:

1. I became much more aware of when I was confronting a defense, interpreting a behavior pattern, or offering a suggestion.
2. After coding videotapes, I could catch a patient behaving defensively much quicker.
3. I could see my errors and my patient's evasions that previously I would never have caught.
4. I began to distinguish a patient's healthy, adaptive affect from defensive affect.
5. It became clear that therapists avoid feelings as much as their patients.
6. Repeatedly, I found my subjective impression of what happened in the sessions to be inaccurate.

In these and many other ways, the coding of the videotaped therapy process made an incredible contribution toward learning how to do and how to improve doing therapy. This was one of the ways my research has had a profound influence on my practice.

EARLY PROCESS RESEARCH AND ITS EFFECT ON CLINICAL PRACTICE

At the Beth Israel Medical Center in New York City, under the direction of Arnold Winston, my colleagues and I derived research hypotheses directly from our clinical experience. For example, we learned from clinical work that if defenses were high, then improvement was more difficult to attain. Also, if the patients were able to reach deep feelings, we could more easily note improvement. Drawing from this clinical experience, I put all my research energy into focusing on how the degrees of affect and defense contribute to outcome.

There were many years between my first envisioning how to do psychotherapy process research and obtaining the actual research data for each study. As noted above, my colleagues and I had to develop relevant coding systems; compile videotapes of completed and evaluated sessions; train coders; and then code the tapes. Finally, data then had to be analyzed. It took 10 years from start to finish, and I was understandably eager to see the results (that I felt certain would come out in the predicted direction!).

I have a vivid memory of watching the old deck-writer printer crank out our long-awaited results onto rolls of 24-in.-wide, green-lined computer print-out paper. After 10 years of waiting, the results were devastating! In the first study, neither affect nor defense showed any relationship to patient improvement at outcome. The correlations were zero. It seemed impossible that this could have happened. Clinically, it seemed so obvious that more defensive patients did more poorly and more affective patients did better. The data made no sense. I had to remind myself what a former research mentor had taught me: "The data are your friend!" Nevertheless, I went home that day feeling that my "friend" had betrayed me.

A few nights later, laying awake and staring at the ceiling, it occurred to me that an upcoming study might help us understand what had led to these confusing findings; this study isolated affect and defense only when they followed an interpretation of the patient–therapist relationship. The data for this study were collected by Franklin Porter (1987), and the results were going to be ready in the next 2 or 3 weeks. It occurred to me that these context-specific variables might help us understand the puzzling and counterintuitive findings.

In the end, these hunches paid off. The results supported the original hypothesis, but they did so in a more sophisticated manner than my clinical intuition had indicated. The study showed strong differences in outcome when interpretations were followed by deep experiencing of affect versus when interpretations were followed by defensive behaviors. I deduced from this study that the relation between process and outcome must not be overly generalized. The efficacy of affect and defense must be assessed in context of the therapist intervention.

Our conscious minds indeed limit what we can see. "How we need the objectivity of science," I thought. The data were indeed my friend after all, and had provided me with greater understanding of the clinical process than my subjective impression—my bias—could have discerned alone. In fact, these findings made much sense in retrospect. It taught me that we need the objectivity and methodology of science to refine and sharpen the focus of our intuition. We need the honeybee as well as the unicorn.

Since then, these findings have guided my clinical work. When I give an interpretation, I now pause, and wait to see what kind of response the patient makes. Is it an opening to feeling, or a shutting down of defensiveness? That information tells me whether to proceed along affective lines, or to further explore the resistance.

Then at the 1997 Annual Conference for the Society for Psychotherapy Research, I encountered a study by Perry (1997) that showed that the degree of defensiveness did in fact negatively predict outcome in depressed patients. I was confused because I had not found that defenses predicted outcome. What was wrong? After some discussion, it occurred to me that my subject population comprises individuals with personality disorders, and it may therefore represent a much more heterogeneous group than those diagnosed as depressives—at least in terms of the defenses that are used. Maybe depressive clients use a more consistent group of defenses, which are then more predictive of response to treatment. In such ways, my clinical consciousness is constantly refined and made more sophisticated —or at least humbled—by research.

THE FIRST CLINICAL TRIAL: THE EFFECTS OF PROCESS AND OUTCOME RESEARCH ON PRACTICE

The next big impact of research on our clinical work concerned the role of confrontation and value of the anxiety-provoking approach. In the early 1980s, my colleagues and I strongly believed in the anxiety-provoking and confrontational approach taught us by Habib Davanloo, one of the pioneers in brief psychotherapy (Davanloo, 1980). We did not believe Davanloo blindly, but were eager to submit his therapy model to empirical study. In fact, I have always been skeptical about these charismatic clinicians who tell us they have "the right and only way." Each method must be studied as objectively as possible. Nevertheless, I had been willing to gamble my research efforts on Davanloo's anxiety-provoking approach to short-term therapy because his videotapes were the most powerful I had ever seen, and his method appeared a to be a potent one to study.

The Beth Israel Medical Center Research Program had been established by Arnold Winston in 1982 to study these confrontive and provocative short-term methods (McCullough & Winston, 1991; Winston et al., 1989). Sixty-four patients received a standard assessment battery and were randomly assigned to one of two treatment conditions that varied the amount of confrontation and focus on affect. All 40 sessions of each therapy were videotaped, and 4 of the sessions were coded for psychotherapy process variables.

I was the research director of this project, from 1985 to 1990. For two of these years, Habib Davanloo trained us in his method, which was called short-term dynamic psychotherapy (STDP; Davanloo, 1980). The research therapists worked tremendously hard to copy the master as closely as possible, sometimes trying to mimic Davanloo's every move. In addition, we used this confrontive short-term therapy almost exclusively in private practice. There was no denying that we were biased in favor of this method.

To test our therapy in a randomized clinical trial, Arnold Winston decided on a comparison model that was a less confrontive, more traditional version of active focused psychotherapy called brief adaptive psychotherapy (BAP). Those of us devoted to Davanloo's confrontational approach were quite skeptical about this other model. After all, we saw our confrontational methods as intense and progressive. The changes in our patients seemed dramatic. In our biased minds, our intense and confrontive approach simply had to lead to more improvement. However, it is noteworthy that the BAP group felt equally devoted to their less confrontive model of treatment and held the same skepticism about us.

Alas, 7 years later all our hunches proved wrong. The results of the clinical trial demonstrated what all other psychotherapy research demonstrated, that is, that there were no significant differences in outcome between the milder confrontive group (the BAP group) and the strongly confrontive group (the STDP group; Winston et al., 1994, 1991). Just as had happened earlier with the affect–defense results, we were again astonished! How could our intuition be so off? But there it was. The average treatment outcome showed little difference between the two groups.

There was one aspect of the data, however, that was interesting. The outcomes in the BAP group fell within a fairly narrow range, but the STDP group outcomes had a much wider variability. Even though all patients showed some degree of improvement since receiving treatment, some of the STDP group became dramatically better, while some became only slightly better. It would have been interesting to study these variations in outcome in the two groups. However, I moved to the Center for Psychotherapy Research at the University of Pennsylvania and did not have time to pursue this. In fact, I forgot about this finding until the second clinical trial yielded a similar pattern of results 7 years later (which I discuss below).

The wide variability in outcomes led us to look at another clinical phenomenon that we had been avoiding: the sometimes poor response to the highly confrontive treatment. There were several STDP research patients who dropped out, whereas no patients had dropped out of our private practices. On reflection, we realized that when we performed live research interviews that were publicly viewed, we held firmly to the "book" of the anxiety-provoking model and confronted the patient's defenses continuously and repeatedly. In contrast, when patients in our private practice reported discomfort with such confrontation, we tended to shift our styles so that they would not feel so badgered or harassed.

The results of the rigidly confrontative versus flexible empathic approaches differed dramatically. As noted, a number of our research participants dropped out, and they were so furious, in fact, that they never returned. This was the case even though we had explained in advance that we were testing a confrontive model and would offer them a different treatment if they didn't like it.

We were very concerned about these dropouts. First, as healers, we should do no harm. These people were suffering and badly in need of help, yet our interventions had alienated them. The negative reaction of the research patients was extremely important data, but even that alone was not sufficient to change our position. It was too easy to believe that if only we could get Davanloo's technique "right" the patients might have responded better.

Although the private patients responded positively to the combination of some confrontation with support, did this change our position? Curiously it did not. We simply thought we were being "incompetent" therapists and placating our patients; we held onto our bias that we had to be "tough" for patients to change. Our clinical experience, as salient as it was, did not lead to behavior change in the therapists. We were sufficiently wedded to our beliefs that it took more research data to convince us to shift to gentler, less confrontive methods.

Intensive Study of Confrontation on Patient Response

As a result of these surprising outcomes and our curiosity and concern about patient responses, we decided to further explore the process of confrontation. Although we had begun to have doubts about confrontation, we were still not ready to give up on its power. It was possible that our research therapists were not as skilled in confrontation as Davanloo.

We resolved to test his theories in a number of stepwise process studies. The first was conducted by Monica Salerno at Columbia Teacher's College and was supervised by my colleague, Barry Farber, and me (Salerno, Farber, McCullough, Winston, & Trujillo, 1992). Salerno et al. examined whether a therapist's confrontation yielded more affect or more defense in the minute following the confrontation. To our surprise, and counter to our hypotheses, a clarification was more often followed by affect than a confrontation. Well, we thought, hanging onto our biases, maybe several minutes of sustained confrontation would be needed to break through to deep affect.

Therefore, the next dissertation, again conducted at Columbia Teachers College and supervised by Barry Farber and me (Makynen, 1992), was designed to examine confrontations that were sustained over many minutes —as Davanloo's method endorsed. We were certain we would see increased affective responding in the longer confrontive periods. But we were wrong again! Sustained minutes of confrontation did not elicit more affect. Counter to our hypotheses, and counter to our clinical intuition, sustained minutes of clarification elicited greater affect in the patients. The Makynen study strongly contributed to the growing need for graded and empathic procedures for recognition and relinquishing of defenses. In exploratory analyses of the coding data, confrontations given *along with a supportive or empathic statement by the therapist* resulted in a greater likelihood of expression of affect, a higher rating of therapist alliance (especially in lower functioning or more "difficult" patients), and a better probability of improvement at outcome. Patients seemed to be more receptive to the painful information contained in a therapist's confrontation or interpretation when it was paired with a statement that reflected empathy, understanding, support, or care.

The final dissertation to confirm these initially counterintuitive findings was conducted by Christine Joseph from Rutgers University and was supervised by Stan Messer and me (Joseph, 1988). Following these studies of patient response to certain therapist interventions, Joseph then decided to look at patient–therapist interaction from the opposite perspective. She compared the likelihood that a given therapist intervention (e.g., questions, clarifications, confrontations, interpretations, self-disclosure, support, etc.) would precede affective responding versus defensive responding. We hypothesized that confrontation would significantly elicit affective responding. But Joseph, like Makynen (1992) and Salerno et al. (1992), demonstrated that, of all the eight interventions, confrontation more often elicited defensive behavior. Clarification was the only variable that significantly elicited affect. Apparently, the therapist's listening carefully and reflecting back what the patient said prepared the patient to respond in a less defensive and more open and affective manner.

Studies such as these have led me and my colleagues to seriously question the anxiety-provoking techniques as the best—or only—method for altering defenses. Our inclination as clinicians, to back off and be more gentle, was supported by these studies. Therefore, when anxieties emerged, no longer did therapists have to intensify the confrontation of defenses to achieve "breakthroughs" to feeling, as with Davanloo's (1980) anxiety-provoking theory. Our studies and the studies of others at that time (e.g., Wallerstein, 1986, on the Menninger study; research on common factors) were demonstrating that emotional depth could also be elicited by support, validation, and the provision of a safe and encouraging relationship in which the patient could face difficult issues.

These accumulating research results were hard to ignore. By 1989, I finally yielded to the data and began to develop a new treatment model based on these results. In 1990, I tested early versions of this new and gentler model on a few patients, with dramatic success. After 15 to 17 sessions, several of these patients said, "I'm a whole new personality" or "My friends tell me I'm a completely different person." These results led to modification of the treatment model to an anxiety-regulating approach rather than an anxiety-provoking one. Instead of confronting patients, more clarification was used, and confrontation was accompanied by more supportive interventions.

Intensive Study of Affective Responding

Further research from the Beth Israel lab (McCullough et al., 1991) demonstrated that the patient's affective response to transference interpretations significantly predicted improvement at outcome.

The strength of this relationship was heightened by the fact that transference interpretations followed by affect were a rather uncommon occurrence. (There was a total of 61 in 64 coded sessions; i.e., less than one per session. No such responses occurred in the four poorest outcomes cases.) This finding emphasized (a) the efficacy of eliciting patient affect under specific therapeutic conditions (e.g., interpretation) and (b) the need to understand how to remove the obstacles and how to increase the occurrence of such responses.

In another study, Taurke et al. (1990) demonstrated that the ratio of affect to defenses expressed was predictive of improvement. (The greater the ratio of expressed affect to defenses, the greater the improvement at outcome.) Patients started with an average of one episode of expressed affect per every five defensive responses at admission. At termination, the five most improved patients showed an average of one affective response for every two defensive responses. The five least improved patients showed no change in the 1:5 affect-to-defense ratio shown at admission. This study provided direct support of Malan's (1979) conceptual scheme that lowering defensiveness in relation to affective expression contributes to improvement in outcome.

Viewed as a whole, these studies on confrontation, clarification, defenses, and affects underscore the need for techniques to elicit affective expression, as well as the need for techniques which *overcome the defensive obstacles* to affective expression. Thus, the objectives in the short-term anxiety-regulating model (the restructuring of defenses and affects) follow directly from the above research.

Thus, research can indeed influence practice. Many of my colleagues and I have found that research and discovery led to several major changes in the model of therapy we use. Many of us shifted from Davanloo's (1980) confrontational model to a more empathic model, counterintuitive to logic when we began the study. We learned how crucial affect is to change, as well as how therapists avoid affect as much as do patients. We developed ideas for using videotape for improving research as well as training. We were all shifting the way we worked on the basis of research we could no longer ignore. Those of us who have had hands-on experience with observation of videotapes and the study of therapy microprocesses as I have been describing have been greatly influenced in the way treatment is conducted.

THE SECOND CLINICAL TRIAL: OUTCOME RESEARCH THAT FURTHER AFFECTED CLINICAL UNDERSTANDING

In 1990, at the Department of Psychiatry, the University of Trondheim in Norway, a research study led by Martin Svartberg and Tore Stiles ran a clinical trial to test my newly developed STDT model against cognitive therapy (CT). The main purposes of the study were to examine (a) the comparative outcomes of my anxiety-regulating form of STDP and a CT based on Beck and Freeman (1990) and Young (1990); (b) the course of improvement both during and after treatment; and (c) a series of process variables and their impact on outcome. Fifty patients meeting DSM–III–R (*Diagnostic and Statistical Manual of Mental Disorders*, 3rd ed., rev.; American Psychiatric Association, 1987) criteria for Cluster C personality disorders (i.e., avoidant, dependent, obsessive, passive–aggressive, and self-defeating) were randomized to 40 sessions of either STDP or CT. All sessions were videotaped.

The group of Norwegian research therapists who were studying my treatment became just as zealous about my therapy model as the Beth Israel group had been about Davanloo's. Affirmation, empathy, and support combined with confrontation now seemed to us to be so obviously superior to other methods in restructuring defenses that we believed we had a very strong and progressive model of treatment to test.

We were equally skeptical that CT could perform as well as the powerful methods that had evolved in STDP for the treatment of patients with long-standing character problems. But, like the Beth Israel research groups a decade before, the cognitive therapists were biased toward their treatment and felt just as skeptical about us! Maybe we need our biases to keep up morale during the lengthy and tedious research process. At any rate, a number of years were required to provide therapy to a total of 50 patients. Finally in 1997, the results came in.

Like most other psychotherapy research to date, and like our previous clinical trial at Beth Israel in New York, the results of the Norwegian clinical trial indicated that at termination there were no significant differences between STDP and CT in terms of rates of improvement during treatment for symptoms or interpersonal functioning.

I was frankly disappointed. I complained to the study's director and said, "But Martin, you said your impression was that the STDP group performed better!" "Yes, I did," he replied, "but that was my subjective impression, and the data tells us differently. You ought to be pleased that your model demonstrated efficacy like all the others."

Well, I was somewhat pleased, but also somewhat discontented. I had spent 10 years attempting to develop a model that would combine the strongest treatment components I could identify. For a while, I attempted every form of rationalization: Were the two treatment groups different enough? Did the STDP therapists perform the treatment adequately? (Indeed, for the most part, they did excellent work.) So, on reflection, I had to accept these initial results that both groups improved similarly—at least at termination.

I believe it was Newton who said that we must take our theories lightly. Over the years, I have been initially disappointed by results time and again. But the data keeps me on track. What I am learning from empirical study is that the answers I seek are not going to be as forthcoming, or as easy to identify as I had initially thought.

At present there are other studies that may provide more information. The first will be the results of the follow-up study—will the STDP group outperform the cognitive group in maintenance of treatment effects?

The second study that needs to be done is to examine the similar findings of the two clinical trials. In both clinical trials there was a wide variability in the STDP outcomes and a narrow variability in the comparison group. This means that the cognitive group (like the BAP group) had consistent outcomes falling within a narrow range. It also means that the STDP groups had widely varying outcomes; STDP patients had improved, but some patients had shown dramatic improvement and others, minimal improvement in contrast to the cognitive group. The more affectively intense STDP group had less consistency in outcomes.

I had not explored this finding 8 years earlier. If I had, I might have learned something that would have improved this second clinical trial. This time I would like to examine this difference in variability of outcomes more closely to see whether the best outcomes in the STDP group are correlated with the therapists who best adhere to the treatment model and whether the least improved outcomes are linked to the poorest adherents to the treatment model. I hope that if we can identify the treatment processes predicting the best and least improved, we can work toward better training of therapists. Someday, we will have treatment models that produce dramatic effects, and my hunch is that continued research on treatment microprocesses will lead us toward isolating active ingredients that can differentiate high-quality from low-quality therapy.

Process of Discovery: Effect of Clinical Practice on Research

The above discussion gave an overview of the research studies that led to revisions in my evolving treatment model. Now I examine this interaction from the opposite direction, that is, how clinical work has affected research, for the clinical discovery process provides fertile soil in which our research hypotheses grow. In the following sections, I try to convey how this discovery process takes place by using some recent examples of surprising or serendipitous clinical experiences.

Discovering Wasted Therapy Time

At a symposium (Thomas, 1996) at the Annual Convention of the American Psychological Association in Toronto, Ontario, Canada, Simon Budman (a well-known researcher and teacher of time-limited treatment) said that after watching many videotapes of psychotherapy, he found that most of the time, not much happens—therapy was not very interesting. When I heard him say this, I initially wanted to disagree. After all, ample research has demonstrated that therapy leads to improvement. However, I have also reviewed hundreds of videotapes, and I had to admit that the sad truth is that much—if not most—of time spent in therapy is—well —wasted. There is an enormous amount of chaff around the wheat. There appears to be far too much noise in the system.

Let me define what I mean by *wasted*. Wasted time means when the activity is not constructive to anything or, worse, when it is destructive. I do not consider time wasted that is given to being together to build trust and alliance, nor to letting things sink in, nor to letting patients go slow because they have been racing all their lives. Wasted time means doing something that is truly unnecessary that does not contribute to the resolution of the problems at hand. We need to begin to examine "effective" versus "ineffective" portions of therapy and try to determine the optimal ratio of change-inducing (or merely comforting) time to what might be, in fact, wasted time. If therapy still manages to be effective in its current incarnations, how much more effective might it be if we were able to distill the essence of the active ingredients?

Revising My Subjective Impression: Studying My Own Videotapes

Every Wednesday afternoon at the Psychotherapy Research Program at Harvard Medical School, a group of experienced clinicians volunteer time to code videotapes of psychotherapy.

The tapes that we had been rating for several months were those conducted by the research therapists. The outcomes were impressive— especially because these were therapists treating their first short-term cases. For each case, we rate among other things the degree to which a patient experiences affect on a 1–100 point scale (see the Achievement of Therapist Objectives Scale manual; McCullough, Meyer, Cui, Andrews, & Kuhn, 1997). Even though these patients improved, the patients' ratings of affect experiencing were low to moderate (20–40). These results suggested that intense levels of affect experiencing were not needed for successful therapy to occur. Our intuition had told us quite differently, for we had believed that we needed intense levels of affect to modify character disorder. Now in retrospect, it seems obvious that people have a hard time "digesting" intense levels of affect, and moderate levels appear to be sufficient for change.

Nevertheless, the coders were lacking practice in rating intense examples of affect. One of the most frequent coding mistakes made by trainees is giving high ratings to moderate levels of affect because they have never seen what high levels of affect look like. I knew that in my own treatments I worked at a much more intense level, so watching my tapes might be instructive.

To demonstrate affective intensity, I decided to have the coders rate a case of mine called the *betrayed idealist*: a successful outcome of a 20-year-old man whose depression since childhood was resolved in 20 sessions and has been maintained for over 3 years. I was excited to show them examples of intense grief, anger, compassion, and tenderness. But I was in for a surprise. Although I have edited many of my tapes for workshops, I had never taken the time to scrutinize every minute of an entire 25-session treatment. I tend to excerpt the most important few minutes. Therefore, my subjective impression of my sessions was startlingly different from what we viewed. True, I held the focus well, and as I had thought, I worked intensely with the affect. My patient's peak affective moments were rated 90 out of 100, whereas the peak moments of the novice therapists did not go above 60. What was distressing was that the percentage of time that I spent doing these very good things was remarkably low. The amount of time I spent rambling on about nothing very important was surprisingly high. Although I was on topic, and I was being supportive in my ramblings, after two or three sentences by me, the patient clearly tuned out, picking his nails, or looking out of the window, waiting for me to stop talking. At that point, nothing worthwhile was happening, and I could do nothing but admit that the time was wasted.

Furthermore, my *average* ratings of my patient's degree of affective experiencing were only 8 points higher than those of the therapists I supervised (research patient average response = 30, range = 5–60; my patients' average response = 38, range = 15–90). Before this research experience, I would never have believed that I was wasting time in therapy. My subjective impression was that I was active every minute. But apparently, the quantity of activity outweighs the quality.

The point is that this "clinical discovery" strongly altered my subjective impression of my delivery of treatment, and it merits further study. When are we, or are we not wasting a patient's time? What might process–outcome results reveal about time that we might call "wasted"? What might the patients tell us about time being wasted or not?

That is the purpose of the study of short-term approaches, to identify powerful change mechanisms initially and roughly in our videotape review and then with more refinement in our research.

Changing My Style Based on Colleagues' Videotapes

Watching colleagues' tapes can have a powerful impact as well. Last year I attended the Short-Term Psychotherapy Conference in New York City, where two tapes were shown, one by Isabel Sklar and one by Diana Fosha. Both therapists are specialists at dealing with affect and were adept at gentle, quiet focus on sorrow in a way that deepened the patient's experience and was extremely moving to watch.

I was on the panel that day, and I commented, "One of the hazards of doing short-term therapy is that therapists become so active that we do not shut up long enough to let the patient feel. After watching these two therapists work, I am going home tomorrow and lower my voice and talk less!" The audience laughed, but I meant what I said. I returned to my office the following Monday morning to see a very defensive man I call *the banker*. I tried to speak less and have longer silences. Within 15 minutes, this reserved, unemotional man started sobbing. I stared at him in disbelief, barely able to absorb the effect of what had transpired. I may have been blocking his sad feelings for weeks by intellectualizing!

I then decided to test this same technique with another reserved, unemotional man. We were on our 50th session and not much was happening, which in my short-term model makes me uncomfortable. I hoped this quieter approach would have an impact. But as I softened my voice and began to speak more slowly, he leaned far back in his chair and eyed me suspiciously, "Why are you talking so softly? What are you up to? [Angrily] Are you being seductive with me?" My clinical hypothesis instantly required revision.

But it was grist for the therapeutic mill. What became evident is that there are optimal levels of silence that sometimes effectively elicit emotion but that at other times elicit paranoia. Watching my skilled colleagues made me vividly aware of how much we have to learn about handling affect well.

Discovering Therapist Avoidance of Feelings

The extensive review of videotapes has highlighted another major problem in the delivery of treatment: handling patients' affect. For years I can remember my colleagues and I walking through the corridors of Beth Israel Medical Center in New York City, scratching our heads and wondering how to handle a certain problem. One of the most frequent questions was the following: "How do you intensify affect?" Affect seemed so elusive, and patients so quickly shifted away from feeling into defensiveness.

Until we carefully scrutinized the videotapes, we had not realized that, alas, it was not only the patient but also the therapist who shifted away from the affective intensity. I have watched the videotapes of myself as well as of dozens of highly experienced senior clinicians, and at times we all "lighten up," shirk the feeling, or blatantly change the subject when the patient begins to experience feelings. If the patient said, "I'm feeling sad," rather than the therapist responding, "Tell me more about your sad feelings," we would say, "I wonder what brings that up now (which leads to an analytical examination) or "You're avoiding your anger by talking about sadness (could be true, but the sadness should be explored as well). At other times, the therapist would talk over the patient, ignoring the sad feelings!

Recognition of this avoidance pattern has been humbling. Apparently, it is easier to preach about strong affect than to practice eliciting it. It also suggests the need for careful research about therapists' avoidance of intense affect.

As the above examples indicate, the open examination of clinical interventions and errors appears to be a valuable tool for a clinical researcher to develop and revise hypotheses and to build and rebuild theories. To advance the field, it seems essential to study these microprocesses.

Effect of Research on Training

Another form of cross-pollination of research and clinical work involves the use of coding procedures as training tools for teaching psychotherapy. Evaluating videotapes for research has awakened me to the tremendous value of videotape for teaching. I now use videotapes in all the classes and workshops I conduct.

When one is immersed in the complexity of the session, it is very difficult to process all the details. The valuable result of watching a videotape is that one learns to process more readily, and to more quickly pick out patterns during the session. The video-watcher seems to develop a therapeutic "observing ego." Viewers can hone their skills as master therapists and researchers as the years go by. I would not want to do research or clinical work on psychotherapy without ongoing videotape review.[1]

Recommendations for Integrating Research and Practice

The ultimate goal of psychotherapy research is not only to develop methods or analyze data but also to continually contribute to our under-

---

[1] I began watching videotapes of psychotherapy in the late 1970s. I recently calculated that I have spent an average of 200 hours of videotape review per year (4 hours per week), for 15 years, for a total of about 3,000 hours. (About 30% are my own tapes, and the rest are tapes of supervisors, colleagues, and supervisees.) During that same time I have probably spent about 12 hours per week (three times as much) in clinical work. I now feel addicted to watching a small portion of my tapes each week because it has felt so beneficial to my growth and development as both a therapist and a researcher. I can more quickly identify effective interventions, catch my errors, note difficulties I might have missed, see whether I stay on focus, or catch myself when I inappropriately "lighten up" the patient's affective experience.

standing of the healing of emotional disorders. Therefore, I offer the following recommendations:

1. Videotape analysis should become a standard training tool.
2. Practical clinical tools should be developed from the research process.
3. Single-case experimental designs that focus on microprocesses of treatment should be conducted to better guide clinical practice.

Use of Videotape for Training: Airline Pilot Standards

The master–apprentice model has long been the method of teaching in the arts, music, and crafts, but psychotherapy is the one field in which the student almost never sees the master doing the work. All too often, beginning psychotherapists are assigned live patients without ever once observing a psychotherapy session being conducted, or without ever having a opportunity to *practice*, or even to observe a senior therapist. The senior psychotherapist, for reasons of confidentially and comfort of the patient, has typically remained largely hidden to the trainee.

With the advent of the videotape, fields such as athletics and surgery have shown us the tremendous value of "the instant replay" or videotape review. In psychotherapy, the videotape now permits observation and practice to happen without anyone getting hurt.

The methods for training airline pilots offer a model for how the videotape might be used. Before a pilot is entrusted with taking a plane into the air, hundreds of hours of practice in the test cockpit are required. It might be worthwhile to consider having therapist trainees log hours at the video machine. As well-documented single-case designs (with videotaped sessions) begin to accumulate, practice programs could be developed for therapists-in-training and standards could evolve for hours logged at the videotape machine, not simply in passive watching, but in interactive coding, responding to and anticipating of the "next move to be made." Furthermore, we need research on this form of training to identify the most effective ways of teaching psychotherapy.

Development of Clinical Tools

One of the clinical tools that has evolved from our Psychotherapy Research Program at Harvard Medical School is a problem and symptom instrument checklist: the Psychotherapy Assessment Checklist Forms (PAC-Forms). This is a patient self-report checklist of symptoms and medical history (e.g., main problems, depression, anxiety, etc.) similar to the checklist that one fills out for a medical examination (e.g., history of mumps, measles, etc.) The PAC-Forms are an abbreviated version of our much more extensive research assessment battery, and they enable private practitioners to easily and quickly acquire information that can guide their diagnostic evaluation on the five axes of the *DSM–IV* (*Diagnostic and Statistical Manual of Mental Disorders*, 4th ed.; American Psychiatric Association, 1994), plus a number of other problem areas. We have made this instrument available to clinicians for a small donation to our research program, and all proceeds go toward generating transcripts of research sessions.

Other clinical tools being developed from our research program are books and articles that describe the clinical process in great depth (McCullough et al., in press; McCullough, 1998). It is well-known in the psychotherapy research field that research articles as they are written have not been helpful in informing or guiding clinical treatment. Although videotapes developed for training are ideal for such purposes, issues of confidentiality have slowed their dissemination. For these reasons, I am developing a series of books that will provide exposure to the minute-by-minute dialogue between the patient and therapist through extensive transcripted material from many sessions of several short-term treatments. Transcripted materials are beginning to be published, but they are necessarily often highly edited and condensed. These books will contain unedited transcripts of sessions—including therapist successes as well as errors. In addition, the transcripts will be interspersed with lively discussions, disagreements and debates between myself (as supervisor), the research therapist, and invited experts with differing theoretical orientations. To ensure that the methods presented have contributed to—or at least have not detracted from—a successful treatment outcome, these cases will be selected from those single-case experiments conducted at the Psychotherapy Research Program at Harvard Medical School that have objectively demonstrated outcomes and follow-ups.

The Single-Case Experiment

The ultimate interplay of research and clinical work converges in well-designed single-case experiments. In large clinical trials, I have found it very difficult to find the time to examine each session in depth and to study the treatment that is provided. Single-case methodology offers a well-developed approach for the in-depth study of microprocesses. However, as an alternative to a control group, single-case design typically depends on reversibility or withdrawal of treatment to demonstrate effects and to control for threats to internal validity. This has posed an obstacle for therapies in which learning takes place, because treatment effects generally are not reversible; insight once gained or affect once experienced cannot easily be forgotten. Hilliard (1993) noted that "when effects are not reversible, the threats to internal validity cannot be as easily ruled out" (p. 378).

As an alternative to reversibility, researchers have recommended that single-case designs be developed that demonstrate the magnitude and immediacy of change, that is, rapid, dramatic change can imply a treatment effect (e.g., Hersen & Barlow, 1976; Kazdin, 1981). Therefore, in our psychotherapy research program, we are working to develop more rigorous single-case designs for psychodynamic (nonreversible treatment effect) approaches. These methods attempt to capture the magnitude and immediacy of change by systematically varying several aspects of the treatment by (a) staggering the onset of active, focused treatment (e.g., to begin with a supportive or placebo condition); (b) staggering the onset of focus on a specific psychodynamic conflict; and (c) varying the type and amount of treatment intervention provided on that focus (e.g., degree of defense or affect restructuring needed to resolve conflicts about grieving).

In such a multiple baseline approach, treatment would be tailored to the specific patient as similarly as possible to the naturalistic provision of treatment (to enhance external validity); interventions would be varied over time, and response to interventions would be assessed continuously (to enhance internal validity). Such designs not only could aid researchers in teasing out potent interventions and change mechanisms but also would have direct relevance to the practicing clinician.

CONCLUSION

My colleagues and I have just finished 2 decades of therapy outcome research. Process research is just getting off the ground. Over the span of years, the knowledge gleaned from the systematic study of clinical work has the power to shape and refine our treatment models, to help generate more sophisticated hypotheses, and to guide our clinical work. Research studies take years, but search and discovery can happen daily—or even hourly. It is in the daily examination of what we do that we build the hypotheses we need to test repeatedly. Research refines our thinking and feeling, but it is in our hearts that it all begins.

In writing this chapter, I began with what was conscious—the methodical bee—but in trying to talk about my own process, I came to find the mystical unicorn emerging. So I conclude, as does Hudson in his book:

> And yet still I must believe that one never does or can find the whole in all its aspects, and that there never after all will be a philosopher who did not reach his truth ... except by some partiality and one-sidedness—and that, far from mattering, this is the right and the only way. (Hudson, 1972, pp. 177–178)

REFERENCES

American Psychiatric Association. (1987). *Diagnostic and statistical manual of mental disorders* (3rd ed., rev.). Washington, DC: Author.

American Psychiatric Association. (1994). *Diagnostic and statistical manual of mental disorders* (4th ed.). Washington, DC: Author.

Beck, A. T., & Freeman, A. (1990). *Cognitive therapy of personality disorders*. New York: Guilford Press.

Davanloo, H. (Ed.). (1980). *Short-term dynamic psychotherapy*. New York: Jason Aronson.

Hersen, M., & Barlow, D. H. (1976). *Single case experimental designs: Strategies for studying behavior change*. New York: Pergamon Press.

Hilliard, R. B. (1993). Single-case methodology in psychotherapy process and outcome research. *Journal of Consulting and Clinical Psychology, 61*(3), 373–380.

Hudson, L. (1972). *The cult of the fact: A psychologist's autobiographical critique of his discipline*. New York: Harper & Row.

Joseph, C. (1988). Antecedents to transference interpretation in short-term psychodynamic psychotherapy (Doctoral dissertaton, Rugers University, 1990). *Dissertation Abstracts International, 50,* 04B.

Kazdin, A. E. (1981). Drawing valid inferences from case studies. *Journal of Consulting and Clinical Psychology, 49*(2), 183–192.

Makynen, A. (1992). The effects of continued confrontation on patient affective and defensive response. (Doctoral dissertation, Columbia University Teachers' College, 1992). *Dissertation Abstracts International, 54,* 01B.

Malan, D. M. (1979). *Individual psychotherapy and the science of psychodynamics*. London: Butterworth.

Marziali, E. (1984). Prediction of brief psychotherapy from therapist interpretive interventions. *Archives of General Psychiatry, 41,* 301–304.

McCullough, L. (1991). Psychotherapy Interaction Coding System manual: The PIC System. *Social & Behavioral Science Documents, 18,* 50.

McCullough, L. (1998). Short term psychodynamic therapy as a form of desensitization: Treating affect phobias. *In session: Psychotherapy in Practice, 4*(4), 35–53.

McCullough, L., Kaplan, A., Andrews, S., Kuhn, N., Wolfe, J., & Lanza, C. (in press). Transforming Affect: *A workbook for short term dynamic psychotherapy*. New York: Guilford Press.

McCullough, L., Meyer, S., Cui, X. J., Andrews, S., & Kuhn, (1997). *The Achievement of Therapeutic Objectives Scale manual (ATOS)*. Unpublished manuscript. (Available from the STDP Program, Box 466, Dedham, MA 02026).

McCullough, L., & Winston, A. (1991). The Beth Israel Psychotherapy Research Program. In L. Beutler & M. Crago (Eds.), *Psychotherapy research: An international review of programmatic studies* (pp. 15–23). Washington, DC: American Psychological Association.

McCullough, L., Winston, A., Farber, B., Porter, F., Pollack, J., Laikin, M., Vingiano, W., & Trujillo, M. (1991). The relationship of patient–therapist interaction to outcome in brief psychotherapy. *Psychotherapy, 28,* 525–533.

Perry, C. (1997, June 24). *Defenses predict depressive symptomatology.* Paper presented at the annual conference of the Society for Psychotherapy Research.

Porter, F. (1987). The immediate effects of interpretation on patient in-session response in brief dynamic psychotherapy. (Doctoral dissertation, Columbia University Teachers College, 1987). *Dissertation Abstracts International, 48,* 87–24076.

Salerno, M., Farber, B., McCullough, L., Winston, A., & Trujillo, M. (1992). The effects of confrontation and clarification on patient affective and defensive responding. *Psychotherapy Research, 2*(3), 181–192.

Taurke, E., Flegenheimer, W., McCullough, L., Winston, A., Pollack, J., & Trujillo, M. (1990). Change in affect-defense ratio from early to late sessions in relation to outcome. *Journal of Clinical Psychology; 46,* 657–668.

Thomas, J. L. (Chair). (1996, August). *The many models of brief psychotherapy.* Symposium conducted at the 104th Annual Convention of the American Psychological Association, Toronto, Ontario, Canada.

Wallerstein, R. S. (1986). *Forty-two lives in treatment: A study of psychoanalysis and psychotherapy.* New York: Guilford Press.

Winston, A., Laikin, M., Pollack, J., Samstag, L., McCullough, L., & Muran, C. (1994). Short-term psychotherapy of personality disorders. *American Journal of Psychiatry, 151*(2), 190–194.

Winston, A., McCullough, L., Pollack, J., Laikin, M., Pinsker, H., Nezu, A. M., Flegenheimer, W., & Sadow, J. (1989). The Beth Israel Psychotherapy Research Program: Toward an integration of theory and discovery. *Journal of Integrative and Eclectic Psychotherapy, 3,* 345–357.

Winston, A., McCullough, L., Trujillo, M., Pollack, J., Laikin, M., Flegenheimer, W., & Kestenbaum, R. (1991). Brief psychotherapy of personality disorders. *Journal of Nervous and Mental Disease, 179*(4), 188–193.

Young, J. E. (1990). *Cognitive therapy for personality disorder: A schema-focused approach.* Sarasota, FL: Professional Resource Press.

7

RESEARCH AND PRACTICE AS ESSENTIAL TENSIONS: A CONSTRUCTIVIST CONFESSION

ROBERT A. NEIMEYER

When the editors of this volume invited me to contribute an account of my own experience of the relationship of psychotherapy research to practice, I hesitated. It was not that I found the topic uninteresting; quite the contrary, I found it hard to let go of the idea, no matter how many days I tried to ignore the intriguing invitation that kept beckoning to me whenever I opened my e-mail file. The problem was that the task of "going public" with my own (increasingly discordant) inner dialogue about the "sometime relationship" of research and practice was, well, a bit threatening. In my life as a therapist and researcher, I found myself tacking back and forth between the slippery subtlety required to conduct therapy and the apparently necessary formalization required to investigate it. Moreover, the dialectical tension represented by these two contrasting stances has— if anything—grown across time, so that I could not pretend to have resolved the issue, either for myself or others. Thus, in sheepishly accepting the invitation to write from within this tension, I had the nagging concern that the chapter might read like something of an Augustinian *Confessions* without the benefit of final redemption!

What follows is an externalization of my inner dialogue about the research and practice dialectic, which has yet to achieve any firm synthesis. Any resolution that I struggle to impose is at best provisional and might well take a somewhat different form by the time this book is in print. If I have any consolation about this state of affairs, it derives from my suspicion as a constructivist (R. A. Neimeyer & Mahoney, 1995; R. A. Neimeyer & Raskin, in press) that the same might be said of any form of human knowledge, which is inherently fragmentary, perspectival, historically situated, and embedded in our ongoing conversations and debates with others who support or challenge our constructions—even if these "others" are other aspects of ourselves. But I'm getting ahead of myself. In the interest of constructing a coherent narrative, I'll begin at the beginning, when I more or less simultaneously got bitten by the "science bug" while developing a serious case of phenomenology. Unfortunately, both appear to be chronic conditions, and although the symptomatology has shifted over the years, and my immune system has strengthened against the more virulent forms of each, I have continued to be comorbid for both right up to the present day. Fortunately, the reader probably need not worry about contracting a similar condition from reading this chapter, as I suspect that there is a strong constitutional factor that determines who is susceptible. So think of this as an exotic case study of "expressive–compulsive disorder with mixed features," and use your own good judgment about whether to share your prognosis with the patient!

RESEARCH VERSUS PRACTICE: A DIALOGUE IN TWO VOICES

A Naive Beginning: Crisis Intervention

I first recall recognizing the now familiar bifurcation between my researcher and practitioner selves when I was completing my undergraduate study at the University of Florida. Majoring in psychology and minoring in philosophy (with a particularly strong attraction to European existentialism and phenomenology), I was also volunteering as a crisis intervention worker in the Alachua County Suicide and Crisis Intervention Center, which was then a model program of its kind in the nation. As a "green" telephone counselor with a reputation for having good "active listening" skills, I was nonetheless impressed with the obviously more advanced crisis management skills of the senior care team members, who not only trained and supervised volunteers like me but also actually conducted face-to-face interventions with potentially suicidal clients. These counselors—typically graduate student interns in counseling and clinical psychology—modeled, and the rest of us emulated, a direct but caring way of assessing a client's risk of self-harm, of defining the precipitating problem, and of formulating action plans that would help clients achieve a new and more viable equilibrium. Although fairly straightforward as a form of therapeutic interaction, the style of these volunteers was sufficiently different from the instinctive ways that untrained persons dealt with such "life and death" situations that I became fascinated with the prospect of studying the issue. Because I had recently gotten interested in death attitudes as measured with personal construct methods, I focused mainly on those attitudes toward death that might distinguish crisis workers with different levels of experience from untrained psychology students (R. A. Neimeyer & Dingemans, 1980). Although this research was not on counseling per se, it was on counselors and laid the foundation for later work that more directly addressed therapist variables and clinical skills.

The problem with this initial study of counselors would be a familiar one for many researchers—it left me with more questions than answers, insofar as it did not directly address the distinctive response styles that seemed to define effective crisis counseling. These questions were sharpened when I graduated and entered the clinical doctoral program at the University of Nebraska, where I sought out the local crisis intervention centers to extend my skills in working with severely distraught individuals. What I found was mildly shocking to me: In place of the intensive 3-month training and close in-center supervision that characterized the Gainesville center, the Lincoln crisis services offered much more limited training (in one case, a single weekend workshop) before having volunteers take calls in their homes, without any serious form of supervisory oversight. Moreover, in witnessing the few role-plays of counseling situations that time permitted, I was painfully aware that most of the volunteers had incomplete mastery of even the most basic active listening skills, to put it charitably. For example, enacting the part of a severely depressed and potentially self-destructive college student in one such scenario, I was stunned when the counselor made short work of my presenting problem, encouraging me to "shave off my beard, get some new clothes, find a girlfriend, and everything would be all right." She was perfectly serious. Three days later, she was taking real crisis calls from clients like the one I had played! Faced with this discrepancy in preparedness of volunteer counselors, I at first experienced a working coalition between my germinal researcher and clinician identities. The dialogue between them, if it had been spoken aloud, might have sounded something like the following:

Clinician: A few of these crisis counselors are good, but some of them are downright *scary*. Did you hear the male counselor in that last role-play ask the female caller to meet him somewhere for a drink, so they could "talk things over more freely?" That doesn't fit any definition of "active listening" that I've ever heard.

Researcher: The problem here is one of quality assurance. What these services need is some objective criterion of counselor performance that helps them ensure, first, that their skills training is having some effect and, second, that the paraprofessionals have at least a rudimentary grasp of basic crisis intervention skills before they go on-line.

Clinician: Well, I certainly have some impressions about how many of these trainees can respond more appropriately . . .

Researcher: If you have some impressions, operationalize them. We can then establish a pool of items that discriminate appropriate from inappropriate counselor responses, construct and validate an inventory of suicide counseling skills, and build it into future paraprofessional training and selection efforts.

Clinician: Sounds like a good place to start.

As a result of this straightforward collaboration between my clinical and research roles, I constructed the Suicide Intervention Response Inventory (SIRI), a measure of the respondent's ability to select an appropriate response to crisis counseling scenarios. This led logically enough to a series of studies that established the validity and reliability of the SIRI (R. A. Neimeyer & MacInnes, 1981; R. A. Neimeyer & Oppenheimer, 1983), explored its factor structure (R. A. Neimeyer & Hartley, 1986), examined the acquisition of suicide management skills among medical students and psychiatric residents (R. A. Neimeyer & Diamond, 1983), and compared the 10 most common errors made by medical and nonmedical crisis interventionists (R. A. Neimeyer & Pfeiffer, 1994b). This latter research was particularly interesting in demonstrating that medical and counseling students erred in quite different ways when they did so, with medically trained interventionists reacting in a defensive, distancing, advice-giving, and essentially authoritarian fashion, whereas counselors fell into a pattern of excessive passivity, failing to sufficiently structure an interaction with a suicidal or disorganized client. For instance, medical students were seven times more likely than counselors to dismiss patient complaints with advice such as, "You've got to look on the bright side" or to retreat into a professionalistic response to an angry client who questioned why the helper should care about him by responding, "I've been trained to care about people. That's my job." In contrast, nonmedical counselors were less likely to prompt a silent client or secure a "no suicide" contract. These findings raised some interesting questions about selection and socialization of professionals in both fields, who may eventually face similar veiled communications of client despair in the course of their practices. Ultimately, this line of research also revealed limitations of the original SIRI, leading to the development of a revised version that removed the "ceiling effect" that prevented its application to more skilled psychotherapists (R. A. Neimeyer & Bonnelle, 1997; R. A. Neimeyer & Pfeffer, 1994a).

If I had limited my involvement in counseling and psychotherapy research to the study of the selection of facilitative responses to standard counseling scenarios, I might have remained unabashedly optimistic about the synergistic integration of the research and practice aspects of my professional identity. Unfortunately, other roughly simultaneous developments in my Boulder model graduate training were perturbing this comfortable synthesis, not the least of which was my immersion in the role of psychotherapist.

Clinical Complexities: The "Real World" of Psychotherapy

Like most psychotherapy trainees, I approached my first appointment with a client with a mixture of fear and fascination. Although my 4 years of experience in crisis intervention had given me a "leg up" on some of my more hapless peers in terms of basic counseling skills, I soon learned that the more intimate and sustained engagement in human change that took place in longer term psychotherapy required more than simply helping people get through one crisis after another. My first client, a nurse undergoing the breakup of a long-term relationship, seemed to invite and appreciate my helping her sift through the nuances of her relationship history, winnowing out themes that characterized not only her foundering romance but also her past relationships with men and her aspirations for the future. In the course of our 20 or so sessions, she movingly expressed her pain and uncertainty, collaborated with me in constructing metaphors that captured some of the subtler aspects of her experience, and made some courageous decisions about how to relate to her partner and when to "let go." We grew to like and respect one another, and we shared both laughter and tears in our termination session, as we wished each other well on our respective life trajectories.

My second case was another matter. My sense of false confidence in receiving a second referral form with a check mark next to "relationship problems" soon faded, as I confronted an angry and combative married couple in which the husband had recently disclosed his affair with another man. Unschooled in systemic thinking, I initially tried to defuse the tension by separating the warring spouses and seeing each individually before reconstituting a conjoint session. In doing so, I found the husband's germinal search for a sense of identity as a bisexual man far easier to identify with and validate than his wife's seemingly paranoic battle with the world and her attempts to "bully" him into being something he apparently was not. Although well intentioned, the therapy was a disaster, culminating in an individual meeting with the wife in which she so loudly and vehemently attacked my competence and compassion that the therapist conducting the adjacent therapy in our clinic disbanded her session because of her client's distress over what was happening next door. I was forced to concede that I never succeeded in getting inside the perspective of the "betrayed" wife, who came to view me as just another man who neglected her emotional needs while having secret liaisons with her partner.

What these two sessions taught me was that (a) morphologically similar presenting problems could, on closer inspection, dissolve into quite different sets of issues, (b) the "same" therapeutic model did not usefully generalize across different client contexts, (c) some worlds of meaning were easier for me to enter into than others, and (d) I was inevitably part of the therapeutic equation, for better or worse. Fortunately, my deepening familiarity with personal construct theory (Kelly, 1955) provided a conceptual scaffolding that made sense of the individuality of clients, and the personalism of my encounter with them. Thus, even if I was not uniformly successful as a therapist, I at least had recourse to a sophisticated theory that helped me understand some of what was transpiring in therapy and, when I was fortunate, engage in "course corrections" that led to a better working alliance with diverse clients.

At about this same time, my major professor, Al Landfield, came into possession of a remarkable series of previously unknown reel-to-reel tapes of George Kelly, the founder of personal construct theory, conducting psychotherapy. For a budding construct theorist like myself, this was roughly tantamount to a psychoanalytic trainee finding a long-lost Edison cylinder recording of Freud performing psychoanalysis! As a result, I was given an opportunity to transcribe and analyze scores of hours of the "master's" therapy, conducted some 20 years before. From the outset, the exercise was riveting, as I listened back across the years to Kelly's efforts to "join" with a defensive and resistant client, articulate the largely preverbal constructs that regulated the client's life, and foster new possibilities in his relationship to other persons in his world. The therapy presaged many later developments in psychotherapy, from the cognitive–behavioral to the interpersonal–analytic and existential–phenomenological, and often impressed me with Kelly's clinical acumen. At the same time, Kelly sometimes faltered, made little headway, or persisted with a therapeutic strategy that seemed to have already proven itself a failure. I was left with an image of a maverick therapist whose interventions typically were congruent with his theory, revealing both its power and, perhaps, its limitations (R. A. Neimeyer, 1980).

During this period, the inner dialogue between my researcher and clinician aspects grew more strained, as the latter reveled in the clinical complexities of Kelly's work and my own,[1] while the scientist in me "played it safe" with the SIRI research and a developing series of studies on friendship formation from a personal construct perspective. In a sense, the dialogue effectively ceased for a few years, as each compartmentalized "voice" found its own audience in conversations, conferences, and journals, without the apparent necessity of talking (or listening) to the other.

A New Hope: The Coming of Cognitive Therapy

I entered graduate school at the time Beck's (1976) first influential formulation of cognitive therapy principles was breaking on the psychological scene, and I was applying to internships when his magnum opus on the treatment of depression (Beck, Rush, Shaw, & Emery, 1979) was finding its way onto professional bookshelves and into graduate syllabi throughout the country. Given my fairly deep immersion in personal construct theory, Beck's perspective struck me as familiar in some respects (e.g., its assumptions that people respond to the meanings they attach to events, rather than to events in themselves, and that individuals develop idiosyncratic schemas on the basis of past experience) and as novel in others (e.g., its cornucopia of concrete techniques for revising cognitive structures). Like a competent speaker of Italian studying Spanish, I began a fairly serious study of the theory and research beginning to develop within the Beck perspective, and I became sufficiently "bilingual" in the two language systems to have cordial conversations with cognitive therapy "insiders," even while retaining a personal construct "accent."

This fortuitous occurrence set the stage for the next phase of my development as a psychotherapy researcher, which took place during my intensive internship year at the University of Wisconsin's medical center. In those days, Wisconsin offered a wide array of psychotherapy training experiences, ranging from family therapy with Carl Whitaker to Tavistock-style group therapy with Jim Gustafson as well as traditional psychoanalysis with Joe Kepecs. Adding to this clinical richness was a vital psychotherapy research program spearheaded by Marge Klein, and involving Al Gurman and John Greist as collaborators. I eagerly dived into all of these opportunities, which offered a new prospect for some form of rapprochement between my scientist and practitioner identities.

What emerged was my involvement in a well-controlled outcome study of treatments for depression, comparing group therapy (whose con-

---

[1]Like all stories, this one is a simplified account of a complex history. There were obviously many other persons and authors who influenced my emerging identity as a psychotherapist, ranging from clinical supervisors such as Clifford Fawl and Gerry Weinberger to philosophers such as Martin Buber (1970) and Maurice Merleau-Ponty (1962). In selecting a few highlights, I am only trying to illustrate some of the prominent factors that contributed to my inner dialogue about the feasibility of capturing the idiosyncrasies of practice in the nomothetic net of research.

tent partially reflected Gurman's interests in cognitive formulations) with two forms of physical exercise: relaxation–meditation and running (both of which derived from Greist's personal and professional interests in non-traditional treatments). I became a junior member of the research team, consulting on methodology and serving as a therapist in both the group psychotherapy and running conditions (if nothing else, managing to maintain my running program through a very cold and snowy Wisconsin winter!). My distinctive contribution to the study was the design of a specialized repertory grid, a personal construct measure that assesses the content and structure of a respondent's belief system (Kelly, 1955; R. A. Neimeyer, 1993b). In the modified form we used, the grid required participants to evaluate several aspects of their personal identity on a sample of relevant, personally generated constructs (e.g., trustful vs. mistrustful, ambitious vs. lazy), and the resulting ratings were used to derive several measures of cognitive features theoretically relevant to depression within Beck's formulation (e.g., negativity toward the self and future, polarized or dichotomous thinking). Preliminary analyses of the pretherapy data generally supported a cognitive conceptualization of depression, with each of these features showing significant associations with level of depression as measured by the Symptom Checklist (R. A. Neimeyer, Klein, Gurman, & Greist, 1983).

However, results of the outcome study itself were sobering. Although comparable improvement on a number of symptom measures was noted in all three conditions, the exercise-based treatments produced more durable gains than did the group therapy. More perplexing at the time was the nonspecificity of the outcomes, with no indication that the psychotherapy condition—even with its cognitive emphasis—had a greater impact on cognitive features of depression than did the activity-based treatments with which it was compared (Klein et al., 1985). My overall experience with this clinical trial prompted some rethinking on my part, which might have been externalized in the form of the following dialogue:

> Researcher: Hmm. There's food for thought here. We "did everything right," from a methodological standpoint, carefully establishing reliable research diagnostic criteria for our sample, randomizing participant assignment to conditions, training and monitoring therapists in each modality, minimizing attrition, and evaluating participant response on a host of well-validated and reliable outcome measures. So why the "no difference" conclusion?

> Clinician: Well, the most obvious possibility is that all of the treatments had a positive effect on participants. I can certainly say from my personal experience that the impact of a supportive group that encouraged members to evaluate their depressogenic cognitive and behavioral pat-

terns was at least matched by the sense of accomplishment that clients felt in accompanying us in 3 months of "one on one" runs through the wintry woods along Lake Mendota.

Researcher: But you're comparing apples with oranges! If the rationales underlying each of the treatments make any sense, you'd expect more differential change, at least on the measures of cognitive and interpersonal functioning, physical well-being, and tension measured by the repertory grid and other instruments. And yet these treatment-specific differences were few and far between. Surely you are not willing to endorse some form of unsatisfying "common factors" argument that ignores the mechanisms of change presumed to be activated by each treatment?

Clinician: Well, not yet, anyway. Part of the problem may be that the treatments themselves were not that "clean." Although I hate to admit it, and tried to keep it to a minimum, I sometimes listened to running-condition clients' brief accounts of their weekly travails as we puffed our way through the snow, and I even gave vague encouragement to group-condition clients who spontaneously shared their newfound enthusiasm for aerobics with other group members. Maybe what is needed is experimentation with even clearer forms of treatment that are tightly derived from well-developed alternative theories. If the truth be known, our integration of cognitive concepts in the groups was less than complete. In fact, we gave at least equal "air time" to exercises designed to promote group cohesion and emotional self-awareness. The overall ratio of cognitive to "noncognitive" interventions might prompt even Tim Beck to engage in depressive self-talk!

Researcher: Thanks for the belated confession. In the future, I'm obviously going to have to watch you and your clinical colleagues a little more closely! And just to be on the safe side, I'm going to tighten down on the measurement aspects not only to make sure that you are doing what you say you're doing but also to assess the presumed specificity of your interventions.

As a result of this experience, I developed greater optimism about the "researchability" of psychotherapy, and a keener interest in the workings of cognitive therapy in particular. But I also experienced a subtle shift in the "power relations" between my scientist and practitioner selves, perhaps paralleling that of the field of psychotherapy research as a whole: My research role had begun to assume a kind of supervisory stance in relation to my practice persona, and it was clear for the next few years who was "calling the shots," at least when the video camera was running in the context of the subsequent series of studies.

The Uneasy Coalition: A Constructivist in Cognitive Clothing

My postdoctoral move to a research associate position at the University of Rochester gave me the opportunity to mount large-scale clinical trials of my own, supported by the treatment staff and facilities of the university's Mt. Hope Family Center. I therefore launched a research program that continued after I left Rochester to take a faculty position at the University of Memphis in 1983. The core of the program concerned the implementation of "pure-bred" cognitive therapy in a group format, something that was fairly novel in those days, combined with an intensified effort to identify the "mechanisms of change" responsible for clinical improvement. I was particularly compulsive in designing a "squeaky clean" study that recruited experienced therapists, carefully diagnosed clients, randomized assignment to cognitive therapy and waiting-list conditions, manualized treatment, checked treatment implementation, and assessed outcome with the best available scales, which were completed both by clients and clinicians who did not know the treatment conditions.

One significant feature of this study was the opportunity it afforded to expand my earlier experimentation with repertory grid measures of cognitive structure, teasing out both theoretically "symptom-linked" measures of negativity about the self and future and "vulnerability-linked" measures of tendencies to construe the self in dichotomous terms. These measures were grounded not only in a cognitive therapy perspective but also in a personal construct model of depression that I was attempting to formalize at the time (R. A. Neimeyer, 1984, 1985b). The two approaches shared many content emphases (e.g., anticipatory failure, negative self-construing, dichotomous thinking), but the personal construct view also added a dimension concerned with structural features of the construct system that was relatively absent in traditional cognitive therapy (constriction and system disorganization at deeper levels of depression). Although the personal construct view failed to have much impact on the work of Beck and his associates, it did prove fertile in guiding research in group therapy for depression (Winter, 1992) as well as studies of the predictors of suicide risk among psychiatric patients (Hughes & Neimeyer, 1990, 1993; Prezant & Neimeyer, 1988). A subsequent factor analytic study demonstrated that the grid-based measures indeed tapped theoretically distinct features of the self-schemas of depressed individuals, which were clearly distinguishable from the more content-laden measures of cognitive errors and psychiatric symptomatology used in the majority of research (R. A. Neimeyer & Feixas, 1992).

Measurement issues aside, the overall results of this study were encouraging, documenting the reduction in both depressive symptomatology and suicide ideation in cognitive therapy clients relative to controls (R. A. Neimeyer, Heath, & Strauss, 1985). Moreover, both measures of self-negativity and polarized construing changed in predictable directions, providing at least some support for the presumed mechanisms of change posited by a cognitive model. This apparent success ushered in a series of studies of cognitive predictors of treatment response in cognitive and interpersonal therapies (R. A. Neimeyer & Weiss, 1990) and the role of homework as an "active ingredient" in cognitive–behavioral therapies for depression (R. A. Neimeyer & Feixas, 1990). At the same time, I collaborated with colleagues in following up research on exercise-based treatments for depression, in an attempt to demonstrate or rule out a cardiovascular training effect as a sufficient explanation for the clinically substantial changes observed in participants (Doyne et al., 1987; Ossip-Klein, Bowman, Osborn, McDougal-Wilson, & Neimeyer, 1989). In general, these studies further intensified the preoccupation with methodological control evident in my earliest forays into the outcome arena. For example, the R. A. Neimeyer and Feixas (1990) study of homework and no-homework versions of cognitive therapy was hailed as virtually unique in the psychotherapy literature in ensuring a "fair" clinical trial, by not only ensuring "delivery" of the intended intervention by the therapists but also checking "receipt" of the core message by the clients (Lichstein, Riedel, & Grieve, 1994). Thus, by conventional standards, the research program overall was clearly progressive.

And yet, all was not well for me as a principal investigator. Despite the success of these studies and the extensions of them into inpatient psychiatric settings (R. A. Neimeyer, Robinson, Berman, & Haykal, 1989; Nottingham & Neimeyer, 1992), I was troubled by concerns that were not being adequately addressed in my research-based practice. Stated in dialogic form, the misgivings might have sounded something like this:

Researcher: Well, so far so good! Sure, some of our unpublished studies may have had a hard time distinguishing between the cognitive therapy and no-treatment controls, but, hey, that could happen to anybody. Overall, this therapy clearly looks efficacious, and the tighter our design, the better the results. No wonder the pendulum is swinging in our direction throughout the whole field of psychotherapy research. History is on our side!

Clinician: I don't buy it. To begin with, although our cognitive groups may often, but not always, outperform no-treatment conditions, it is much less clear in our own research that they are superior to viable alternative treatments like interpersonal therapy (Klerman, Weissman, Rounsaville, & Chevron, 1984) or even competently conducted nonprofessional mutual support (Bright, Baker, & Neimeyer, 1999)! What's more, in my private practice I find that I rarely use straightforward cognitive interventions—even such basic concepts as "cognitive distortions" strike me as offensive and disrespectful, and the whole therapy as I have seen it practiced by its proponents seems preoccupied with minute details—a kind of psychotherapy devoid of *W* responses and absorbed in little *d*s, to use a Rorschach metaphor.

Researcher: You're analogizing the epitome of scientific psychotherapy to that unholy instrument!? Now I know you've really gone over to the other side. Surely you cannot seriously call into question the whole contemporary *zeitgeist* toward focused, directive, cognitive–behavioral self-control therapies as the leading exemplars of empirically validated treatments? What do you want psychology to do, just adopt an antiscientific "anything goes" mentality, on the presumption that any hare-brained treatment is as good as any other? Is that what you're advocating?

Clinician: Not at all. But we might start with the assumption that there are good reasons that intelligent and ethical therapists have spent their entire lives practicing within the framework of psychodynamic, humanistic, and systemic therapies, apparently to the benefit of their clients. It's not at all clear to me that cognitive–behavioral perspectives have a corner on the market of truth or efficacy, and the smugness I sometimes detect in their advocates is galling for this very reason. And as to that "contemporary *zeitgeist*" business, social studies of science give us ample reason to believe that the field may be shaped as much by sociological factors as by scientific ones.[2] More subtly, I suspect that the development of highly individualistic and "efficient" therapies centered on self-control, rational restructuring of troublesome emotions, and pursuit of mastery and pleasure experiences is given impetus by a deeply inscribed cultural discourse that constructs "personhood" in terms that lend credence to such mod-

---

[2]Sociologists of science have long contended that scientific fields are at least partly determined by "noncognitive" factors, such as charismatic leaders, trendsetting research, group dynamics, institutionalization, power hierarchies, and the like (Mulkay, 1979; Mullins, 1979). In their more radical moments, such theorists have virtually deconstructed the dialogue of rationality that gives science its special warrant and have questioned its pride of place among human forms of knowledge production (Woolgar, 1989). My own sociometric studies of the development of personal construct theory (R. A. Neimeyer, 1985a) and psychotherapy (R. A. Neimeyer & Martin, 1996) as scientific specialties leads me to similar, if less radical, conclusions.

els. Finally, the longer I practice a cognitive model of therapy, the more difficult I find it to keep from "constructivizing" it by relativizing all the terms, looking for the personal logic inside the apparently "dysfunctional" thinking, considering the discursive foundations of the client's narrative within his or her family and culture, and . . .

Researcher: Hold on a minute! I'm not even sure what you mean by that last part, much less how you would operationalize it to the point that it could be scientifically falsified. If you seriously want to follow this cockeyed line of thought, you should at least provide some evidence for the heretical claim that cognitive–behavioral therapies are no better than (shudder) "general verbal" approaches. What does the literature say about that?

Clearly, this portion of the dialogue could be expanded into a much more thorough discussion of the salient contrasts between constructivist therapies and their cognitive cousins, which differ importantly at epistemological and strategic levels (R. A. Neimeyer, 1993a). Briefly, traditional cognitive therapies view beliefs as valid to the extent that they correspond with a "real world" as revealed through the senses, and these therapies elevate rational disputation of erroneous beliefs as the sine qua non of mental health. Language, in this view, at most mediates between internal representations and external reality. The therapeutic practices that cohere with this perspective tend to focus on the bit-and-piece correction of faulty beliefs and on training in approved skills, targeted toward the amelioration of troublesome emotions. The therapist thereby assumes an authoritative, directive role, and the client that of a student. Constructivist approaches tend to depart from this characterization in virtually every respect, beginning with their commitment to a coherence theory of truth that emphasizes the struggle of people to construct integral belief systems that are consensually validated by relevant others. Accordingly, clients are viewed as striving to construct meaningful narrative accounts of their experience, irrespective of standardized canons of "truth" or "rationality," drawing on the resources of linguistic and symbolic systems that constitute a social reality rather than reflecting an objective world. Therapy in this view becomes more creative than corrective, with emotional shifts and nuances being taken as valuable guides into tacit domains of meaning that may be adequately represented only in metaphoric terms. The therapist appropriately adopts a "not knowing" stance, accentuating the entailments and dilemmas implied by the client's constructions and the recursive processes by which they are sustained in interaction with intimate others and with culture, more generally (Mahoney, 1991; R. A. Neimeyer, 1995b, 1998a).

The upshot of these conceptual considerations was that I became increasingly skeptical of the realist metatheory underpinning cognitive–behavioral therapy. Its advocates, on the other hand, seemed to take this metatheory for granted, and argued for the superiority of their preferred treatment as the only scientifically defensible one. In an attempt to address this question of the unique efficacy of cognitive–behavioral therapy, I therefore collaborated with two colleagues in conducting a comprehensive quantitative review of the outcome literature on cognitive–behavioral and alternative treatments for the disorder I knew best—depression. The results were thought provoking and spurred me in new directions.

From a Distant Perch: A Meta-Analytic Overview of Treatments for Depression

In the late 1980s, Leslie Robinson, Jeff Berman, and I teamed up to review all controlled studies of psychotherapy for depression, a review that grew to include all comparative trials of psychotherapy and pharmacotherapy as well (Robinson, Berman, & Neimeyer, 1990). We identified over 50 studies that met inclusion criteria and applied well-honed meta-analytic techniques to examine differences in outcome attributable to treatment format (group vs. individual), therapy type (e.g., cognitive, behavioral, general verbal), and a number of other variables, ranging from the length of therapy to the theoretical allegiance of the investigator. In short, we attempted to step out of the immediacy of conducting such treatments and designing primary studies of particular interventions; instead, we tried to see what might be learned from the efforts of scores of investigators over more than 20 years of researching treatments for the most common (and best studied) of psychological disorders.

The process of reviewing the literature was as revealing as the results themselves. We soon learned that the majority of studies were conducted by investigators who had a clear allegiance to one of the therapy models being evaluated (typically cognitive–behavioral), often signaled by their detailed and enthusiastic presentation of their preferred perspective in the introduction to the study, as well as in their own previous publications. By contrast, their comparison condition (when an "active" alternative treatment was included in addition to a no-treatment control) was thinly described in placebolike terms—*emotional support, group discussion, didactic education,* and the like. Often, no reference was even given for such comparison treatments, strongly suggesting that these conditions were intended as "straw man" opponents, devoid of the active ingredients presumed by the investigators to make therapy of any kind credible to therapists or beneficial for clients. Serious comparisons to plausible alternative therapies (e.g., psychodynamic therapy, crisis intervention, process-oriented group work) were so rare as to preclude their separate review. However, there was more heterogeneity and verisimilitude in the provision of different therapy formats, as well as in the typical number of sessions and size of groups, making analysis of these factors feasible.

In keeping with the findings of earlier meta-analysts, we found clear evidence that psychotherapy for depression was effective and, in fact, equal to antidepressant medication in efficacy (Robinson et al., 1990). Moreover, potentially more cost-effective group therapies were as beneficial as individual treatments, a finding that might encourage their more widespread use in the current climate of cost containment (R. A. Neimeyer et al., 1989). Furthermore, briefer therapies tended to fare as well as longer term alternatives, although the length of treatments included in these studies rarely exceeded more than a few months (Robinson et al., 1990). But most striking, the slim advantage of cognitive–behavioral therapies over their alternatives quickly dissipated when we controlled for investigator allegiance by partialing out the variance attributable to manifest researcher preference before calculating our *d* statistics (Robinson et al., 1990). In other words, once experimenter bias was accounted for, the presumed frontrunners among scientific therapies fared no better than the often marginally credible alternatives with which they were commonly compared. Thus, although psychotherapy in general seemed beneficial in addressing the cognitive, behavioral, interpersonal, and vegetative features of depression, there was little evidence that any one treatment outperformed another.

The upshot of this review lent credence to my clinical misgivings about the presumed hegemony of the dominant psychotherapy paradigm in academia and encouraged my investigation of alternatives. In a sense, my clinical voice was given more "airtime," and my researcher identity assumed a more supportive role, one less constrained by the dominant paradigm. My collaborative research on different treatments for another pressing clinical topic—sexual abuse—was one result.

Coming Home: Evaluation of a Constructivist Treatment for Survivors of Sexual Abuse

At about the same time that Jeff, Leslie, and I were embarking on our review of the depression literature, my colleague Pam Alexander and I launched a series of studies with several of our students—notably Stephanie Harter, Victoria Follette, and Marlin Moore. Pam's background interest in incest research and mine and Stephanie's in personal construct theory came together to produce a study of the long-term effects of sexual abuse, which suggested that the impact of incest was less a function of the abuse event per se than of the constructs of self and others that the survivor formed as a result (Harter, Alexander, & Neimeyer, 1988). Buoyed by this demonstration of the relevance of constructivist concepts and methods to a topic typically studied from mainly an epidemiological perspective, we soon expanded the paradigm in the direction of psychotherapy research.

What emerged was the first controlled study of the efficacy of any form of psychotherapy for survivors of intrafamilial sexual abuse (Alexander, Neimeyer, Follette, Moore, & Harter, 1989). In it, we sought to compare a clinically respected but empirically unevaluated process group format modeled on the work of Courtois (1988) with an alternative group structure, one derived explicitly from a constructivist base. It is interesting to note that the latter "interpersonal transaction" (IT) group format (Landfield, 1979) had developed from my earlier studies with my brother on the acquaintance process, although this area at first seemed remote from the area of psychotherapy research (G. J. Neimeyer & Neimeyer, 1981, 1985; R. A. Neimeyer & Neimeyer, 1983). This experience of the convergence and divergence of themes, topics, and lines of investigation across the course of a career brings to mind the unanticipated intersections in Darwin's "networks of enterprise," which he traced so elaborately in his scientific diaries (Gruber, 1989). This rediscovery and reinterpretation of aspects of one's own past work has convinced me that nothing is ever wasted in a scholarly career, as even apparent cul-de-sacs and abandoned directions feed directly or indirectly into new and seemingly unrelated lines of investigation. This serendipitous process alone should give us pause in describing science as a wholly logical and predictable method for constructing progressive research programs, a view supported by postpositivist philosophers of science (Feyerabend, 1978; Polanyi, 1958).

Borrowing the structure of the IT group each therapy session began with a series of "rotating dyads" in which each group member briefly discussed an assigned topic (e.g., who I was as a child and who I am now) with every other member, allowing the discussion to evolve across the series of interactions. The resulting similarities, differences, and insights were then discussed more fully in a subsequent whole-group phase of each meeting (R. A. Neimeyer, 1988a). In its clinical application for the treatment of incest survivors, topics selected were of high relevance to sexual abuse (e.g., problems with trusting too much and trusting too little, ways you would like to be similar to and different from your mother). These topics were then arranged across sessions to encourage progressively deeper levels of disclosure and processing as group cohesion built across time (Harter & Neimeyer, 1995). Like constructivist therapy in general, the emphasis throughout the IT experience was placed on the nonconfrontive exploration of personal meanings, the implications of one's current construction of self and personal relationships, and the development of a more hopeful account of one's past, present, and future. By comparison, the process group format used spontaneous whole-group interactions to elucidate the (sometimes problematic) interpersonal style of members and to understand its relationship to their abuse experience. Thus, our goal in the study was to evaluate the relative advantages of two promising formats, each of which was coherent with the theoretical perspective of one of the two principal investigators, and to establish the efficacy of both approaches relative to a waiting-list control condition.

In summary, results of a large, well-controlled study supported the comparable effectiveness of both treatments in reducing core symptomatology associated with a history of sexual trauma (Alexander et al., 1989; Harter & Neimeyer, 1995). However, more focused analyses revealed some specific advantages for the process group format in improving overall social functioning for group members, as well as particular benefits of the more structured and perhaps less threatening IT format in ameliorating the anxieties of more severely traumatized women (Alexander, Neimeyer, & Follette, 1991).

A unique feature of this study was its attempt to integrate research on group dynamics within the basic framework of the outcome investigation. To accomplish this, we constructed a specially adapted form of repertory grid to assess each participant's perception of each other group member as well as each therapist, at both early and later stages in the group's development. This allowed us to tease out the positivity of group members toward one another and toward therapists, as well as their level of identification with each, and to relate these process factors to outcome for individual members. We found that members' positivity and identification with one another early in the group experience were associated with more favorable outcomes, but that across time, these intermember processes were displaced in importance by members' ability to identify with the therapists (R. A. Neimeyer, Harter, & Alexander, 1991). Moreover, the predictive power of these grid-based variables was impressive, substantially exceeding the usual amount of variance accounted for by process factors in the group psychotherapy literature. A reexamination of these "round-robin" grids through the powerful statistical lens of Kenny's (1991) social relations model (SRM) provided a still more detailed view of the contribution made to these group perceptions by individual perceivers, targets, and their unique dyadic relationships (Johnson & Neimeyer, 1996), the first full implementation of SRM methods in the field of psychotherapy research.

The experience of this multifaceted research program again bootstrapped my internal dialogue to new levels. Specifically, the infusion of constructivist concepts into the design of both the treatment (the IT group) and the methods (the group grid) of the study encouraged a more collaborative relationship between my clinical and empirical aspects, as reflected in the following dialogue:

> Clinician: Hey, that was refreshing! I thoroughly enjoyed the supervision of the IT groups, which seemed to give the female therapists a chance to relate personally as well as professionally to the women in their groups, rather than being straitjacketed by protocols designed to constrain

them to more technical roles. And the group grids really did seem to pick up on aspects of group process typically ignored in most outcome research, which tends to use groups for convenience rather than for their unique curative power. The respectful and serious implementation of the group process format also left me feeling good about what the rest of the participants received, including those who were offered involvement in the same kind of groups a few months later.

Researcher: You and I are on the same wavelength again. Those same factors increased the internal and external validity of the design, and the resulting theory-grounded methods provide the only empirically validated therapies for this all-too-common clinical population. What more could a scientist–practitioner ask for?

Clinician: Well, I hate to spoil the party, but there is something. I keep having this nagging feeling that these outcome studies, even with their process embellishments, seriously underspecify what is actually happening in the therapy room. Results like those we reported may provide a generic warrant for a certain form or format of therapy, but how much do they really describe the delicate interchange between client and therapist that transforms the experience of both? Moreover, in a supervisory context, aside from telling me whether a trainee is in the general ballpark of the therapy being conducted, how much guidance do such "empirically validated treatments" provide about what a therapist should be doing at this particular moment with this particular client? This moment-to-moment engagement is ultimately where the "rubber meets the road," and yet this is where nearly all psychotherapy research falls curiously silent.

Researcher: You expect a lot! I don't think we even have a vocabulary to articulate the sorts of processes you're talking about, much less the statistical methods to track them. I'm ready to lend a hand here any way I can, but I'm not sure that you're asking the kinds of questions I'm prepared to answer. It sounds like you need to spell out your concerns a little more clearly and get back to me when you get them sorted out.

Clinician: Maybe you're right. I'm not really sure I've addressed these sorts of processes to my own satisfaction, much less framed them in a way that you can sink your teeth into them. Give me some time to work on this, and I'll keep you posted.

My pessimism about the sensitivity of psychotherapy research to the moment-to-moment nuances of therapeutic engagement stemmed primarily from my involvement in outcome research. But I began to suspect that the same difficulty arose for most of the field of process research, which tends to reduce client and therapist "verbalizations" to a handful of coarse but somewhat reliable categories (e.g., question, statement, exploration of feeling) or to a single dimension of presumed "depth" of processing. Both strategies seem to simplify the complexity of artful interaction almost to the point of absurdity, a point that has been honestly acknowledged by some of the leading process researchers in the field (Hill, 1995).

Actually, my long involvement in research on personal relationships (R. A. Neimeyer & Mitchell, 1988) had led to the same impasse. Once we had convincingly demonstrated the role of functional and structural similarity in construct systems as a factor in friendship formation and development, I was left yearning for a more processual view of how interpersonal constructions, communications, and impressions of the partner and oneself evolved across the course of relating. Although our attempts to map changes in partner perceptions using content coding of ongoing impression diaries shed some light on this question (R. A. Neimeyer, Brooks, & Baker, 1996), ultimately the subtleties of interaction seemed to elude such methods. A brief but ambitious attempt to track mutual dependencies in self-disclosure on a speaking-turn-by-speaking-turn basis proved no more satisfying (Bright, Neimeyer, & Baker, 1990). Our lag–sequential analyses of dozens of unstructured, naturalistic interactions demonstrated that such communications were interdependent but failed to address *how* or *why* they were, much less to reflect the idiosyncrasies of particular dyads that were obvious to any observer of the videotapes. Thus, this became another of the scores of "file drawer" studies that I eventually lost interest in trying to publish. I suspect that a systematic analysis of the "blind alleys" in any research program or career would reveal more about the nature of science as practiced than would the usual analyses of the published literature.

Thus, although the two sides of my psychologist identity found a way to have a respectful conversation in the context of our research on the treatment of sexual abuse, a deeper chasm seemed to open that each reluctantly acknowledged. It was ultimately the clinician who first decided to explore that chasm by more closely scrutinizing his own experience of therapy through constructivist goggles.

Trouble in Paradise: The Linguistic Turn

The first sign of this trouble in the newfound alliance between my researcher and therapist aspects arose when I started attending more closely to what I was really doing in therapy. It was not that my familiar personal construct metaphors for describing the structures and processes of individual change were wrong, really, but that they were, well, too *personal*. In other words, although they revealed the constraints and possibilities for change deriving from my client's construction of self and world, they seemed to miss or at least shift the emphasis from what transpired *between* us in the process of "doing" therapy. Gradually, it began to dawn on me that there was a theme running through the work of those construct theorists (Feixas, 1992; Mair, 1989; Procter, 1987) and other constructivists (Anderson & Goolishian, 1992; Efran, Lukens, & Lukens, 1990; Greenberg & Pascual-Leone, 1995) who I was finding most interesting—namely, a focus on the conversational construction of meaning in individual and family therapy.

Although the focus on therapy as conversation at one level seems obvious, it in fact had significant implications for my level of analysis of the therapeutic transaction. To begin with, it prompted me to take a fresh look at my own contribution to the conversation, revealing a number of fairly reliable gambits that I drew on to "sculpt" the flow of our dialogue toward useful recognitions and possible reconstructions. This more contextualized analysis of my own therapy led me to notice different intentions in my interventions—intentions to *nuance* a promising implication in a client's passing remark, to *contrast* aspects of his or her experience that seemed to exist in some dialectical tension, to *weave* together strands of conversation that were thematically connected, to *analogize* a vaguely understood experience to a metaphorically congruent domain that was more concretely symbolized, to *structure* diffuse material in ways that clarified its implications for action, and to *ambiguate* other client utterances in ways that opened them to novel alternative readings (R. A. Neimeyer, 1996). What this conversational shift reinforced was a microanalytic approach to therapy that viewed every utterance as an intervention, tacitly guided, which in some way "perturbed" the flow of interaction toward fresh possibilities—or stale reiteration.[3] Striving to capture this more discursive view, I came to define therapy as follows:

> the variegated and subtle interchange and negotiation of (inter)
> personal meanings . . . in the service of articulating, elaborating, and

---

[3]It is important to note that this shift does not necessarily lead to a view of therapy that privileges the role of talk over action. In an expanded definition, *languaging* can be defined as "any form of symbolic display, action, or communication within human communities—verbal or nonverbal—intended to establish, question, or otherwise negotiate social and personal meanings and coordinate behavior" (R. A. Neimeyer & Mahoney, 1995, p. 406). As such, it includes not only the words and grammar used by each participant in dialogue but also the coverbal intonation, nonverbal signs (e.g., eye contact, leaning forward), and even contextual cues (e.g., dim lighting, office setting) that highlight, qualify, or undercut the spoken word and establish a symbolic frame that encourages certain forms of interaction, but not others. Each of these factors can be viewed as a conscious or nonconscious intervention that shapes the client's processing as well as the therapist's (R. A. Neimeyer, 1988b) Some idea of what this "rational–linguistic" approach to therapy looks like in practice is provided by a detailed illustration of my work in the context of grief therapy (R. A. Neimeyer, in press-b).

revising those constructions that the client uses to organize his or her experience and action. Such a definition emphasizes several features of the psychotherapy process, including the delicacy with which the therapist must grasp the contours of the experiential world of the client, the dialogical and discursive basis of their interaction, and the contributions of both to their mutual inquiry. . . . Although psychotherapy conceived along these lines can have many concrete objectives, at an abstract level all of these involve joining with clients to develop a refined map of the often inarticulate constructions in which they are emotionally invested and that define what they regard as viable courses of action, and then extending or supplementing these constructions to enlarge the number of possible worlds that they might inhabit. (R. A. Neimeyer, 1995c, p. 2)

As I began to dwell more consistently within this therapeutic frame, I started to recognize its continuity with the work in narrative therapy (Freedman & Combs, 1996; Parry & Doan, 1994) that had fascinated me for some time. Like constructivists, narrative theorists had rejected an objectivist epistemology and were concerned with the personal and collective construction and deconstruction of meaning in human interaction. But the greater inflection that they placed on the temporal development of life stories offered a useful counterbalance to the more structural concerns of many constructivist therapists and provided a complementary set of metaphors for understanding the processes of human change. At a concrete level, a narrative perspective prompted me to pay more explicit attention to clients' use of such devices as storytelling, journal writing, and poetic self-exploration in therapy, all of which fit comfortably with a constructivist style of intervention (R. A. Neimeyer, 1995a). At a more abstract level, a narrative view opened upon a horizon of larger cultural narratives, inscribed at the level of language and social convention, which often were implicated in the construction of problem-saturated identities on the part of persons seeking psychotherapy (White & Epston, 1990). Recursively, these more culturally informed narrative views suggested methods to help clients liberate themselves from the dominant stories that constrained their lives and to discover in their "sparkling moments" of self-affirmation the seeds of new and more hopeful identities and relationships (Monk, Winslade, Crocket, & Epston, 1996; R. A. Neimeyer, 1993c).

How has this most recent turn affected the tenor of my inner dialogue? In some respects, it is too early to tell. It has certainly encouraged me to take a harder look at qualitative as well as quantitative analyses of the process of meaning reconstruction, particularly in the context of my current research on bereavement and loss (R. A. Neimeyer, 1998b; R. A. Neimeyer & Stewart, in press) Clearly, it has also reinforced my interest in social constructionist thought, with its deep-going implications for deconstructing notions of "individuality," "disorder," and "personality" in psychotherapy (R. A. Neimeyer, 1998c, in press-a). But ultimately, I suspect I will discover the fuller implications of this linguistic shift for the "sometime relationship" between my scientist and practitioner aspects only in hindsight.

CONCLUSION:
RETROSPECT AND PROSPECT

Engaging in this extended confessional has been a bit discomfiting—stripping away the public pretense that research programs develop smoothly in the planful and rational fashion that the leading ideologues of scientist–practitioner training seemed to envision. However, it has also been liberating—giving me the opportunity to formulate a meaningful, if somewhat labrynthian account of the major shifts I have undergone over my first 20 years of conducting and studying psychotherapy. Although I am no longer Catholic enough to believe that this confession alone will absolve me of all sins I might have committed along the way, I appreciate the opportunity to look back with some degree of candor across the years and to imagine where my ongoing internal (and external) dialogue might lead me in the future.

Where do I find myself at the present moment, as I contemplate the relation between scientific research and practice? I see the two existing in some essential tension, neither collapsing into the other, and each having its own inherent logic, coherence, and, at epiphanous moments, even eloquence. While I continue to respect the integrity of both the researcher and the clinician roles as well as the importance of their interchange, I also have grown more playful and provisional in enacting each one, as well as more generous in allowing myself to explore the affordances and the limitations of each without immediately having to answer to the other. Like a speaker of both Spanish and English, I am prone to take up one or the other in different conversational contexts, drawing on the somewhat different resources of each "language" to envision and navigate the world of psychotherapy a bit differently. Moreover, I have come to view both my research and practice incarnations as developing entities, fraught with their own occasional internal contradictions, each striving to be more precise, evocative, and rich in its engagement with its subject matter. Thus, I have come to accept (at least for now) that neither represents a complete language, that neither can claim superiority to the other, and that both are evolving toward ends that can be neither envisioned from my current standpoint, nor achieved in any final sense in my lifetime. But such seems to be the nature of human knowing, whatever its particular form or focus.

Although this multilingualism represents a provisional accommodation that is currently functional for me, I recognize that there are others who might view it as anathema, who might advocate a much tighter synthesis of science and practice, view one as leading the other, or enact only one pole or the other of the dialectic. Certainly, the "polyvocality" I am currently drawn toward poses the risks of fragmentation associated with other postmodern perspectives (Gergen, 1991) and denies one the reassuring certainty of having a single, integral position. It also fails to specify in any absolute sense the future direction that should be pursued by the field of psychotherapy research, inasmuch as these directions necessarily arise from the internal and external conversations in which different investigators are situated. But I draw encouragement from the recognition that I am not in this alone and that the readers and contributors to this volume are struggling with similar tensions in their own lives and work. Ultimately, I am optimistic that this struggle will yield new possibilities for psychotherapy research and practice, in a way that will make each more relevant to the other.

REFERENCES

Alexander, P. C., Neimeyer, R. A., & Follette, V. M. (1991). Group therapy for women sexually abused as children: A controlled study and investigation of individual differences. *Journal of Interpersonal Violence, 6*, 219–231.

Alexander, P. C., Neimeyer, R. A., Follette, V. M., Moore, M. K., & Harter, S. L. (1989). A comparison of group treatments of women sexually abused as children. *Journal of Consulting and Clinical Psychology, 57*, 479–483.

Anderson, H., & Goolishian, H. (1992). The client is the expert: A not-knowing approach to therapy. In S. McNamee & K. J. Gergen (Eds.), *Therapy as social construction* (pp. 25–39). Newbury Park, CA: Sage.

Beck, A. T. (1976). *Cognitive therapy and the emotional disorders.* New York: International Universities Press.

Beck, A. T., Rush, J., Shaw, B., & Emery, G. (1979). *Cognitive therapy of depression.* New York: Guilford Press.

Bright, J. I., Baker, K. D., & Neimeyer, R. A. (1999). Professional and paraprofessional group treatments for depression: A comparison of cognitive–behavioral and mutual support interventions. *Journal of Consulting and Clinical Psychology, 67*, 491–501.

Bright, J. I., Neimeyer, R. A., & Baker, K. (1990). *Self-disclosure reciprocity during initial acquaintance: A lag-sequential analysis.* Unpublished master's thesis, University of Memphis, Memphis, TN.

Buber, M. (1970). *I and thou.* New York: Scribner.

Courtois, C. A. (1988). *Healing the incest wound.* New York: Norton.

Doyne, E. J., Ossip-Klein, D., Bowman, E., Osborn, K., McDougall-Wilson, I., & Neimeyer, R. A. (1987). Running versus weight lifting in the treatment of depression. *Journal of Clinical and Consulting Psychology, 55*, 748–754.

Efran, J. S., Lukens, M. D., & Lukens, R. J. (1990). *Language, structure, and change.* New York: Norton.

Feixas, G. (1992). Personal construct approaches to family therapy. In R. A. Neimeyer & G. J. Neimeyer (Eds.), *Advances in personal construct psychology* (Vol. 2, pp. 217–255). Greenwich, CT: JAI Press.

Feyerabend, P. (1978). *Against method.* London: Verso.

Freedman, J., & Combs, G. (1996). *Narrative therapy.* New York: Norton.

Gergen, K. J. (1991). *The saturated self.* New York: Basic Books.

Greenberg, L., & Pascual-Leone, J. (1995). A dialectical constructivist approach to experiential change. In R. A. Neimeyer & M. J. Mahoney (Eds.), *Constructivism in psychotherapy* (pp. 169–191). Washington, DC: American Psychological Association.

Gruber, H. (1989). Networks of enterprise in creative scientific work. In B. Gholson, W. R. Shadish, R. A. Neimeyer, & A. C. Houts (Eds.), *Psychology of science: Contributions to metascience* (pp. 246–265). New York: Cambridge University Press.

Harter, S. L., Alexander, P. C., & Neimeyer, R. A. (1988). Long-term effects of incestuous child abuse in college women. *Journal of Consulting and Clinical Psychology, 56,* 5–8.

Harter, S. L., & Neimeyer, R. A. (1995). Long term effects of child sexual abuse: Toward a constructivist theory of trauma and its treatment. In R. A. Neimeyer & G. J. Neimeyer (Eds.), *Advances in personal construct theory* (Vol. 3, pp. 229–269). Greenwich, CT: JAI Press.

Hill, C. E. (1995). Musings about how to study therapist techniques. In L. Hoshmand & J. Martin (Eds.), *Research as praxis* (pp. 81–103). New York: Teachers College Press.

Hughes, S. L., & Neimeyer, R. A. (1990). A cognitive model of suicidal behavior. In D. Lester (Ed.), *Current concepts of suicide* (pp. 1–28). Philadelphia: Charles Press.

Hughes, S. L., & Neimeyer, R. A. (1993). Cognitive predictors of suicide risk among hospitalized psychiatric patients: A prospective study. *Death Studies, 17,* 103–124.

Johnson, M. E., & Neimeyer, R. A. (1996). Perceptual sets and stimulus values: The social relations model in group psychotherapy. In J. L. Nye & A. M. Brower (Eds.), *What's social about social cognition?* (pp. 154–174). Thousand Oaks, CA: Sage.

Kelly, G. A. (1955). *The psychology of personal constructs.* New York: Norton.

Kenny, D. A. (1991). A general model of consensus and accuracy in interpersonal perception. *Psychological Review, 98,* 155–163.

Klein, M. H., Greist, J. H., Gurman, A. S., Neimeyer, R. A., Lesser, D. P., Bushnell, N. J., & Smith, R. E. (1985). A comparative outcome study of group psychotherapy vs. exercise treatments for depression. *International Journal of Mental Health, 13,* 148–177.

Klerman, G., Weissman, M., Rounsaville, B., & Chevron, E. (1984). *Interpersonal psychotherapy of depression*. New York: Basic Books.

Landfield, A. W. (1979). Exploring socialization through the interpersonal transaction group. In P. Stringer & D. Bannister (Eds.), *Constructs of sociality and individuality* (pp. 133–151). London: Academic Press.

Lichstein, K. L., Riedel, B., & Grieve, R. (1994). Fari tests of clinical trials: A treatment implementation model. *Advances in Behavior Research and Therapy, 16*, 1–29.

Mahoney, M. J. (1991). *Human change processes*. New York: Basic Books.

Mair, M. (1989). *Between psychology and psychotherapy*. London: Routledge.

Merleau-Ponty, M. (1962). *Phenomenology of perception*. London: Routledge.

Monk, G., Winslade, J., Crocket, K., & Epston, D. (1996). *Narrative therapy in practice*. San Francisco: Jossey-Bass.

Mulkay, M. J. (1979). *Science and the sociology of knowledge*. London: Allen & Unwin.

Mullins, N. C. (1979). *Theories and theory groups in contemporary American sociology*. Chicago: University of Chicago Press.

Neimeyer, G. J., & Neimeyer, R. A. (1981). Functional similarity and interpersonal attraction. *Journal of Research in Personality, 15*, 427–435.

Neimeyer, G. J., & Neimeyer, R. A. (1985). Relational trajectories: A personal construct contribution. *Journal of Social and Personal Relationships, 2*, 325–349.

Neimeyer, R. A. (1980). George Kelly as therapist: A review of his tapes. In A. W. Landfield & L. M. Leitner (Eds.), *Personal construct psychology* (pp. 74–101). New York: Wiley.

Neimeyer, R. A. (1984). Toward a personal construct conceptualization of depression and suicide. In F. R. Epting & R. A. Neimeyer (Eds.), *Personal meanings of death* (pp. 41–87). Washington, DC: Hemisphere.

Neimeyer, R. A. (1985a). *The development of personal construct psychology*. Lincoln: University of Nebraska Press.

Neimeyer, R. A. (1985b). Personal constructs in depression: Research and clinical implications. In E. Button (Ed.), *Personal construct theory and mental health* (pp. 82–102). London: Croom Helm.

Neimeyer, R. A. (1988a). Clinical guidelines for conducting interpersonal transaction groups. *International Journal of Personal Construct Psychology, 1*, 181–190.

Neimeyer, R. A. (1988b). Integrative directions in personal construct therapy. *International Journal of Personal Construct Psychology, 1*, 283–298.

Neimeyer, R. A. (1993a). An appraisal of constructivist therapy. *Journal of Consulting and Clinical Psychology, 61*, 221–234.

Neimeyer, R. A. (1993b). Constructivist approaches to the measurement of meaning. In G. J. Neimeyer (Ed.), *Constructivist assessment: A casebook* (pp. 58–103). Newbury Park, CA: Sage.

Neimeyer, R. A. (1993c). Constructivist psychotherapy. In K. T. Kuehlwein & H. Rosen (Eds.), *Cognitive therapies in action: Evolving innovative practice* (pp. 268–300). San Francisco: Jossey-Bass.

Neimeyer, R. A. (1995a). An invitation to constructivist psychotherapies. In R. A. Neimeyer & M. J. Mahoney (Eds.), *Constructivism in psychotherapy* (pp. 1–8). Washington, DC: American Psychological Association.

Neimeyer, R. A. (1995b). Client-generated narratives in psychotherapy. In R. A. Neimeyer & M. J. Mahoney (Ed.), *Constructivism in psychotherapy* (pp. 231–246). Washington, DC: American Psychological Association.

Neimeyer, R. A. (1995c). Constructivist psychotherapies: Features, foundations, and future directions. In R. A. Neimeyer & M. J. Mahoney (Eds.), *Constructivism in psychotherapy* (pp. 11–38). Washington, DC: American Psychological Association.

Neimeyer, R. A. (1996). Process interventions for the constructivist psychotherapist. In H. Rosen & K. T. Kuehlwein (Eds.), *Constructing realities* (pp. 371–411). San Francisco: Jossey-Bass.

Neimeyer, R. A. (1998a). Cognitive therapy and the narrative trend: A bridge too far? *Journal of Cognitive Psychotherapy, 12,* 57–65.

Neimeyer, R. A. (1998b). *Lessons of loss: A guide to coping.* New York: McGraw-Hill.

Neimeyer, R. A. (1998c). Social constructionism in the counselling context. *Counselling Psychology Quarterly, 11,* 135–149.

Neimeyer, R. A. (in press-a). Narrative disruptions in the construction of the self. In R. A. Neimeyer & J. Raskin (Eds.), *Constructions of disorder.* Washington, DC: American Psychological Association.

Neimeyer, R. A. (in press-b). The language of loss. In R. A. Neimeyer (Ed.), *Meaning reconstruction and the experience of loss.* Washington, DC: American Psychological Association.

Neimeyer, R. A., & Bonnelle, K. (1997). The Suicide Intervention Response Inventory: A revision and validation. *Death Studies, 21,* 59–81.

Neimeyer, R. A., Brooks, D. L., & Baker, K. D. (1996). Personal epistemologies and personal relationships. In B. Walker & D. Kalekin-Fishman (Eds.), *The construction of group realities* (pp. 127–160). Malabar, FL: Krieger.

Neimeyer, R. A., & Diamond, R. (1983). Suicide management skill and the medical student. *Journal of Medical Education, 58,* 562–567.

Neimeyer, R. A., & Dingemans, P. (1980). Death orientation in the suicide intervention worker. *Omega, 11,* 17–25.

Neimeyer, R. A., & Feixas, G. (1990). The role of homework and skill acquisition in the outcome of cognitive therapy for depression. *Behavior Therapy, 21,* 281–292.

Neimeyer, R. A., & Feixas, G. (1992). Cognitive assessment in depression: A comparison of some existing measures. *European Journal of Psychological Assessment, 8,* 47–56.

Neimeyer, R. A., Harter, S., & Alexander, P. C. (1991). Group perceptions as predictors of outcome in the treatment of incest survivors. *Psychotherapy Research, 1,* 149–158.

Neimeyer, R. A., & Hartley, R. (1986). Factorial structure of the Suicide Intervention Response Inventory. *Suicide and Life-Threatening Behavior, 16,* 434–447.

Neimeyer, R. A., Heath, A., & Strauss, J. (1985). Personal reconstruction during group cognitive therapy for depression. In F. R. Epting & A. W. Landfield (Eds.), *Anticipating personal construct psychology* (pp. 180–197). Lincoln: University of Nebraska Press.

Neimeyer, R. A., Klein, M. H., Gurman, A. S., & Greist, J. H. (1983). Cognitive structure and depressive symptomatology. *British Journal of Cognitive Psychotherapy, 1,* 65–73.

Neimeyer, R. A., & MacInnes, W. D. (1981). Assessing paraprofessional competence with the Suicide Intervention Response Inventory. *Journal of Counseling Psychology, 28,* 176–179.

Neimeyer, R. A., & Mahoney, M. J. (Eds.). (1995). *Constructivism in Psychotherapy.* Washington, DC: American Psychological Association.

Neimeyer, R. A., & Martin, J. M. (1996). Looking back, looking forward: Personal construct therapy in sociohistorical perspective. In W. Dryden (Ed.), *Developments in psychotherapy* (pp. 140–166). London: Sage.

Neimeyer, R. A., & Mitchell, K. A. (1988). Similarity and attraction: A longitudinal study. *Journal of Social and Personal Relationships, 5,* 131–148.

Neimeyer, R. A., & Neimeyer, G. J. (1983). Structural similarity in the acquaintance process. *Journal of Social and Clinical Psychology, 1,* 146–154.

Neimeyer, R. A., & Oppenheimer, B. (1983). Concurrent and predictive validity of the Suicide Intervention Response Inventory. *Psychological Reports, 52,* 594.

Neimeyer, R. A., & Pfieffer, A. M. (1994a). Evaluation of suicide intervention effectiveness. *Death Studies, 18,* 131–166.

Neimeyer, R. A., & Pfieffer, A. (1994b). The ten most common errors of suicide interventionists. In A. Leenaars, J. T. Maltsberger, & R. A. Neimeyer (Eds.), *Treatment of suicidal people* (pp. 207–224). Washington, DC: Taylor & Francis.

Neimeyer, R. A., & Raskin, J. (Eds.). (in press). *Constructions of disorder.* Washington, DC: American Psychological Association.

Neimeyer, R. A., Robinson, L. A., Berman, J. S., & Haykal, R. F. (1989). Clinical outcome of group therapies for depression. *Group Analysis, 22,* 73–86.

Neimeyer, R. A., & Stewart, A. E. (in press). Constructivist and narrative therapies. In C. R. Snyder & R. E. Ingram (Eds.), *Handbook of psychotherapy.* New York: Wiley.

Neimeyer, R. A., & Weiss, M. E. (1990). Cognitive and symptomatic predictors of outcome of group therapies for depression. *Journal of Cognitive Psychotherapy, 4,* 23–32.

Nottingham, E. J., & Neimeyer, R. A. (1992). Evaluation of a comprehensive inpatient rational–emotive therapy program. *Journal of Rational–Emotive and Cognitive–Behavior Therapy, 10,* 57–81.

Ossip-Klein, D., Bowman, E., Osborn, K., McDougal-Wilson, I., & Neimeyer, R. A. (1989). Effects of running and weight lifting on self-concept in clinically depressed women. *Journal of Consulting and Clinical Psychology, 57,* 158–161.

Parry, A., & Doan, R. (1994). *Story re-visions.* New York: Guilford Press.

Polanyi, M. (1958). *Personal knowledge.* New York: Harper.

Prezant, D. W., & Neimeyer, R. A. (1988). Cognitive predictors of depression and suicide ideation. *Suicide and Life-Threatening Behavior, 18,* 259–264.

Procter, H. G. (1987). Change in the family construct system. In R. A. Neimeyer & G. J. Neimeyer (Eds.), *Personal construct therapy casebook* (pp. 153–171). New York: Springer.

Robinson, L. A., Berman, J. S., & Neimeyer, R. A. (1990). Psychotherapy for the treatment of depression: A comprehensive review of controlled outcome research. *Psychological Bulletin, 108,* 30–49.

White, M., & Epston, D. (1990). *Narrative means to therapeutic ends.* New York: Norton.

Winter, D. A. (1992). *Personal construct psychology in clinical practice.* London: Routledge.

Woolgar, S. (1989). Representation, cognition, and self: What hope for an integration of psychology and sociology? In S. Fuller, M. DeMey, T. Shinn, & S. Woolgar (Eds.), *The cognitive turn: Sociological and psychological perspectives on science* (pp. 201–224). Dordrecht, The Netherlands: Kluwer Academic.

8

WHAT DO YOU BELIEVE IN? CLINICAL CONVICTION OR EMPIRICAL EVIDENCE?

REINER W. DAHLBENDER AND HORST KAECHELE

Participants and Scenery: As they have many times before, two psychoanalysts meet at an international psychotherapeutic conference somewhere in Germany in the late 1990s. Their names are Kalle and Ziffel, just like the two protagonists in Bertold Brecht's *Fluechtlingsgespraeche* (Brecht, 1990). Kalle is an immigrant of German origin who is living in the midwestern United States. Ziffel is working in a university town in the south of Germany. Like strangers in the night, they meet, discuss, and separate, again until their next opportunity to meet and discuss.

[Both are laughing and shaking hands very familiarly.]

Ziffel: Halloo, halloo!

Kalle: Guten Tag! It has been a while since we last met.

Ziffel: Yes indeed! I am actually surprised to meet you. I thought you would not come.

Kalle: Well, I was not sure if I would be able to make it, but then

. . . . You know, my parents were from a village in the eastern part of Germany. I felt like I should see this place now that it has become possible.

Ziffel: Oh, I see—for sentimental reasons. Hmm, why not!

Kalle: Yes for some. Quite a bit has changed over here. [laughing] In an older magazine I read about this year' s love parade at Berlin. It must have been a most impressive event and very controversial at the same time.

Ziffel: A Berlin love parade? No, I only know that Berlin has become a gigantic building site after the reunion. But I must admit I am not wild about love parades even if they are much better than the parades and celebrations in the old days.

Kalle: That's true.

Ziffel: [with a little smile on his face] As a psychoanalyst I prefer to think of Berlin as the city that hosted the first psychoanalytic institute with formal organized training.

Kalle: I see. Well, the Germans always have had a special talent for any form of organization. It was a problem only when they had to make a revolution and some other—but we probably shouldn't get involved too much in big politics.

Ziffel: There is enough politics in our field at present.

Kalle: Anyway, you seem as if you want to tell me more about this institute.

Ziffel: Oh you *are* really empathetic. As a psychotherapy researcher, you are surely interested that they have, very early on, begun to do some—let's say *evaluative*—research. But I am still pondering why these guys like Fenichel and the others in the Berlin Institute didn't influence the psychoanalytic movement more by their rather systematic report on the outcome of psychoanalytic treatment (Fenichel, 1930).

Kalle: Hey, wait a minute, wait. What are you talking about? I never heard about this report.

Ziffel: [a little provocative] I really do not *expect* you to read all the old stuff in our field.

Kalle: Ha, ha.

Ziffel: No matter. It seems that you haven't even read the psychotherapy researchers' bible, the *Handbook of Psychotherapy and Behavior Change* (Bergin & Garfield, 1971). I mean, have you seen the evaluation of the clinical work of the Berlin Institute of Psychoanalysis from 1920 to 1930, which is referred to in the first edition of this handbook?

Kalle: That is a little unfair. At least I try to cover the recent issues of our *Psychotherapy Research*.

Ziffel: Okay, but sometimes it is worthwhile to remember that clinicians such as Fenichel, Rado, and Mueller-Braunschweig had their own way of accounting for what they were doing. They felt that reporting in a systematic fashion was a necessary part of their clinical work. And this, this seems to be lost in our times.

Kalle: Hmm. But it is just accounting, just poor counting without much statistics!

Ziffel: Now you are unfair. We are talking about the 1920s and 1930s; nonparametric statistics had not yet been invented, by the way.

Kalle: Okay, I guess you really want me to admit that the Berlin Institute and its members played an impressive role in the scientific development of psychotherapy in Germany.

Ziffel: Exactly. In a way, they were important historical figures. And later after the war—I guess you also do not know that— Schultz-Hencke wanted to replace some of Freud's metatheoretical constructs . . . (cf. Thomae, 1963, 1969)

Kalle: [interrupting] Really? I never heard of him.

Ziffel: Harald Schultz-Hencke was thrown out of the paradise of membership in the International Psychoanalytic Association for his then politically incorrect claims. The fact is that he convinced the local general insurance company to support an outpatient clinic. There, his collaborator, Annemarie Duehrssen, later conducted Germany's first controlled field study on the success of unlimited psychoanalytic-oriented psychotherapy sessions once or twice a week.

Kalle: At least I know of that study. As far as I can remember, she demonstrated an enormous effect on days of hospitalization and days off work. And that's why the German general insurance system started to include payment for the treatment of neurotic and psychosomatic disturbances.

Ziffel: Yeah, you are getting better. And that would ultimately lead to the decision of 1967 (see Thomae & Kaechele, 1987). But it took more than just one study to get nationwide psychotherapy coverage implemented.

Kalle: What do you mean by this suggestive remark?

Ziffel: I think we have to talk about the role of the clinical experts in this process of societal recognition. One study does not make a summer; many formal and informal encounters between therapists and funding agencies were needed to develop what today would be called *standards of treatment*. These guidelines for conducting analytic psychotherapies were based less on formal research evidence than on the consensus achieved by psychoanalytic leaders, such as Cremerius, Duehrssen, Ehebald, Faber, Goerres, Haarstrick, and Thomae. These leaders composed a formal statement that in postwar Germany the reinstallment of psychoanalysis would need the support of the German Research Foundation (Goerres, Heiss, Thomae, & Uexkuell, 1964). And by jove, they got support for the postdocs' training analyses for quite a number of years.

Kalle: Are you joking? Just like President Yeltsin officially declared the reinstallment of psychoanalysis in Russia in 1996 (Reshetnikow, 1996).

Ziffel: *Nyet*, I am not. It really is true that today we are in a position in Russia to experience exactly the same phenomena, for probably different reasons, that occurred in Germany after World War II. Clinicians are making politics, not waiting for research findings, but convincing, and arguing with politicians and other representatives of the public.

Kalle: So, in a way, this historical agreement answered the question of who pays how much for what treatment? In this sense, we are talking about a more general topic: How consensus should be achieved on the distribution of the resources of a society.

Ziffel: Uhm! What happened in West Germany was that a group of highly influential clinicians were able to establish a financially well-bolstered psychotherapy delivery system. I like to call it the "6–300 toll-free system."

Kalle: As a fairly healthy person, I never had a chance to experience that system. But it sounds interesting. Could you explain this "6–300" business to me, please?

Ziffel: Well, all you need to do is catch yourself a "psychogenic disorder" and visit a doctor. After some frustrating efforts on his side to find a somatic reason for your complaints, he will refer you to a licensed psychotherapist—either a medical specialist for psychotherapeutic medicine or a specialist psychologist. He may offer you a quick emergency shot of 6–25 sessions, or he may talk you into a peer-review based and monitored long-term therapy lasting from 50–300—or even more—sessions. Thus, 6–300, toll-free.

Kalle: Good Lord, I hope I never shall need it. You mean these groups have successfully developed this insurance-based delivery system for psychotherapy without the companies clamoring for much further formal research on outcome?

Ziffel: Now you have it. Except for the good start with the Duehrssen study, which is scarcely mentioned in the 1971 handbook review, there was very little research on efficacy or on effectiveness, or on process (Duehrssen, 1962, 1972; Duehrssen & Jorswieck, 1965). In the "old days" the public obviously regarded clinicians as experts who did not need much formal research. There was no so-called evidence-based practice like the ones Grawe and others are clamoring for today (Grawe, Donati, & Bernauer 1994; Roth & Fonagy, 1996).

Kalle: As I see it, Duehrssen's time there wasn't much formal research anyhow. So today, the salient questions are these: Are we any better off with all our research? Do we know enough to implement evidence-based psychotherapy today?

Ziffel: You are much too fast. Evidence-based practice is not easy to achieve and—

Kalle: —I know. And it is surely more than just using techniques with demonstrated efficacy in experimental settings. Evidence-based practice has something to do with the interdependencies of the state of research and its consequences for practice; it has to teach soberness about what we know and what we don't know. So improvements in the therapy delivery system will not automatically result from just following experimentally based treatments. Do you agree?

Ziffel: There is no doubt about that. But let's turn to the German psychotherapeutic history again. The events we spoke of before were true milestones for the field, and these stones were carried by a psychoanalytic professional community at a time when behavioral therapy was just in its infancy at some of the clinical psychology departments in Germany. At that time, the demand for scientific credibility naturally included clinical expertise and wisdom.

Kalle: I heard about that well-known wizard, Alexander Mitscherlich (Mitscherlich, 1966–1997); he amounted to more than an army fighting for recognition of psychoanalytic thinking, not only in psychosomatic medicine but also in many walks of life of the German postwar "fatherless society."
          [Both are silent for a short while. Suddenly Kalle starts laughing.]

Kalle: Ha, I just had a nice idea: You could place Annemarie and Alexander on one of the cleared pedestals in East Germany where Marx and Lenin had to step down. A nice idea. But let's be serious again. Do you want to say that we have excluded clinical expertise from our scientific discourse?

Ziffel: Perhaps I want to say that. If you, for example, look closely at the 4th edition of our handbook (Bergin & Garfield, 1994), you will find "clinical experience" as a very relevant therapist variable. But the psychotherapy researchers' bible does not present *clinical experience* as an esteemed research tool. Hmm ... you will not find a special chapter on this theoretically striking topic. At least Robert Holt made it quite clear in the late 1950s that clinical prediction cannot be replaced by statistical prediction without considerable losses (Holt, 1958).

Kalle: Do you suggest that formal psychotherapy research has narrowed our perspective?

Ziffel: It certainly has narrowed our visions. We no longer maintain that psychotherapy would be a good thing for most people.

Kalle: Aren't you also relieved that this burden has been taken from our shoulders? That we are no longer the rescuers of society as we were in the late 1960s?

Ziffel: Hmm? So far so good. I don't know. However, there is a considerable gap between many clinicians' conviction that a sizable proportion of people need longer psychotherapies and the dearth of systematic research on long-term psychotherapy as a respectable object of investigation. Luckily, Ken Howard's consumer-oriented research policy will help to demonstrate that some patients do need longer term therapies (Howard, Lueger, Maling, & Martinovich, 1993).

Kalle: Don't tell me—I have read Seligman's enthusiastic evaluation of the *Consumer Reports* findings. Recently, in a Society for a Scientific Clinical Psychology (SSCPnet) posting, Ken Howard pointed out that something must be wrong in our field that the professional psychotherapy researchers are highly self-critical, and outsiders like Martin Seligman are pouring out praise on the wonders of psychotherapy.

Ziffel: This is very surprising, as Seligman has published a book titled *What You Can Change and What You Can't* (Seligman, 1994) in which he limited his wisdom to the findings of randomized controlled studies. And now, he has changed from Saulus to Paulus. In his discussion of the report, he stated that for the validation of psychotherapy, as practiced daily, researchers involved in efficacy studies are using the wrong method because they leave out too many crucial elements (Seligman, 1995).

Kalle: It sounds as though we have new wizards. Am I right; are you attacking my most favorite design—the randomized controlled trial?

Ziffel: I'm not really sure. At least there are different kinds of therapeutic gold. In any case, we are talking about subtle changes in society and in the psychotherapy research community. My training suggests that an experienced clinician would have a say in the evaluation of research findings and would estimate their relevance for practicable application. For example, take the findings of the National Institute of Mental Health study in which even a planned dose of 16 sessions was seldom realized —no wonder that with 12 sessions a high relapse rate occurred.

Kalle: Now you are criticizing the overestimation of formal research findings?

Ziffel: Indeed. We might be in danger of reducing the process of knowledge creation to only laboratory research conditions. Only rarely do we discuss those serious problems concerning external validity. Perhaps we tend to forget what we all should know, that experimental validity has its own threats (Kazdin, 1994).

Kalle: Three cheers for meta-analysis! But, hmm? I mean, meta-analysis has indeed had remarkable impact on psychotherapy research. However, today many psychotherapy researchers still tend to overestimate the expected objectivity of this research tool. Sociologists are not so keen on secondary studies. For them, meta-analysis is just one instrument among others. We ought to be aware of its limitations. I share the common critical view, especially concerning the necessity of selecting clinically relevant, methodologically adequate, and properly conducted studies (Roth & Fonagy, 1996).

Ziffel: Oh no, stop! Let's not talk about effect sizes, average Z scores, interval scales, dependent data, average clients, and so forth (Wilson & Rachman, 1983). [laughing] You see, I also have learned my lessons!

Kalle: [ironically] Yeah, I see. [now more seriously] No, don't be afraid, my friend, I didn't want to go any deeper into these methodological considerations. And I agree that we, in principle, know about the opportunities and also the deficiencies of this as well as our other methodological and statistical tools.

Ziffel: And what is causing your concern?

Kalle: [lost in thought] Hmm, perhaps? [ironically again] Meta-analysis is good for this kind of horse-race research: "Is an average patient with an average, let's say, anxiety disorder, better off with Type A, Type B, or Type C treatment, or perhaps a simultaneous or in succession combination of B and C?" To me, it seems that we are still discussing more about methodology and statistics and too little about psychotherapy and how its functioning ought to be conceptualized (Kazdin, 1994).

Ziffel: You mean, we still know too little to really understand psychotherapy?

Kalle::   Exactly! Our heads are occupied mostly by very simple linear models such as "less of this causes more of that." But we still do not have a theory that grasps the complexity of psychotherapeutic change processes. There are only few and very preliminary attempts to formulate something like a common theory of psychotherapeutic change.

Ziffel: Oh, I've got an idea! We could adapt the current results of neurobiological brain research that suggest a much more synergetic perspective (Haken & Haken-Krell, 1997; Spitzer, 1996; Stadler & Kruse, 1995)! From this perspective, that is, the internal representations of the generalized significant social interactions of our development, which at least partly cause our symptoms, could be changed if both patient and psychotherapist are able to modify those control parameters that are responsible for new emotional, cognitive, and behavioral qualities in a close interpersonal relationship.

Kalle: You're talking about chaos theory, bifurcation, and that stuff, right?

Ziffel: Yeah. You need not agree with this specific theory. I just wanted to give you an idea of a theory that might be useful to conceptualize the dynamic processes of psychotherapeutic change.

Kalle: It is true, chaos theory has been usefully applied in many other areas. Maybe it will help in our field too, but at present, we are at the very early stages. But, in my opinion, we should neither fall into a black-and-white pattern between a theoretical and a methodological orientation nor between different research strategies.

Ziffel: Uhm, I might have been misunderstood. To make it clear, I do not see a black-or-white pattern either. For me, there is no reason for a flight from systematic clinical research into laboratory statistical pragmatism, which usually does not pay much attention to complicating factors such as comorbidity and so on. There is no reason for flight because there are issues that can only be clarified by empirical research based on methodologically well-designed and elaborated statistical approaches—whereas the empirical research based on clinical experience is doomed to fail.

Kalle: I believe that many issues are only accessible in natural settings.

Ziffel: Can you give me an example?

Kalle: Sure! The psychoanalytic concept of free association is one. It has been tested in quite a number of experimental studies

(Bordin, 1966; Kroth & Forrest, 1969); however, none of these studies could clarify the role of free association as a clinical tool because they were analogue studies with limited validity for the clinical situation. From your own experimental study, I know how difficult it is to catch the therapeutic dialogue with elements of free-flowing thought (Heckmann, Hoelzer, Kaechele, & Robben, 1987). We need much more of the kind of research that tries to study the clinical everyday reality as well as possible. And we need different kinds of research for different purposes.

Ziffel: So we agree on this decisive issue. Couldn't it be that we might need clinical expertise to cover those domains of knowledge that are hard to study by experimental procedures?

Kalle: After all, a lot of medicine is not evidence based (Windeler & Holle, 1997). For example, most surgical techniques are based on the expertise of rather skillful surgeons. On the basis of the personal skills of many other surgeons, they have been modified and so, step-by-step, in everyday practice they have proved effective. In medicine, there is a long tradition of action- and experience-based decisions.

Ziffel: But is this desirable? I hate going under the knife on the basis of only one guy's opinion!

Kalle: Desirable or not, it is simply a fact. And this is another fact: Most patients see a second or even a third surgeon before they make up their minds.

Ziffel: That seems very wise! ... By the way, I remember a young patient I met at the hospital. He was suffering from an acute myeloproliferative leukemia. A few years after a bone-marrow transplantation at one of the most famous and successful transplantation centers, his blood cells started proliferating again. Because he had developed quite a few complicating factors, his doctors denied his request for a second transplantation despite the fact that a donor was available. He went to another statistically less successful hematological unit that was known for very high clinical standards and successful transplantations even in very severe cases. There things went well, and he got his second chance. It's always wise to seek a second opinion. While the first doctor might not treat you in light of some perhaps questionable group statistics, the next might look at your personal situation more completely and treat you despite the risk of a failure. No easy decisions!

Kalle: [ironically] That's it for today's topic: empirical evidence versus clinical expertise.

Ziffel: Ha, ha! I'll try to return to our field. ... Do you think it is possible to apply the randomized controlled trial model to long-term treatments with hundreds of sessions?

Kalle: Isn't one consideration the fact that we do not know enough about the natural course of a disorder? Well, I would not wait long if I were elected as a waiting-group patient in a research trial. Rolf Sandell reported on a perplexing finding. In his study on long-term treatments, waiting-list patients received more informal treatment while waiting than did the patients in his experimental group (Sandell, Blomberg, & Lazar, 1997). Long-term follow-up sometimes demonstrates striking findings, not only about the service delivery system.

Ziffel: You mean the patients' impatience does in fact spoil our wonderful randomized controlled trial design? So what would you suggest? What do you think of the single-case studies that most psychoanalysts retreat to?

Kalle: I am afraid that single-case studies don't have much impact on the governmental agencies or on our scientific adversaries—they are a treat for our hearts, they are a "high noon" of inner psychoanalytic scientific achievements (Dahlbender, 1993; Fonagy & Moran, 1993; Leuzinger-Bohleber & Kaechele, 1988).

Ziffel: Perhaps the situation is not as critical as it looks. Systematic observational studies on a large natural sample are a good answer. The Stuttgart Center for Psychotherapy Research has collected systematic prospective evaluative data on the psychodynamic treatment of 1,200 patients with eating disorders (Kaechele, 1992).

Kalle: Whew! Who gave you the money?

Ziffel: A German Ministry for Research and Technology program administrator was wise enough to consider treatment not only as crisis intervention but also to regard long-term relapse prevention as the major aim of psychotherapy. Thus, the ultimate question would be, How much treatment would be sufficient to provide long-term protection against symptomatic relapse?

Kalle: So we are happily back to Freud! I mean, this was one of his core ideas. Freud was aware that we have no means by which to totally eradicate the propensities for psychic disturbances; life always can confront us with situations in which our capacities for successful coping are not enough.

Ziffel: The Freudian enterprise always stood for more than just rapid symptom relief with short-lived follow-up results. And at present, indeed, there seems to be a little "crisis" in our high estimate of the impact of short-term therapy. Some protagonists—I think of George Silberschatz—are really shocked by the limited life span of their once impressive outcomes (Silberschatz, 1997).

Kalle: I must admit that there is a smile even on the clinical side of my face.

Ziffel: As long as it is not a mocking smile, its okay. Mocking the clinicians' convictions usually was the business of psychotherapy researchers, wasn't it? Lawrence Kubie once said something like, "Love and cherish the therapist, but for heaven's sake do not trust him" (Kubie, 1952). Is this the way to bridge the worlds?

Kalle: Isn't this only a romantic wish for the peaceful meadows. . . . Only lambs, no wolves?

Ziffel: The reality—in Germany, at least—is that the influential meta-analysis by Klaus Grawe and his coworkers had its impact because the pending legislation in which psychologists would become part of the medical system was about to get over the hurdles. Klaus Grawe's claim that the chairs for psychotherapy were occupied by the wrong people, as all of them happen to be psychoanalytically trained, was no longer a statement justified by the meager meta-analytic differences—it was sheer politics (Tschuschke & Kaechele, 1996).

Kalle: You mean making a clever selection of studies, a purposeful interpretation and translation for the public, especially for politicians, is sometimes very creative and innovative?

Ziffel: Exactly!

Kalle: Are you still suffering from those conclusions?

Ziffel: Well . . . to me it was a new experience to be called a misplaced person.

Kalle: I am glad that you did not suffer so much from that attack. By the way, as you know yourself, the clinical significance of the differences in effect sizes between various treatments reported by various meta-analyses still awaits corroboration by Phase IV studies.

Ziffel: That makes me feel better! And what do you mean by clinical significance? Is it perhaps what clinicians think that is significant?

Kalle: Don't be silly. This kind of circularity may suffice for psychoanalysts following the famous definition that psychoanalysis is what psychoanalysts do. No, we are in a better position. After many years in the medieval darkness of statistical significance testing, a few of us have discovered that true significance resides in meaningful changes according to the practical value, or importance, of a treatment (Kazdin, 1994).

Ziffel: To me, it seems we agree that we need a continuous discussion among us of clinical and research viewpoints (Kaechele & Kordy, 1993). Meta-analytic findings that run counter to my clinical experience will have a harder subjective screening before I am able to assimilate them. And if I do not find sufficient support. . . .

Kalle: You are aware that you are in danger of remaining in conservative, sometimes even ideological, tracks?

Ziffel: Yes, at least in principle.

Kalle: Perhaps I should admit this too? Hmm?

Ziffel: Clinical work is constantly teaching me new things, and these clinical findings have a huge impact on me personally. Each of my patients has left a mark on me and on formal research —and also consensus on so-called professional standards—do have a hard time matching this.

Kalle: You know, I also work as a clinician. Still it seems to me that formal research findings widen my scope. In the clinical situation, I too often find myself lost in a jungle of so-called certainties that offer not much more comfort than singing in the night when it is dark. Therefore, to me, formal research holds a strong promise of overcoming present limitations of daily routines. Too often I feel myself practicing at a suboptimal level and would hope to be supported by well-established evidence. The main dilemma in our present situation seems to be that the gulf between the *laboratory charades*—as Kubie termed a lot of experimental work in 1952—and the clinical situation is still too large.

Ziffel: Yes, we need more experience in bridging these domains, more training on how to do this instead of the precarious use of laboratory findings for making professional politics. And we need ways of professional monitoring and of auditing service delivery (Roth & Fonagy, 1996). Otherwise, the majority of our colleagues will remain as uninterested in research findings as they are at present.

Kalle: So, maybe, we have to develop a personal culture of multiple identity? It may seem risky to try to work as a clinician as a researcher, and as an administrator. However, this might lead to a professional identity diffusion. . . .

Ziffel: [interrupting and laughing] Ha, ha, beware of your Axis II diagnosis!

Kalle: Don't worry! I mean, we will have different options in the different roles, and we will have to make different commitments.

Ziffel: At the very beginning, even the decision to see a patient entails 1 hour less of research, and to distribute money to research may mean less money for any immediate gain for patients; so our aim should be to raise more money for patients by creating good, clinically meaningful research and acting as responsible administrators.

Kalle: Quite a sizable number of conflictual tasks.

Ziffel: Do you need a psychotherapy session from time to time?

Kalle: Yes, I am afraid I do.

Ziffel: We could make toll-free appointments, even for longer times. Let's first check your prerequisites like goals, motivation, willingness to take part in research projects, and so forth.

Kalle: I'll see. I think we should join the conference routine again. See you again, next time, next place—

Ziffel: —next mood, next controversy. Goodbye.

Kalle: *Auf wiedersehen!*

REFERENCES

Bergin, A. E., & Garfield, S. L. (Eds.). (1971). *Handbook of psychotherapy and behavior change: An empirical analysis* (1st ed.). New York: Wiley.

Bergin, A. E., & Garfield, S. L. (Eds.). (1994). *Handbook of psychotherapy and behavior change: An empirical analysis* (4th ed.). New York: Wiley.

Bordin, E. (1966). Free association: An experimental analogue to the psychoanalytic situation. In L. A. Gottschalk & A. A. Auerbach (Eds.), *Methods of research in psychotherapy* (pp. 189–208). New York: Appleton-Century-Crofts.

Brecht, B. (1990). *Fluechtlingsgespraeche* [Refugees' talks]. Frankfurt am Main, Germany: Suhrkamp.

Dahlbender, R. W. (1993). Single case analytic evaluation of in-patient psychotherapy in a patient with colitis ulcerosa. *German Journal of Psychology, 17,* 156–159.

Duehrssen, A. (1962). Katamnestische ergebnisse bei 1,004 patienten nach analytischer psychotherapie [Follow-up results of 1,004 patients after analytic psychotherapy]. *Zeitschrift fur Psychosomatische Medizin, 8,* 94–113.

Duehrssen, A. (1972). *Analytische psychotherapie in theorie, praxis und ergebnissen* [Analytic psychotherapy in theory, practice, and outcome]. Göttingen, Germany: Vandenhoek & Ruprecht.

Duehrssen, A. M., & Jorswieck, E. (1965). Eine empirisch-statistische untersuchung zur leistungsfaehigkeit psychoanalytischer behandlung [An empiri-cal–statistical study of the efficiency of psychoanalytic treatment]. *Nervenarzt*, *36*, 166–169.

Fenichel, O. (1930). Statistischer bericht ueber die therapeutische taetigkeit 1920–1930 [Report on the therapeutic activities in 1920–1930]. In S. Radó, O. Fenichel, & C. Mueller-Braunschweig (Eds.), *Zehn jahre Berliner Psychoanalytisches Institut, Poliklinik und Lehranstalt* (pp. 13–19). Vienna, Austria: Internationale Psychoanalytische Verlag.

Fonagy, P., & Moran, G. (1993). Selecting single case research designs for clini-cians. In N. E. Miller, L. Luborsky, J. P. Barber, & J. P. Docherty (Eds.), *Psychodynamic treatment research: A handbook for clinical practice* (pp. 62–95). New York: Basic Books.

Goerres, A., Heiss, R., Thomae, H., & Uexkuell, T. V. (1964). *Denkschrift zur lage der aerztlichen psychotherapie und der psychosomatischen medizin* [Memorandum on the situation of medical psychotherapy and psychosomatic medicine]. Wiesbaden, Germany: Steiner.

Grawe, K., Donati, R., & Bernauer, F. (1994). *Psychotherapie im wandel: Von der konfession zur profession* [Psychotherapy in change: From confession to profes-sion]. Göttingen, Germany: Hogrefe.

Haken, H., & Haken-Krell, M. (1997). *Gehirn und verhalten: Unser kopf arbeitet anders als wir denken* [Brain and behavior: Our brain works different from what we think]. Stuttgart, Germany: Deutsche Verlags-Anstalt.

Heckmann, H., Hoelzer, M., Kaechele, H., & Robben, H. (1987). Resistance and transference as two main constituents in an "experimental analogue" of free association. In W. Huber (Ed.), *Progress in psychotherapy research* (pp. 582–593). Louvain-la-Neuve, Belgium: Presses Universitaire de Louvain.

Holt, H. (1958). Clinical and statistical prediction: A reformulation and some new data. *Journal of Abnormal and Social Psychology, 56*, 1–12.

Howard, K., Lueger, R., Maling, M., & Martinovich, Z. (1993). A phase model of psychotherapy: Causal mediation of outcome. *Journal of Consulting and Clinical Psychology, 61*, 678–685.

Kaechele, H. (1992). *Planungsforum "psychodynamische therapie von ebstörungen"* [Planning forum "Psychodynamic treatment of eating disorders"]. Center for Psychotherapy Research, Stuttgart, Germany.

Kaechele, H., & Kordy, H. (1993). Aims of psychotherapy research in the nineties. In B. Strauss, C. Bahne Bahnson, & H. Speidel (Eds.), *New societies—New models in medicine* (pp. 160–168). Stuttgart, Germany: Schattauer.

Kazdin, A. E. (1994). Methodology, design, and evaluation in psychotherapy re-search. In A. E. Bergin & S. L. Garfield (Eds.), *Handbock of psychotherapy and behavior change* (pp. 19–71). New York: Wiley.

Kroth, J. A., & Forrest, M. S. (1969). Effects of posture and anxiety level on effectiveness of free association. *Psychological Reports, 25*, 725–726.

Kubie, L. S. (1952). Problems and techniques of psychoanalytic validation and progress. In E. Pumpian-Mindlin (Ed.), *Psychoanalysis as science: The Hixon* lecture on the scientific status of psychoanalysis (pp. 46–124). New York: Basic Books.

Leuzinger-Bohleber, M., & Kaechele, H. (1988). From Calvin to Freud: Using an artificial intelligence model to investigate cognitive changes during psychoanalysis. In H. Dahl, H. Kaechele, & H. Thomae (Eds.), Psychoanalytic process research strategies (pp. 291–306). Berlin, Germany: Springer.

Mitscherlich, A. (1966–1967). Krankheit als konflikt: Studien zur psychosomatischen medizin [Illness as conflict] (Vols. 1–2). Frankfurt am Main, Germany: Suhrkamp.

Reshetnikow, M. (1996). The first hundred years of psychoanalysis: Its Russian roots, repression and Russia's return to the world's psychoanalytic community. Unpublished manuscript, East European Institute of Psychoanalysis, St. Petersburg, Russia.

Roth, A., & Fonagy, P. (Eds.). (1996). What works for whom? A critical review of psychotherapy research. New York: Guilford Press.

Sandell, R., Blomberg, J., & Lazar, A. (1997). When reality doesn't fit the blueprint—Doing research on psychoanalysis and long-term psychotherapy in a public health service program. Psychotherapy Research, 7, 333–344.

Seligman, M. E. P. (1994). What you can change and what you can't. New York: Knopf.

Seligman, M. E. P. (1995). The effectiveness of psychotherapy. American Psychologist, 50, 965–974.

Silberschatz, G. (1997). Differences between short and long term therapies: A comparison of outcome and follow-up data. Paper presented at the 20th Ulm Workshop on Empirical Research in Psychoanalysis, Ulm, Germany.

Spitzer, M. (1996). Geist im netz [Brain in the net]. Heidelberg, Germany: Spektrum Akademischer Verlag.

Stadler, M., & Kruse, P. (1995). (Eds.). Ambiguity in mind and nature. Berlin, Germany: Springer.

Thomae, H. (1963). Die neo-psychoanalyse Schultz-Henckes: Eine historische und kritische betrachtung [The neo-psychoanalysis of Schultz-Hencke: A critical and historical review]. Psyche, 17, 44–128.

Thomae, H. (1969). Some remarks on psychoanalysis in Germany, past and present. International Journal of Psycho-Analysis, 50, 683–692.

Thomae, H., & Kaechele, H. (1987). Psychoanalytic practice: Vol. 1. Principles. Berlin: Springer.

Tschuschke, V., & Kaechele, H. (1996). What do psychotherapies achieve? A contribution to the debate centered around differential effects of different treatment concepts. In U. Esser, H. Pabst, & G. W. Speierer (Eds.), The power of the person-centered-approach: New challenges—perspectives—answers (pp. 159–181). Cologne, Germany: GwG-Verlag.

Windeler, J., & Holle, R. (1997). Beurteilung klinischer studien: Hinweise zum kritischen literaturstudium [Judgment of clinical studies: Remarks for a critical study of the literature]. *Der Internist, 38,* 337–343.

Wilson, G. T., & Rachman, S. J. (1983). Meta-analysis and the evaluation of psychotherapy outcome: Limitations and liabilities. *Journal of Consulting and Clinical Psychology, 51,* 54–64.

9

RESEARCH AND PRACTICE: DOES CULTURE MAKE A DIFFERENCE?

JULIA SHIANG

When I was asked to write this chapter, the image that first came to mind was something I had seen on a walk in the hills that I had taken earlier in the day. The California spring rains had just arrived (in December, a fact difficult for me to reconcile as a New Englander), and the streams were swollen with gushing water. The usual walking path was covered with bands of water running every which way, intertwining, dispersing, coming together again, disappearing, and then pooling in quiet moments of suspension. As the path ran downward, so, too, did the water career downhill to eventually gather in a swirling pool of churning froth.

My experience of trying to integrate research and practice, practice and research, often feels much as if I were a leaf in the midst of this water —twisting, turning, being submerged, popping up, being allowed to contemplate at the edge of the moving water for a moment, being carried forward by the client's needs, the client's view of things. I test a hypothesis that grows out of theory and research (i.e., "Is this person developmentally

I acknowledge the helpful discussions of this chapter with colleagues, espcially Dr. Leigh McCullough; an anonymous anthropological reviewer; and Dr. Bob Hsiang, Karen Bissiri, Sonja Bogumill, Helena Young, Christine Dasoff, and Dr. David Mohr.

stuck? Is this person secure in attachments with others?"), sometimes knowing I am in part of the stream that is helpful but at other times finding myself catching my breath, fearful of drowning in water that is too deep. The constant here is that the water continues along its path, just as the client continues along his or her path, moving, sometimes kicking up some froth, sometimes lying low. And my work is to make sense of it, by the intertwining of research and practice. The problem is that my job as a researcher is to make sense of the phenomena, whereas my job as a clinician is to be therapeutic. Where do these roles intersect and inform each other? The interweaving of the two isn't an easy process.

What follows is an exploration of the incorporation and development of a greater awareness that clients' and therapists' culture play in the therapeutic process. By culture, I mean the following:

1. What are the cultural beliefs and behaviors of the client, and how do they shape or influence the client's problem presentation?
2. What are the cultural beliefs and behaviors of the researcher or clinician, and how do they influence his or her work?
3. What are the dynamics of working out the therapeutic alliance based on these two sets of cultural beliefs and behaviors?

Research in these areas is critical to understanding the relative impact of these factors on the therapeutic process. Considering these issues has forced me to ask, What insights, failures, and questions have arisen from my own clinical work in this arena? How do research findings inform the clinical process and vice versa? The process of writing this chapter has allowed some aspects of my ways of doing "things"—research and practice —to become more conscious. This is a step in further developing choices that are more conscious as my own awareness develops over time and experience. This is hard work; it requires discipline and an observing, compassionate ego. A counterweight that helps me achieve a balance in my professional career has been my daily experience of being enriched through marriage and raising three children. It is through interactions with my family in everyday moments (Pine, 1992) that I am continually reminded of how cultural settings are negotiated in life.

RESEARCH INTERESTS

I'll start with some information about my research background and resultant biases. I took an undergraduate degree in biochemistry and learned about the scientific method. Although I didn't stay in biochemistry, its method and training had an important influence on the way I think about problems and problem solving. At first, everything in this world seemed crystal clear—either it was true or false—there was no room for ambiguity. Science appeared to be based on the cold, hard facts. But as I did more and more experiments, I began to realize that the way we filtered the "facts" had a great deal to do with the nature of our assumptions. This training in methodology was excellent preparation for developing critical thinking, but after college I realized that 20-hour centrifuge experiments through the night were not for me. I wanted to be more directly involved with people and their concerns.

I became interested in the open classroom movement in England and found a job teaching 6-, 7-, and 8-year-olds in the same class. Through this firsthand experience with the nitty-gritty of teaching, I began to see that when the culture of the school and the culture of the parents did not match, the child was usually in academic and emotional trouble. Funded by the Carnegie Mellon Foundation, I began a program to improve communication between African American parents and their children's teachers (predominantly European American) with an elementary school in the inner city of New Haven, Connecticut. Dr. Jim Comer of the Yale Child Study Center was on our board. In this particular school, about one half of the African American students "flunked" kindergarten, whereas their Caucasian counterparts were mostly passed to the first grade. For 4 years my staff and I worked to bring the goals of learning between the two groups (cultures) into alignment. I learned a lot; working with staff members who slowly made their way off welfare, I witnessed their many adaptations to harsh environments and active discrimination. Although parents' ways of raising their children were essential for living on the street, they were working against the children in the structured environment of school. And I learned that the school personnel, having little exposure to life on the street or the effects of discrimination, had little awareness of how their environment was actively contributing to the children's perpetual failure. Over the 4 long, hard years, the project did manage to reduce the numbers of children failing kindergarten, but for me, the immediate effect was that I had a diagnosable case of burnout. My way out of real life was to enter a graduate program at Harvard University. These previous experiences working with families then became the basis for research with families, and I was lucky enough to team up with Dr. Robert LeVine at Harvard University to study families and aging. When the time came to chose a population to study, I chose to move back toward my own heritage: I would interview Chinese families in the Boston area. I received training in qualitative research tools and a way of thinking that have served me well as a clinician.

As the interviews with Chinese families proceeded, it was clear to me that many families were suffering from depression and problems of adjustment to the United States. I began to get advanced training as a clinician at Yale and at Stanford. For 8 years, I worked in community and hospital settings with families, young adults, and children. After moving to California, I was fortunate to be offered an academic position in the clinical psychology program at the Pacific Graduate School of Psychology and a clinical research position in the Department of Psychiatry and Behavioral Sciences at Stanford University School of Medicine. In both settings, my work has focused primarily on the study of cultural beliefs and behaviors in the areas of psychotherapy, adaptation to the United States, and suicide.

I have been primarily either a clinician (8 years) or a researcher (5 years) these past years. Although it seems that it should be relatively easy to use research findings to match a treatment to a particular psychological disorder, in actuality, the fit to clients who often do not meet the research criteria is much more challenging. I generally use and teach manualized therapies, finding them more effective, but I sometimes worry that I will lose sight of the specific, idiosyncratic needs of the person. From my vantage point, there have existed too few mechanisms or opportunities within the field to actually integrate the researcher and the clinician roles in rigorous and satisfying ways while preserving the integrity of clients' needs.

On reflection, I realize that three overarching themes have evolved to guide my application of research to practice. First, while conducting research concerning culture, I find that I understand human behaviors and motivations more fruitfully by using systemic thinking (where A and B interact and have a reciprocal relationship with each other); consequently, I am less engaged in linear types of thinking (where A leads to B). Correspondingly, as a clinician, I am interested in hearing more about the system in which the person operates—what are people's support systems, what are their relationships to work and family, how do they tell their story?

Second, I find that the discipline required in the ordering and sorting, hypothesis testing, and rethinking that is associated with conducting research serves me well. It acts as an active framework that guides the sorting and organizing of the multiple layers of data that surround a client's presentation. Use of this dynamic framework also serves to confront my own "truths"; it can pull me up short because there are, after all, multiple ways to see the "truth" of each situation.

Third, although I use research findings to guide my pattern of asking questions, I am skeptical about applying them wholesale to the struggles of individual people. This comes from the experience of working directly with clients; they often tell me that something isn't working. I find that sometimes a client's ways of thinking or feeling are not accurately predicted by what the research would suggest; then it is time to lean forward and spend more energy listening to the story of this person and later to go back to the framework that continues to help guide my thinking. While trying to weave back and forth between research findings and my own clinical experience in order to effectively work with the person sitting in front of me, I sometimes feel as if I am the leaf, rushing headlong down a swollen stream. The anxiety of "not knowing" is often present. I start at the landing base where there are developmental theory and social science frameworks that have taught me to categorize, order data, and ask questions; then I am out in the middle of the stream where I hear the specific and peculiar nuances of this person's story; then I work hard to maintain a balance between these two states. Sometimes there is a safety net; other times there isn't. And most often I really don't know the exact impact of all those brilliant interventions.

WHAT DIFFERENCE DOES CULTURE MAKE?

At present, I teach, supervise therapists-in-training, and conduct research on the impact of cultural beliefs and practices on people who have moved from one culture to another—either through migration or by virtue of being socialized into one set of cultural beliefs and behaviors and then needing to adapt to another set of beliefs and behaviors. One research project has found that people who have migrated change their life goals differentially in the areas of work, family, and social life; they adopt more Western values in their work and careers but exhibit relatively less change in their family lives. Some of these patterns of adaptation are associated with high levels of depression (Shiang, Bogumill, Kalehzan, & Benet, 1998). We are interested in learning more about what specific aspects of culture endure in the face of new values and behaviors. What specific kinds of adaptations predict successful functioning in the new culture? And are there predictable conflicts associated with these adaptations?

Another area of inquiry focuses on failures in adaptation. We study patterns of completed suicide among cultural, racial, or ethnic groups in San Francisco and find that Asians use methods of completing suicide that are similar to those used in China. For example, the most common method of completing suicide in precommunist (1949) China was the use of hanging (Shiang, Barron, Xiao, Blinn, & Tam, 1998); this was the predominant method used in the 10-year period of 1987–1997. Caucasians predominantly use methods of gunshot and overdose. These findings suggest that cultural beliefs and practices concerning death and suicide endure through the process of immigration (Shiang et al., 1997).

I am often asked by clinicians and researchers alike: "So what difference does culture make anyway?" Isn't the difference between people really due to biology, the personality, the basic temperament, or psychological motivation?" Culture is frivolous. In my teaching and supervision, I have found that many people find it difficult to clearly articulate aspects of one's own culture; it is something taken for granted and is therefore less defined.

As one student said to me, "I'm American, I don't have a culture. I just do the same as everyone else around me." This person probably doesn't think she has a culture because it is unconscious—she just lives it. Culture is so ingrained that it is difficult to talk about it—we just "do it." This is especially true for people who identify strongly with "mainstream" U.S. culture; the dominant group thinks of itself "without" culture. It is often only when a person identifies with a nondominant aspect of the society does he or she acknowledges a culture.

However, when people visit a culture very different from their own, suddenly their culture (and their relationship to it) becomes apparent. This was true for my 17-year-old Chinese American daughter, who spent 5 weeks in a village in West Africa this summer. She reflected the following:

> Walking down the street, I am expected to greet everyone I meet and to search for a connection to this person—oh, yes, I know your cousin, oh yes, your uncle sells me fish, and so on—and as you can imagine this took time. At first it felt like "wasted" time—we weren't getting my "work" (interviewing mothers about indigenous ways of teaching children) done—but then it slowly dawned on me that this is their "work"—finding ways to be a community. At home, on my own street in Palo Alto, I haven't even met all the people who live on our street. (personal communication, 1997)

In this Senegal community, values, behaviors, and daily actions are oriented primarily to establishing and maintaining contact with others as opposed to accomplishing an instrumental goal. As a colleague trained in sociology once said to me, "I thought my study of Chinese society was mainly about groups. Then when I went to China—it was a rude shock to see that aspects of culture had a huge impact on group functioning—and moreover to realize that my culture was so fundamentally different" (personal communication, 1997). Her assumption that culture was secondary to other sociological phenomena was challenged.

For our research projects and clinical work, it is this invisible culture that we try to bring to light. In both research and clinical work, I am continually asking, "What is culture?" "How does it make a difference in this person's life?" "How do we measure it?" "Does that make it real?" "How does an understanding of culture add to the study of basic psychological phenomena and our work with clients?"

The fact is that all people have culture—held consciously or not—and this culture has an impact on the therapeutic process. It has been suggested that European American culture has had an impact on the definitions used in psychological research and clinical work. Markus, Kitayama, and Heiman (1996) in reviewing core principles of social psychology such as motivation, cognitions, and interpersonal behavior in the most recent edition of the *Handbook of Basic Principles*, suggested that "psychologists may be prematurely settling on *one* psychology, that is, on one set of assumptions about what are the relevant or most important psychological states and processes, and on one set of generalizations about their nature and function" (p. 858). This model is based on the primary assumption that the end-state of all human potential is an autonomous, individuated person. It has formed the bedrock of assumptions upon which most psychological study in the United States has been based. However, it has become increasingly clear over time that this is not the *only* viable bedrock upon which psychological study can be based. In the past 10 years, mainstream psychology has begun to endorse the viability of many definitions of the healthy, good, and moral person.

Betancourt and Lopez (1993) noted that there are more than 100 definitions of culture in the scientific literature. For our purposes, culture is conceptualized as having multiple levels of impact on the human being as well as having a vital, dynamic aspect. *Culture*, as we define it, provides (a) the "things" or material aspects that are necessary for daily living; (b) language (ways of filtering out perceptions); (c) a schema for the acceptable interactional patterns among the individual, family, community, and the larger group or society, such as role definitions; (d) the shared meanings of these things; and (e) the continual, and often unarticulated, manipulation and negotiation of these meanings in both active and passive ways in the individual and the group. To consider how cultural beliefs and behaviors are constituted, let us consider a framework suggested by Markus and Kitayama (1994, p. 342) to study the expression of emotion.

I have adapted this framework (see Figure 9.1) to include the consideration of people that move from one culture into another. The framework describes the components that lead to the individual's instrumental action (see the right side of the figure). These components, in the adapted form of the framework, are as follows:

1. Collective reality made up of core cultural ideas, which form the sense of the good, the moral, and the self-construal.
2. Sociopsychological processes constituted and reinforced by various practices and systems such as caretaking, education, and scripts for social interactions.
3. Change from one culture to another, particularly in the case of being raised in the culture of heritage and then moving out into the culture of settlement. This process requires negotiation and modification of one's cultural ideas as well as an assessment of the ways in which one will accomplish life goals most successfully. These processes often occur in the face of stressors such as learning a new language, creating new support networks, utilizing institutional systems, and status changes. (I have added this process.)

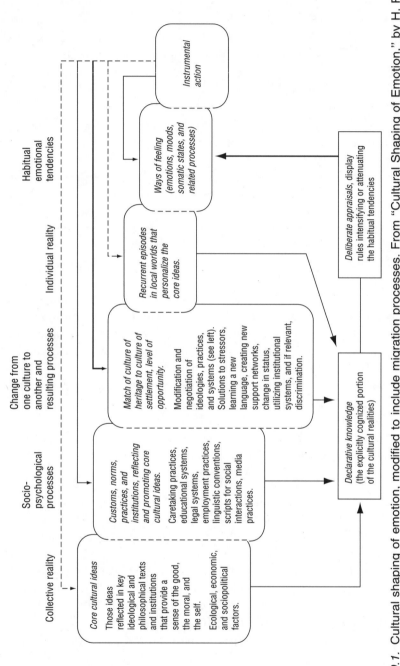

Figure 9.1. Cultural shaping of emotion, modified to include migration processes. From "Cultural Shaping of Emotion," by H. R. Markus and S. Kitayama, in *Emotion and Culture: Empirical Studies of Mutual Influence* (p. 342), edited by H. R. Markus and S. Kitayama, 1994, Washington, DC: American Psychological Association. Adapted by permission.

4. Individual reality includes the way we learn what is normative within the specific dynamic of our own family systems and communities.
5. Habitual emotional tendencies have to do with those tendencies that have been coded as an automatic response in the process of learning over time.

As noted above, these components all lead to an individual's instrumental action. At the bottom of the figure, declarative knowledge is indicated to show that many of these components can be articulated by the people in the group and that these feed into the making of deliberate appraisals. They also state that not all people will have full cultural expertise.

In considering a comparison of different cultural groups, Triandis, Kashima, Shimada, and Villareal (1986) suggested that societies can be placed on a spectrum that ranges from "individualistic" to "collectivistic." Kitayama and Markus (1994) suggested that, in the same vein, individuals can be characterized as lying on a spectrum ranging from "independent" to "interdependent"—each having a specific and different definition of the good, the moral, and the self. In my clinical work I find it useful to use these conceptualizations: Does the client define him- or herself as individualistic or interdependent in the specific problem area? In the research setting, I am attempting to determine to what degree people adhere to these self-construals.

Thus, the definition of *self* is culturally constituted, culturally bound. For the client from a society where the definition of the good, moral person is based on the individualistic or independent model, the goals of autonomy will be given higher priority and the person will give high regard to the promotion of the individual, placing relatively less emphasis on maintaining relationships. If the definition of the good, moral person is based on an interdependent or collectivistic model, then the goals of the person's behaviors focused more on the place of the individual within the group, rather than separate from the group. Relationships with others, especially family, will be at the top of the priority list and, correspondingly, decisions will be made with the needs of the group in mind. Research has shown that most cultures in Asia, Africa, South America, and Southern Europe follow this model (Smith & Bond, 1994). Indeed, the percentage of people who espouse these views actually makes up the majority of people in the world. It has also been suggested that most women in the United States and Northern Europe make decisions in their lives based on the interdependent model (Gilligan, 1982).

In actuality, every person, although he or she might interact daily in a society that is more or less interdependent, will identify with and belong to many groups or categories of people (e.g., wife, younger sister, employer, student). In each group, people might be more or less independent or more or less interdependent in other areas of their lives.

ACCURATE ASSESSMENT OF A CLIENT IN RESEARCH AND PRACTICE

The major questions that arise when clients walk into our clinic are these: How do we assess the person for his or her normative definition of self? How does the person use these in everyday life? How are their beliefs and behaviors maladaptive, and how do their present actions prevent them from achieving what they want in their larger life goals? Obviously, we assume that the client comes into the special situational context of therapy with his or her own cultural framework through which certain realities of class, education, and other factors assert themselves (see above discussion). We try to decipher the cultural dimensions and contexts of the problem as the client presents them. In the clinical setting, it is important to note that any client who is in crisis requires immediate attention and interventions to help alleviate the stress of the crisis.

Sitting across from a client, I initially try to listen for three general categories of information:

1. The values and behaviors of the general categorical groups to which the person says he or she belongs (i.e., heritage, gender, age ["too young, too old"], sexual orientation, etc.) and which of these are most salient. This provides information about the material things, shared meaning, and communication patterns of the groups as well as the definition of the "good, moral self" (see definition above).
2. The person's expressions of the culture. (These may include general, particular, or idiosyncratic aspects.) Another way to understand this is to ask, "What cognitive and affective schemas does the person have for the acceptable goals and expectations related to the problems he or she presents, and what are the contexts for the expression of these values and behaviors?" For example, the person's behavior is often modified by economic circumstances, sexual orientation, and ways of adapting to immediate environmental pressures.
3. Possible conflicts between the person's own goals and the goals of others in the immediate context (family, spouse, school, work). This aspect is critical. For example, a woman might define the "good wife" differently than does her husband. She might experience conflict between the media message of "you can do it all" and her experience of limited

opportunities. What choices does the person have in operating within these systems—in both active and passive ways?

As clients enter therapy, my colleagues and I are concerned with the question of how to accurately measure their values and behaviors. Are there particular changes in values and behaviors that correspond to stresses that result from the immigration process? These questions have led to the development of an area of research focusing on the process of moving from one culture to another. My own motivation to explore this area was bolstered by a serendipitous remark made by a graduate student who convinced me to take the Suinn-Lew Acculturation Scale (Suinn, Ahuna, & Khoo, 1992), a reliable instrument that has often been used to assess the degree to which Asians adhere to U.S. values (higher level = more or greater United States values). It provides a summative score that suggests that the person is more or less acculturated. My student scored the instrument, and then handed it back to me with a quizzical look: "You are less acculturated than I thought you were. You're more Asian." That remark was a bit startling. On reflection, this was an intriguing statement. As we talked about it, she said she perceived me to be quite Western (seeing me at work where I have no "foreign" accent, and where I was urging her to work more independently on her dissertation project), whereas my total score showed that I was more Asian. So, was I hiding something, was I odd or disjointed? Worse still, was I inconsistent across the different aspects of my life? Psychological theory puts a great deal of emphasis on being consistent and having a "core" self across most situations. Worse still, would I fit the label suggested for people like me—living between two cultures—marginalized? Maybe this was because I was raised by Chinese parents within a Confucian context but went to school in a Western–Northern European context. But the more I thought about it, the more I began to realize that my own experience—being attuned to various and differing goals in different contexts—was not "odd," that I do not actually feel marginalized, and that I am quite functional, thank you. Furthermore, in talking with other people about this, it appeared that most people, especially Caucasian women, acted differently in some settings and similarly in other settings. Many mainstream psychological research findings were not describing our experiences.

As a result of this rather casual remark made by a student, my colleagues and I developed a measurement tool called the Cultural Beliefs, Behavior, and Adaptation Profile (Bogumill & Shiang, 1998; Shiang, Bogumill, et al., 1998) to assess similarities and differences in cultural beliefs and behaviors across the different domains of everyday life. This scale provides the profile of a complex "snapshot" of people across several settings in their lives—work, family, social, and daily activities. For example, we found that a person will endorse both the notion that "my own ideas are more important than my friends' ideas when I consider educational deci-sions" (independent in the area of work and education) and "I should take care of my parents when they get old (interdependent in the area of family). We are now in the process of defining a subsample of items to be used to assess a client in the waiting room before interventions start.

INCORPORATING CULTURAL CONSIDERATIONS INTO SYSTEMATIC TREATMENT SELECTION

The general framework we use when considering the influence of a client's culture on determining the treatment plan for interventions is Sys-tematic Treatment Selection (STS; Beutler & Clarkin, 1990). STS pro-vides a way of ordering the often overwhelming amount of information presented by the client that enables clinicians to generate hypotheses about the client and his or her systemic environment. It focuses on four classes of information to be considered in the assessment process:

1. Predisposing client variables
2. Treatment contexts
3. Client–therapist relationship variables
4. Psychotherapeutic strategies and procedures.

Beutler and Clarkin (1990) stated that "effective treatment is a con-sequence of increasingly fine-grained decisions. No effective treatment can be developed from information that is available at one point in time nor from decisions made on the basis of a static set of client characteristics" (p. 20). The four classes of variables in the STS model have the following characteristics: (a) Each is a part of an overall system and each is therefore temporally and sequentially related to the others, (b) the variables are activating characteristics that describe both weaknesses and strengths (e.g., client expectations and coping style can help determine to what degree a client will engage in the therapeutic process), (c) the outcome of the in-teraction between the client's presentation and the prior helping agencies must be considered at every decision point for further interventions, and (d) both individual characteristics as well as the situational context of client and therapist must be considered.

As shown in Figure 9.2, we have modified STS in the following ways:

1. *Predisposing client variables.* Assess for consideration of cultural be-liefs and behaviors, culturally formed syndromes, stressors and adaptations related to culture change, and resource level.

2. *Client–therapist relationship variables.* Assess for stimulus value of both client and therapist, establishing credibility on the part of the ther-apist, careful attention to cultural rules regarding relationships, interven-tions that include the use of education, coaching, multiple roles, and re

ferrals to alternate models of health. Whereas the STS model considers treatment contexts before client–therapist relationship variables, the literature on ethnic matches between client and therapist suggests that relationship variables must be addressed at the beginning of treatment in order to engage clients who have often felt disenfranchised from the system. This is especially so when the therapist is associated with the majority "system" (Western views of mental health, speaks English only, etc.) and the client is from a minority perceived (by self and others) to lack power. Thus, one modification to the model is to focus on developing the therapeutic alliance as a top priority early in the course of therapy, and to continue to "check in" with the client regarding therapist role(s) in the relationship.

3. *Treatment contexts.* Provide education that helps define the purpose of treatment, consideration of a referral to services that might range from indigenous healers to mainstream institutions, consider the active involvement of key community members, and consider interventions that might include multiple approaches to problem solutions.

4. *Psychotherapeutic strategies and procedures.* Based on the above considerations.

APPLICATION TO CASES

I illustrate how the incorporation of cultural considerations in the STS model helps my practice by discussing two cases. The first woman is Kathy (an alias), a 26-year-old Caucasian woman, who has just ended a relationship with her boyfriend of 2 years. She has missed several days of work in the last week and is getting pressure from her boss to finish a major work project that was overdue. She came to the clinic stating that she would never be able to have a satisfying relationship, that she was too feminist for most men, they say she is "aggressive," and that she often "sabotages" her intimate relationships. She intermittently burst into tears and at other times looked inappropriately happy given the content of her discourse. She said that she breaks into tears "for no reason," and cannot sleep. She has lost 10 pounds in the last 3 weeks, has no appetite, and just cannot seem to get rid of the idea that she will never be able to have a long-lasting relationship. At the same time she says she wants to be independent. The precipitating factor that brings her into treatment is the recent breakup with her boyfriend.

The second woman is May Lee (an alias), a 28-year-old Chinese American woman who reports intermittent stomach pain and has missed several days of work in the past 2 weeks. She started the session by saying that after getting a work promotion, she had an "odd" interaction with a

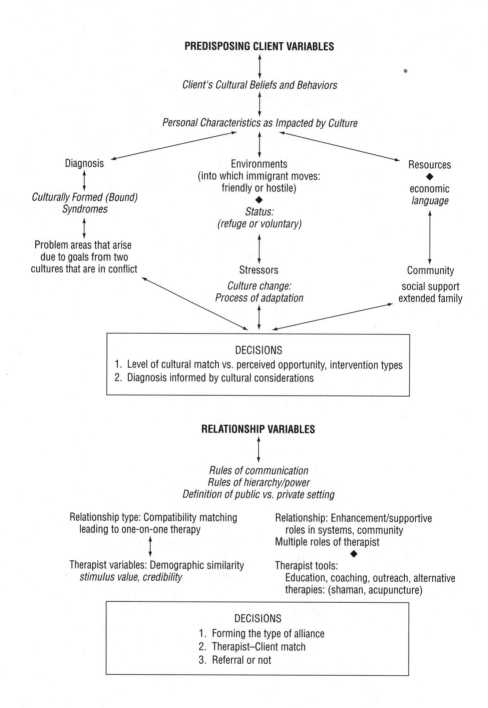

PREDISPOSING CLIENT VARIABLES

Client's Cultural Beliefs and Behaviors

Personal Characteristics as Impacted by Culture

Diagnosis

Culturally Formed (Bound) Syndromes

Problem areas that arise
due to goals from two
cultures that are in conflict

Environments
(into which immigrant moves:
friendly or hostile)

*Status:
(refuge or voluntary)*

Stressors
*Culture change:
Process of adaptation*

Resources

economic
language

Community

social support
extended family

DECISIONS
1. Level of cultural match vs. perceived opportunity, intervention types
2. Diagnosis informed by cultural considerations

RELATIONSHIP VARIABLES

*Rules of communication
Rules of hierarchy/power
Definition of public vs. private setting*

Relationship type: Compatibility matching
leading to one-on-one therapy

Therapist variables: Demographic similarity
stimulus value, credibility

Relationship: Enhancement/supportive
roles in systems, community
Multiple roles of therapist

Therapist tools:
Education, coaching, outreach, alternative
therapies: (shaman, acupuncture)

DECISIONS
1. Forming the type of alliance
2. Therapist–Client match
3. Referral or not

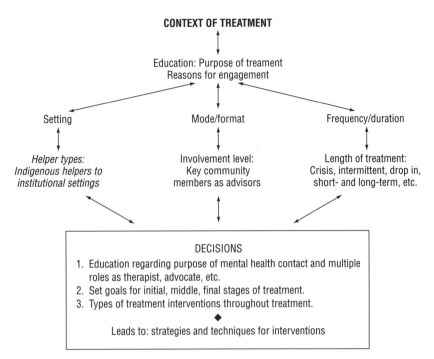

CONTEXT OF TREATMENT

Education: Purpose of treament
Reasons for engagement

Setting

Mode/format

Frequency/duration

Helper types:
Indigenous helpers to
institutional settings

Involvement level:
Key community
members as advisors

Length of treatment:
Crisis, intermittent, drop in,
short- and long-term, etc.

DECISIONS
1. Education regarding purpose of mental health contact and multiple roles as therapist, advocate, etc.
2. Set goals for initial, middle, final stages of treatment.
3. Types of treatment interventions throughout treatment.
◆
Leads to: strategies and techniques for interventions

Figure 9.2. Modified version of systematic treatment selection variables. From "Developing cultural competency in clinical practice: Treatment considerations for Chinese cultural groups in the United States," by J. Shiang, C. Kjellander, K. Huang, and S. Bogumill, 1998, *Clinical Psychology: Science and Practice, 5,* pp. 202–204. Copyright 1998 by the Oxford University Press. Adapted by permission.

coworker who said something to the effect that "all you Asians work too hard." She has not been able to sleep because she is just too "worried." She presented her concerns with little emotional expression, looking sad only when describing her family's move from the People's Republic of China to the United States. When asked about other problems, she said she was trying to decide whether to break off her engagement with her fiancée, saying that her parents don't like him. She has also just been offered a promotion—a good job opportunity—but it would require moving across country and away from her parents. She moved to the United States from the People's Republic of China 5 years ago with her parents, and says that in the People's Republic of China being a good daughter and a good person would mean staying connected to her parents and considering their concerns when choosing a spouse. Here in the United States she is not sure what to do.

Table 9.1 presents some of the ways in which the predisposing client variables and considerations of culture are similar and different for the two women.

TABLE 9.1

Comparison of Systematic Treatment Selection Predisposing Client Variables for Kathy and May Lee

Variable	Kathy	May Lee
Cultural beliefs and behaviors	1. Role definition as a woman, U.S. values. 2. Role as a partner in intimate relationship based on U.S. values.	1. Role definition as woman in Chinese culture, comparison with U.S. culture. 2. Role as daughter in Chinese culture. 3. Role as partner in intimate relationships, Chinese values and comparison with United States.
Personal characteristics	1. Self-doubt in area of relationships. 2. Wishes to be independent. 3. Recent loss. 4. Arousal (high) 5. Reactance level (high) 6. Coping style (internal)	1. "Worries" about relationship and job. 2. Values interdependence with family; values job independence. 3. Anticipating breaking off relationship. 4. Arousal (low) 5. Reactance (low) 6. Coping style (internal)
Diagnosis	1. Mood disorder	1. Physical problems 2. Neurasthenia 3. Mood disorder 4. Conversion disorder 5. Conflict between parents and children in area of expectations for job and relationships.
Environment (stressors)	1. Extra pressure from her job.	1. Recent move out of her parents' home. 2. Job position change. 3. Recent incident of perceived "discrimination" at work.
Resources	1. Friends who socialize about once a week. 2. Health club, but hasn't been going lately.	1. Family. 2. Friends whom she sees about once a week. 3. Chinese cultural social group; attends on the weekends.

Note. For more information on systematic treatment selection see Beutler, and Clarkin (1990).

Treatment Decisions: Cultural Match and Perceived Opportunity to Achieve Goals

After considering the client's personal characteristics, it is possible for the clinician to make two treatment decisions: The first is to assess the degree to which the client's cultural beliefs and behaviors match those of the environment in which he or she is trying to effect some change. The second is to assess the client's perceived opportunity to accomplish the desired change.

My colleagues and I have developed a paper-and-pencil tool to help guide the clinician to make an assessment along two parameters:

Cultural match in beliefs and behaviors: An assessment of the differences between the client's belief system and the U.S. cultural norm yields a determination of difference, ranging from small to large.

Perceived opportunities: An assessment of the perceived opportunities available yields a determination of the client's perception of his or her ability to move forward in addressing his or her problems and goals.

These determinations provide guidance in choosing among the types of interventions available and which ones will potentially have the greatest impact on the client's problems. In addition, they will help the clinician make explicit his or her own understanding of the client's culture (see Table 9.2).

To determine the degree of cultural match in values and practices, the clinician needs to consider (a) does the client identify with the values of the culture of heritage (the homeland) or with the culture of settlement (U.S. norms) in the specific content area that is identified as a problem and (b) what is the U.S. norm? The assessment of the level of cultural match (small to large) is placed along the horizontal axis of the grid.

The term *perceived opportunities* is used because it is the client's view of his or her chances to move ahead that forms the basis of what we might call "hope." Does the client have hope that the problem will change? The level of perceived opportunities (high to low) is placed along the vertical axis of the grid. Sometimes the client's assessment of opportunities is out of line with reality and the mental health worker needs to educate and provide evidence related to the actual level of opportunity. This requires a negotiation between client and clinician; optimism or pessimism about opportunities can reside in either part of the dyad. Sometimes it may be more realistic to come to terms with the fact that the level of opportunities in the specific situation is not as great as desired for (due to discrimination, oppression); reality is more harsh than ideal. In other instances, it may be

TABLE 9.2
Determining Degree of Cultural Match

Perceived opportunity	Level of cultural match: Values and practices	
	δ Client problem: Focus of intervention	Δ Client problem: Focus of intervention
High	Individual type (concrete steps to work with individual to achieve goals)	Individual type (education and developing realistic goals) At level of community and society for both cultural groups Education Advocacy Policy regarding priorities, resources, etc.
Low	At level of community and society Address reasons/practices for low opportunity Interventions at community individual type (education, acceptance, concrete steps to promote change)	At level of society Education Advocacy Realistic assessment of possibility of change Strategies and negotiation Individual Education regarding realistic assessment of situation

DIAGNOSIS, INFORMED BY CULTURE:

RULE OUT _____
CONCERNS/QUESTIONS/ISSUES TO CLARIFY WITH
A. CLIENT: _____
B. CONSULTANT _____

Note. Modified version of clinician practice decision. From "Developing cultural competency in clinical practice: Treatment considerations for Chinese cultural groups in the United States," by J. Shiang, C. Kjellander, K. Huang, and S. Bogumill, 1998, *Clinical Psychology: Science and Practice, 5,* p. 190. Copyright 1998 by the Oxford University Press. Adapted by permission.

that the clinician needs to be educated about the realities of the client's situation. Specific interventions can then be tailored to encourage realistic and long-lasting changes.

In the grid presented, interventions that focus on change at the individual level are greatest when the delta of difference in cultural match is small and the level of perceived opportunities is high (top left quadrant of the grid). For example, if a person wants to advance in the U.S. educational system (where the delta is small and opportunity is high), then perhaps the most effective intervention will be to learn how to fill out college application forms, take entrance examinations, and learn to cope with the understandable anxiety that accompanies the process. However, if the delta of difference in cultural match is large and the perceived opportunities for achieving goals are low (lower right quadrant of the grid), then the individual can be educated about these differences. The most effective strategy for coping with these differences would be at the level of societal change. If, for example, the elderly Chinese find it difficult to use a nursing home as one possibility for care of their elderly, then the most adaptive stance may be to set up their own housing to accommodate the elderly. As successful elderly housing develops to address the needs of specific groups, other elderly housing development ventures may consider tailoring their programs to serve specific populations. What we notice from the types of interventions in each of the quadrants is that interventions in the upper left-hand quadrant would be focused primarily on the individual, whereas interventions in the lower right-hand quadrant would be focused primarily at the societal level (Shiang, Kjellander, Huang, & Bogumill, 1998).

I illustrate use of the grid by considering Kathy and May Lee's problems. One of the immediate problems Kathy said she was concerned about was finishing a work project that is already overdue. Let's say that at assessment, I found out that she is clear about the work requirements of the project (cultural match between her beliefs or behaviors and her boss's beliefs or behaviors: small difference) and that her opportunities to complete the project are high (perceived opportunity high). In this situation, I can focus on the individual level to determine appropriate interventions and a time line by which she can be encouraged to achieve her stated goal. In contrast, a problem presented by May Lee was that there might be some unconscious stereotyping and possible discrimination occurring in her workplace. My assessment showed that it was a problem for May Lee, yet, when she asked her colleagues about it, they laughed and said it was just a joke (cultural match between her beliefs or behaviors and colleague's belief or behaviors: large difference). Her perception was that she would not be able to change the system on her own (perceived opportunity low) and thus, I would work both at the systems level (perhaps, with the client's permission, contact the human resources personnel department of the company and suggest diversity training for the staff) and at the individual level (what options does she have when someone makes a remark that she considers racist?).

Cultural Considerations in Determining a Diagnosis

How is pathology manifested? Is it manifested in identical ways for people of all cultural backgrounds? Are there areas of similarity and areas of difference? This is one of the central issues facing mental health today. When working with people who hold as life goals the interdependent self-construal as compared with the autonomous, independent self-construal (codified in the Northern European American-based *Diagnostic and Statistical Manual* [4th ed.; DSM–IV; *American Psychiatric Association*, 1994]). How do we assign a diagnosis (useful for communication among mental health workers)? How do specific cultural beliefs and practices influence the manifestation of the psychopathology?

First, it is highly likely that Kathy's constellation of symptoms can be easily matched to the mental health disorders based on *DSM–IV*. This nosology was developed with populations that share characteristics similar to those presented by Kathy. A likely diagnosis is that she is experiencing some form of depression. She has suffered several recent losses. Several symptoms (appetite changes, loss of weight, sleeplessness, emotional instability) suggest a *DSM–IV* diagnosis of mood disorder. This diagnosis provides us with a working hypothesis on which to map further information as well as language that can be useful for communicating with other mental health workers. Her wish to be independent suggests that she see herself as a good, moral person when she is acting independently. At the same time, she enters therapy due to losses and problems with relationships. As a clinician, I do not yet have critical information about the quality of the "problems" in her interpersonal interactions. This information must be gleaned from my clinical interactions with the client, her reporting of patterns with others in the past, and corroborating information from other sources.

Assigning a diagnosis to May Lee must be done with caution. May Lee may exhibit a number of the same symptoms as Kathy, but it not clear that we can apply the same procedure of using the *DSM–IV*. First, although May Lee says she is Chinese American, we do not know specifically about the set of beliefs and behaviors that guide her decision making, especially in the area of marriage, work, and balancing family needs with her own desires. If we urge her to be independent, are we encouraging her to do what we think as "right" or "moral" on the basis of our own assumptions? And if we don't, how comfortable are we if we stay open to the possibility that she might make choices to foster interdependence between herself and family? Thus, it is critical to determine whether she adheres to a belief system that emphasizes independence or interdependence in the important areas of her life.

Second, we do not know whether her presenting problems of intermittent stomach pain and sleep disturbance stem from physical concerns, psychological concerns, or both. As researchers, we know that depression does not look the same across all cultures (Kleinman & Goode, 1985). The recent inclusion of culture-bound syndromes in an appendix in *DSM–IV* acknowledges this fact. There is substantial evidence to indicate that some cultures based on the interdependent model express sad feelings in ways that emphasize the unity between mind and body (Kleinman & Goode, 1985). Thus, psychological problems are normally expressed in the physical realm. For example, in the societal context of the People's Republic of China, the diagnosis of neurasthenia (worries, sadness, lethargy, body pain) is a common way to express sadness, troubles, and problems with other people. The symptom constellation associated with neurasthenia has considerable overlap with the Western constellation of mood disorder, but the client often emphasizes somatic concerns in a societal climate in which expressing emotional problems is frowned on (Kleinman, 1986). If May Lee recently arrived from the People's Republic of China, then her symptom expression may understandably be closer to neurasthenia.

To determine whether the *DSM–IV* is appropriate for May Lee or must be modified, the clinician must learn more about her beliefs and behaviors, and about the ways in which she has adapted to living in the United States. In the following section, I provide some of this background.

Chinese Cultural Beliefs and Behaviors

Chinese cultural beliefs hold that the mind and body are intricately linked; psyche and soma are parts of one system (Cheung, 1985; Marsella, 1980). In contrast, Northern Europeans view the mind and body as two separate systems. In the West, treatment is the purview of different institutional systems: For problems of the mind, one seeks treatment from a mental health clinic, whereas for health problems, one seeks treatment at a medical clinic. The power of these beliefs is codified in the language used by each culture. In China, traditional folk beliefs emphasize that "all behaviors and actions come from the heart . . . [and that] thinking is in the heart" (Tung, 1993, p. 486), whereas people in the United States are generally treated *either* for bodily pain *or* for psychological pain. In traditional Chinese culture, somatic complaints are a culturally sanctioned mode of emotional expression (Bond & Hwang, 1986; Cheung, 1985; Kirmayer, 1989; K. Lin, 1981; White, 1982). Chinese populations in Asia have been found to prefer "externalizing idioms of distress" (Hsu, 1985; Kleinman, 1986, 1987; Kleinman & Kleinman, 1985; Lum, 1982; White, 1982). Kleinman noted that the expression of somatic symptoms has been adaptive in specific cultural and social contexts, particularly in the People's Republic of China, which emphasizes group cohesion over individual expression within a specific political climate. Recent Chinese immigrants, who are likely to hold more traditional cultural beliefs, are apt to manifest distress as health concerns (Kleinman, 1977, 1980, 1987, 1988; D. W. Sue & Sue, 1990; Tseng, 1975). Expressing problems in somatic form elicits caretaking from others, maintains valued social harmony, reintegrates the individual into his or her social network, avoids shame and stigma, and reduces the experience of painful emotional intensity (Kleinman & Kleinman, 1985).

In China, the emphasis on presenting distress through the body rather than through emotions is also part of a system that evaluates the presence of a mental illness (rather than somatic illness) as a societal stigma. The person is considered somehow "bad" rather than "good" and the close association of individual actions with family worth creates a situation of serious social consequences for Chinese patients (Katon, Kleinman, & Rosen, 1982; K. Lin, 1981; T. Lin & Lin, 1981). The general stigma associated with mental illness often pushes families to hide such illness until the patient becomes severely mentally ill and the family unable to cope. Consequently, the patients who finally come into the mental health system are often gravely impaired.

This belief system is carried to the culture of settlement, where it can endure for many years after migration. In a study of Chinese families in Canada, researchers found that if a family member had a chronic or intractable mental health problem such as psychosis, the family often ended up completely abandoning him or her in anticipation of rejection by the wider community (T. Lin & Lin, 1981). In fact, it was found that even among third- and fourth-generation Chinese people in the United States, shame and stigma were associated with emotional difficulties (Yamamoto & Acosta, 1982).

The clinician trained in a Western model of health may be tempted to view somatization as a defensive reaction that must be dismantled to make progress in therapy. However, conceptualizing somatic symptoms as disguised intrapsychic conflicts can cause differences in problem conceptualization between the therapist and the client (S. Sue & Zane, 1987; S. Sue, 1988), potentially leaving the client feeling misunderstood. As noted above, such a conceptualization fails to recognize the integration of mind and body espoused by traditional Chinese culture (K. Lin, 1981; Lum, 1982; Marsella, 1980). The preeminence given to intraindividual mental processes by Western psychotherapists may understandably perplex Chinese American clients who are oriented toward traditional values. Symptoms that are conceptualized as conversion disorders are not necessarily a guise for "deeper" psychological problems; they may be the body–psychological concern.

I return now to the issue of determining a diagnosis for May Lee. First, it is necessary to send her to a physician to rule out any physical disorder. If she receives a clean bill of health from her physician, I would first consider an adjustment disorder based on the transition from one culture to another; second, parent–child problems; and third, a mood disorder. If she were to continue in therapy, I would expect her somatic symptoms to decrease and the therapy to focus on ways to determine her own goals in life. The key will be to help her stay in therapy long enough to establish a helpful alliance. In the following section I focus on my experiences in forming the therapeutic alliance.

FORMING THE THERAPEUTIC ALLIANCE: RELATIONSHIP RULES IN TRADITIONAL CHINESE SOCIETIES

To establish a therapeutic alliance, it is critical to find ways to communicate based on the client's rules of relationships. The clinician needs to find ways to build trust; authority, not trust, is automatically attributed to the therapist. In the formal setting of a clinic, the Chinese client who believes in more traditional belief systems will adhere to conventional rules of formal relationships. In these traditional Chinese belief systems, the establishment of initial relationships is defined in terms of a strict hierarchy according to age, generational status, gender, and rules of inclusion or exclusion (Leong, 1986; Shiang, 1992, 1993). In general, human interactions both within the family and with strangers are guided by these rules of hierarchy.

Older people deserve more respect; they are expected to speak first and with wisdom. Older men speak before younger women. Personal disclosure, especially of emotional content, is reserved for only those people in the inner circle of family, "aunties and uncles" (close family friends designated to be "within the family"). The individuals are embedded in a network of close kinship relationships, and family members will be reluctant to reveal "private" matters to strangers (among whom the therapist is one). The individual's attachments and loyalty are, above all, to family members (Shiang, 1992). Once trust and credibility (S. Sue & Zane, 1987) are established, the client may relax the rules and include the therapist as a member of the family. I supervised a beginning therapist working with a client whose background was quite similar to that of May Lee. The therapist noted that her client called her "auntie" when introducing the therapist to her daughter. The supervisor wondered what this meant because it was clear that there was no blood relationship between them (the therapist is Caucasian). I explained that by using the familial term to address the therapist, the daughter would clearly understand that the therapist was to be trusted. This did not mean that the therapist would be invited to the family's Chinese New Year celebration but that the client now considered the therapist as part of the inner circle of trusted and reliable family friends.

ASPECTS OF THE THERAPIST IN FORMING THE THERAPEUTIC ALLIANCE

It is commonly understood that one's own experiences play a part in the kinds of transferences and countertransferences that affect the building of the therapeutic alliance. As an adult, I know that by some standards, my badges of respectability are my associations with Harvard, Yale, and

Stanford. They make me acceptable, especially in some communities. But are there any particularly salient experiences of being a Chinese American that affect the building of an alliance? Are there insights that come with the experience of feeling and being labeled "different?"

To try to address this issue in a personal way, let me tell you a little bit about myself. I am the oldest of five children born to Chinese parents who left their country of origin (the present People's Republic of China) voluntarily to receive training and education in the United States. In 1949, their way back to their country of origin and family was cut off for 30 years, with the rise of the communist leadership in the People's Republic of China. This was particularly difficult for them, as they each defined their sense of self in terms of their relationships to their families. My parents settled in the Boston area, raised their children, worked steady jobs, and call themselves Americans. To others, they speak with a foreign accent; to me, they were brave and did the best they could in the new land.

I was raised in a household with strong Confucian beliefs that emphasized respect for elders and for authority—beliefs that hold that people are basically educable and are capable of doing "good" for others in the world (Munroe, 1977). These beliefs were socialized into me by my strong, determined parents, who made it clear that we children were to succeed in the new land by having jobs, raising families, and contributing to society. In a sense, we felt we had no choice. When the kids at school called me "Chink" and pulled on the edges of their eyes to make them "slanty" like mine, my mother said, "Well, just ask them if they want to learn Chinese, and teach them a few words." Those kids didn't call me names again, and I knew that I had something to offer.

Parallel to these experiences were the general experiences I had and still often have of being different, feeling different, and being treated as if I am different. At the same time, some part of me wished to feel the same, be the same, and not to stand out at all. Sometimes this quality of "difference" has to do with being in the minority in the United States. It was made especially apparent when I was 12 years old. My family moved to Taiwan for 2 years. I remember my shock on experiencing the feeling of being surrounded by people who looked like me—and there were so many people too! But in Taiwan, these dilemmas were not solved because although I looked much like everyone else, I attended the American school and most of my classmates were Caucasian. Moving back to the United States, I experienced an overt act of discrimination. My first boyfriend said he broke up with me because his parents were against his dating an Asian person. Still, some parts of me know that different is good, that it defines a part of me and allows me to survive—and to understand and empathize with others who feel different in some way.

It was clear to me from the very beginning of my professional clinical and academic work that people projected onto me many different "pictures." They, of course, had something to do with the stimulus of "me" but had also to do with assumptions that others had of me as part of a larger Asian category. The immediate stimulus of the other person allows for predetermined conceptions to be reinforced or negated. For example, when clients first meet me, they are "hit in the face" with the fact that I am Asian—most therapists are Caucasian (especially when I was working on the East Coast)—and they sometimes express a small level of surprise. Sometimes they ask where I was born or whether I am Chinese or Japanese. This is when the stereotypes of transference and countertransference fly about the room and, if left unexamined, have real potential to harm the building of the therapeutic relationship.

> *Stereotype 1.* I am the quiet, unassuming, submissive, minority Asian female. This belief is often held by educators and supervisors. My mother taught me to counter this by speaking up.

> *Stereotype 2.* I am sexy, exotic and tricky, and easily tempted. This belief is held by many and has been articulated by a number of people with whom I worked in the inner city as well as by severely disturbed veterans who called me a Vietnamese "gook."

> *Stereotype 3.* I am Asian; therefore, I am pushy, competitive, inscrutable, and moneygrabbing. This is a belief often held by student peers. For my part, I suppose the assertive behavior might be a reaction to the projection of being thought of as submissive.

I have been told, with vigor, that I am a "banana"—yellow on the outside, white on the inside. I have been told that I am not Chinese enough, that I am too foreign, that I do not understand, and that I do not pass. When I say that I am trying to raise my children with some Chinese values, people say they are surprised. When I say that I like rock and roll, that my friends are Jewish, Chinese, and Caucasian, that I like making Armenian Easter eggs but don't celebrate the religious holidays, people often say, "Of course, you're American."

Stereotypes can serve a useful purpose in that they help us order data. However, to apply stereotypes thoughtfully requires a consideration of when to apply them, an understanding of whether and how long they guide the cognitive schemas, whether they have the flexibility to allow for new data, and, when they are applied inappropriately, at what cost to whom?

When I am faced with a person who appears to be judging my acceptability and their willingness to engage with me largely on the basis of stereotyping, my sensitive antennae sharpen their points and I become aware of subtle shades of lumping and clumping, discrimination, and dismissal. It appears to me that using stereotypes and prejudices continues to confirm a preestablished mind-set and, when used to devalue others, acts as self-enhancement strategies for the self. Why, then, would someone want to give up these beliefs and feelings? When faced with this, it is easy then for me to react in kind, to make quick judgments, to dismiss, to feel the anger rise. But it is more difficult to react in this way when the person sitting across from me is a client. Then the management of my feelings, my thinking, and my response is much more complicated. The counter-transference reactions of wanting to treat others as I believe I have been treated is seductive, but ultimately tiring and nonproductive. The reaction of wanting to leave the room is another strategy, and I have, a few times, excused myself from the setting. As a colleague once asked, "Is it possible to detach from my own identity?" In general, though, people are more subtle and less direct about their prejudices, or they are naive about their existence. Often these prejudices are based on a lack of exposure or not incorporating evidence to the contrary in a serious manner. In these cases, I have found that asking clients about their own heritage and whether they have questions about my background allows the issue to be directly addressed. I also consciously put some Chinese artwork and objects in my office—maybe a safety blanket phenomenon—that can also serve as a way to introduce a discussion about differences between myself and others.

CONCLUSION

This process of integrating and intertwining practice and research knowledge is a life task. Clearly it is not a matter of just going in, shutting the door, and conducting one or the other in isolation. It is also a matter of finding ways to integrate self-knowledge, being conscious about automatic thoughts and feelings, and allowing the observing and compassionate self into the everyday work. The conscious involvement of the self allows me to be a leaf in the midst of the water moving downstream—but not without signposts along the way that inform me of how best to consider the important cultural issues. Culture does make a difference in the clients' problems, the therapists' work, and in the twisting and turning of the therapy itself.

REFERENCES

American Psychiatric Association. (1994). *Diagnostic and statistical manual of mental disorders* (4th ed.), Washington, DC: American Psychiatric Association.

Betancourt, H., & Lopez, S. R. (1993). The study of culture, ethnicity, and race in American psychology. *American Psychologist, 48,* 629–637.

Beutler, L. E., & Clarkin, J. F. (1990). *Systematic treatment selection: Toward targeted therapeutic interventions.* New York: Brunner/Mazel.

Bogumill, S., & Shiang, J. (1998, March). *Cultural Beliefs, Behaviors, and Adaptation Profile (CBBAP): Preliminary validation.* Poster session presented at the annual California Psychological Association, Pasadena, CA.

Bond, M. H., & Hwang, K. (1986). The social psychology of the Chinese people. In M. H. Bond (Ed.), *The psychology of the Chinese people* (pp. 213–266). New York: Oxford University Press.

Cheung, F. M. (1985). An overview of psychopathology in Hong Kong with special reference to somatic presentation. In W. Tseng & D. Y. Wu (Eds.), *Chinese culture and mental health* (pp. 287–300). New York: Academic Press.

Gilligan, C. (1982). *In a different voice: Psychological theory and women's development.* Cambridge, MA: Harvard University Press.

Hsu, J. (1985). The Chinese family: Relations, problems, and therapy. In W. Tseng & D. Wu (Eds.), *Chinese culture and mental health* (pp. 95–112). New York: Academic Press.

Katon, W., Kleinman, A., & Rosen, G. (1982). Depression and somatization: A review. *American Journal of Medicine, 72,* 127–135, 241–247.

Kirmayer, L. J. (1989). Cultural variation in the response to psychiatric disorders and emotional distress. *Social Science in Medicine, 29,* 327–339.

Kitayama, S., & Markus, H. (1994). *Emotion and culture: Empirical studies of mutual influence.* Washington, DC: American Psychological Association.

Kleinman, A. (1977). Depression, somatization and the new cross-cultural psychiatry. *Social Science and Medicine, 11,* 3–10.

Kleinman, A. (1980). *Patients and healers in the context of culture: An exploration of the borderland between anthropology, medicine, and psychiatry.* Berkeley: University of California Press.

Kleinman, A. (1986). *Social origins of distress and disease: Depression, neurasthenia, and pain in modern China.* New Haven, CT: Yale University Press.

Kleinman, A. (1987). Culture and clinical reality: Commentary on culture-bound syndromes and international disease classifications. *Culture, Medicine and Psychiatry, 11,* 49–52.

Kleinman, A. (1988). *Rethinking psychiatry: From cultural category to personal experience.* New York: Free Press.

Kleinman, A., & Goode, B. (Eds.). (1985). *Culture and depression.* Berkeley: University of California Press.

Kleinman, A., & Kleinman, J. (1985). Somatization: The interconnections in Chinese society among culture, depressive experiences, and the meanings of pain. In A. Kleinman & B. Good (Eds.), *Culture and depression: Studies in the anthropology and cross-cultural psychiatry of affect and disorder* (pp. 429–490). Berkeley: University of California Press.

Leong, F. T. L. (1986). Counseling and psychotherapy with Asian-Americans: Review of the literature. *Journal of Counseling Psychology, 33,* 196–206.

Lin, K. (1981). Traditional Chinese medical beliefs and their relevance for mental illness and psychiatry. In A. Kleinman & T. Y. Lin (Eds.), *Normal and abnormal behavior in Chinese culture* (pp. 95–111). Boston: Reidel.

Lin, T., & Lin, M. (1981). Love, denial and rejection: Responses of Chinese families to mental illness. In A. Kleinman & T. Y. Lin (Eds.), *Normal and abnormal behavior in Chinese culture* (pp. 387–401). Boston: Reidel.

Lum, R. G. (1982). Mental health attitudes and opinions of Chinese. In E. E. Jones & S. J. Korchin (Eds.), *Minority mental health* (pp. 165–189). New York: Praeger.

Markus, H. R., & Kitayama, S. (1994). Cultural shaping of emotion. In S. Kitayama & H. R. Markus (Eds.), *Emotion and culture: Empirical studies of mutual influence* (pp. 339–351). Washington, DC: American Psychological Association.

Markus, H. R., Kitayama, S., & Heiman, R. J. (1996). Culture and basic psychological principles. In E. T. Higgins & A. W. Kruglanksi (Eds.), *Social psychology: Handbook of basic principles* (pp. 857–913). New York: Guilford Press.

Marsella, A. (1980). Depressive affect and disorder across cultures. In H. Triandis & J. Draguns (Eds.), *Handbook of cross-cultural psychology: Vol. V. Psychopathology* (pp. 233–262). Boston: Allyn & Bacon.

Munroe, D. (1977). *The concept of man in contemporary China.* Ann Arbor, MI: University of Michigan Press.

Pine, F. (1992). *Developmental theory and clinical process.* New Haven, CT: Yale University Press.

Shiang, J. (1992). *Emotions and cognitive beliefs guiding parent–child relations in old age of Mandarin-speaking Chinese families living in the United States.* Unpublished doctoral dissertation, Pacific Graduate School of Psychology, Palo Alto, CA.

Shiang, J. (1993, August). *Transactions, behavior, and emotions in Chinese-American families.* Poster session presented at the 101st Annual Convention of the American Psychological Association, Toronto, Ontario, Canada.

Shiang, J., Barron, S., Xiao, S. Y., Blinn, R., & Tam, C. (1998). Suicide and gender in the People's Republic of China, Taiwan, Hong Kong, and Chinese in the U.S. *Transcultural Psychiatry, 35,* 236–253.

Shiang, J., Blinn, R., Bongar, B., Stephens, B., Allison, D., & Schatzberg, A. (1997). Suicide in San Francisco: A comparison of racial groups. *Suicide and Life Threatening Behaviors, 27,* 80–91.

Shiang, J., Bogumill, S., Kalehzan, M., & Benet, V. (1998). *Psychometric properties of the Culture Beliefs, Behaviors, and Adaptation Profile (CBBAP): Assessment of self-construal, core cultural beliefs and practices, and relationship to depression and distress.* Unpublished manuscript.

Shiang, J., Kjellander, C., Huang, H., & Bogumill, S. (1998). Developing cultural competency in clinical practice: Treatment considerations for Chinese cultural groups in the United States. *Clinical Psychology: Science and Practice, 5,* 182–209.

Smith, P. B., & Bond, M. H. (1994). *Social psychology across cultures: Analysis and perspectives.* Boston: Allyn & Bacon.

Sue, D. W., & Sue, D. (1990). *Counseling the culturally different: Theory and practice.* New York: Wiley.

Sue, S. (1988). Psychotherapeutic services for ethnic minorities: Two decades of research findings. *American Psychologist, 43,* 301–308.

Sue, S., & Zane, N. (1987). The role of culture and cultural techniques in psychotherapy: A critique and reformulation. *American Psychologist, 42,* 37–45.

Suinn, R., Ahuna, C., & Khoo, G. (1992). The Suinn-Lew Asian Self-Identity Acculturation Scale: Concurrent and factorial validation. *Educational and Psychological Measurement, 52,* 1041–1046.

Triandis, H., Kashima, Y., Shimada, E., & Villareal, M. (1986). Acculturation indices as a means of confirming cultural differences. *International Journal of Psychology, 21*(1), 43–70.

Tseng, W. S. (1975). The nature of somatic complaints among psychiatric patients: The Chinese case. *Comprehensive Psychiatry, 16,* 237–245.

Tung, M. (1993). Symbolic meanings of the body in Chinese culture and "somatization." *Culture, Medicine and Psychiatry, 18,* 483–492.

White, G. (1982). The role of cultural explanations in "somatization" and "psychologization." *Social Science and Medicine, 16,* 1519–1530.

Yamamoto, J., & Acosta, F. (1982). Treatment of Asian Americans and Hispanic Americans: Similarities and differences. *Journal of the American Academy of Psychoanalysis, 10,* 585–607.

10

SCIENTIFIC DISCIPLINE CAN ENHANCE CLINICAL EFFECTIVENESS

LORNA SMITH BENJAMIN

The various perspectives represented in this book establish that there are substantial differences of opinion about the proper relation between research and practice in the field of psychotherapy. These issues have also been recently reviewed in a noteworthy collection of articles in the *American Psychologist* (VandenBos, 1996). Views range from the idea that research and practice are not, cannot, and even should not be related (e.g., Guntrip, 1973) to the idea that they can be closely connected. The latter position is part of the so-called Boulder model (Raimy, 1950). Despite official adoption by the American Psychological Association (APA), this "scientist–practitioner" model is by no means universally accepted and practiced.

RESEARCH–PRACTICE DILEMMA

The gap between research in and the practice of psychotherapy is marked at one end of the continuum by clinicians who complain that research findings have little to do with the problems they face when "on-line." For example, research studies often are on highly selected, homogeneous populations that have little to do with the cases clinicians actually have to treat. At the other end, official protocols for psychotherapy research studies require a single "pure" therapy approach. But rather than sticking to a single approach, many clinicians prefer to describe themselves as *eclectic*, maintaining that they use their professional judgment to offer "different strokes for different folks."

Another area of disagreement is on the matter of the required "manualization" of therapies in research protocols. This practice strikes some clinicians as pseudoscience, because they believe it is not really possible to codify exactly what it is that the skilled professional therapist does and why. Such manuals may overstate the facts when they claim to operationalize everything that is important. In support of this skepticism, there is preliminary evidence that adherence to a therapy manual can be associated with poor therapy outcome (Henry, Schacht, & Strupp, 1990). One possible interpretation of this finding is that technical compliance to a manual might interfere with alliance building, a factor that is well-known to show powerful association with good outcome (Gaston, Marmar, Gallagher, & Thompson, 1991). A significant number of practitioners continue to believe that the main way to acquire advanced therapy skills is through the traditional method of apprenticeship and experience. This contingent argues that reading and trying to adhere to a manual will leave out too much that is vital to the therapy experience.

In reply, the advocates of science in therapy sometimes argue that clinicians rigidly adhere to whatever approach they learned during training, whether it works or not. More interested in protecting their professional turf than in serving their customers with best approaches, these clinicians fail to acknowledge and apply new techniques established as safe and effective by research protocols. These critics hold that such clinicians, because of their unwillingness to respond to established facts, deserve to be called to order.

MOVEMENT TOWARD THE RESEARCH END
OF THE CONTINUUM

Recently, a shift to the scientific side of the argument has become apparent. The reason is probably economic. Clinicians are aware of an emerging tendency for third-party payers to reimburse only those therapies for which "efficacy" has been established empirically. This perspective is aided and abetted by a list of empirically validated therapies (EVTs) issued in current draft by the APA's Division of Clinical Psychology's Task Force on Promotion and Dissemination of Psychological Procedures (Task Force, 1995). Approved procedures, which to date are mostly represented by pharmacological and cognitive–behavioral interventions, would be used as criteria by site visitors for APA accreditation of graduate programs, of internship facilities, for approval of continuing education credits, and approval of third-party payers. That ascendant policy suggests that clinicians will continue to ignore research findings "at their peril." However, what it is not clear are the ramifications of clinical practice becoming confined to specific technologies shown to be effective by formal research protocols, (the clinical trials model) and required for certification as EVTs.

Because they are attached to the clinical trial short-term research model, the EVT procedures present a great threat to the practice of a more open-ended, sometimes long-term, psychotherapy.[1] They may result in ruling out longer term psychotherapy as appropriate for training, practice, and reimbursement. Decreased availability of longer term psychotherapy would, I believe, deprive us of the only truly effective way to treat the personality disorders that so reliably compromise recovery from many of the Diagnostic and Statistical Manual of Mental Disorder's (DSM's) clinical syndromes. For example, if recurrent major depressive disorder is accompanied by personality disorder, the depression is more severe and longer lasting (Pilkonis & Frank, 1988). The treatment of generalized anxiety disorder and other Axis I disorders is also compromised if there is comorbid personality disorder. Some of us fervently believe that longer term psychotherapy is a highly appropriate and effective treatment approach for many severely disordered individuals, whether or not they have a recognized personality disorder.

Problems With the Current Emphasis on Research-Based EVT Treatments

To be more useful to clinicians, measures of efficacy should extend beyond symptom reduction in the short term. I have argued elsewhere (Benjamin, 1997) that restricting therapy practice to approaches confirmed as effective by the EVT protocol is penny-wise and pound-foolish. *Efficacy* by EVT standards must be established within a short period of time (e.g., 6 weeks) and linked to specific procedures that address specific symptoms

---

[1]The definition of *long-term psychotherapy* is somewhat elusive. I'll use the term *longer* here to mean "not arbitrarily set to end at a fixed number of sessions, like 3, 8, 10 or 20." The well-recognized danger of not setting a limit is that time and money will be wasted; worse yet, patients become dependent on a therapy that may or may not be helping. I think it is very important that the patient have a sense of control over the treatment. This means they may have continued access, provided they are using the opportunity well. Part of the therapy description should include guidelines for knowing how to define and assess "good use." The decision should include consideration of progress to date, need, and resources. It is reasonable that all involved parties (patient, therapist, whoever is paying for it) have input on the assessment of those factors. Because there does need to be responsible concern for the length of treatment, the term *open-ended* could be misleading. Let *longer term therapy* mean "time-limit negotiated, periodically reviewed, and usually quite a bit longer than the typical brief therapy."

in specific populations. Meanwhile, problems that are best treated by longer term psychotherapy, such as personality disorders, do not remit in 6 weeks. Their costs reverberate through the health care system in many ways other than short-term symptom change. This observation suggests that efficacy measures should extend far beyond symptom change, also including rehospitalization, annual medications costs, all medical system visits, lost work days, and so on. If a broadly based assessment of the total system were mounted, then the longer term psychotherapies might very well be confirmed as quite effective. Indeed, a recently published survey of research from 1984 to 1994 (Gabbard, Lazar, Hornberger, & Spiegel, 1997) started a move in this direction. Their survey suggested that psychotherapy

> appears to have a beneficial impact on a variety of costs when used in the treatment of the most severe psychiatric disorders, including schizophrenia, bipolar affective disorder, and borderline personality disorder. Much of that impact accrues from reductions in inpatient treatment and decreases in work impairment. (p. 147)

In a beginning effort to pursue the idea that efficacy measures should be broader in nature and should extend across time, I have tried to elicit funding for a study that would test whether longer term psychotherapy can be cost-effective if total system costs over a period of 2 years are considered. Even the most preliminary discussions of such a study met interesting obstacles. For example, one very large health insurance company told me their database could not be made to yield information on total system costs for individuals. It was not possible to conduct analyses that required totaling by individuals in a way that would pool costs of medications and inpatient and outpatient visits. In addition, this huge health care provider assured me there were almost no personality disordered individuals in their population of psychiatric patients. A scan of recorded diagnoses "proved" this point. Could it be that only the disorders that have been deemed treatable exist? This is an unexpected version of efficacy. Those problem cases of personality disorder simply do not exist!

Another measure of efficacy that would interest clinicians would be to assess the need for rehospitalization. Avoiding hospitalization or rehospitalization could reduce health care costs. It would be important to explore both the mechanisms and cost-effectiveness of treatments that achieve that goal. Readers educated in the "decade of the brain" may be surprised to learn that Matthews, Roper, Mosher, and Menn (1979) reported that posthospitalization milieu treatment at Soteria House lowered the 2-year risk of rehospitalization in young first-break schizophrenics compared with treatment with neuroleptics. Such findings suggest it probably would be worthwhile to give increased current research attention to the efficacy of day treatment, day hospitalization, and day care. Their history is effectively reviewed by Piper, Rosie, Joyce, and Azim (1996). Among other things, these investigators reported that their 18-week day-treatment with group therapy is quite successful in treating individuals with personality disorders.

Research Studies Should More Directly Encompass Everyday Problems Faced by Clinicians

Still other changes (Benjamin, 1997) in the gold standard might help bring psychotherapy research closer to clinical practices. For example, to speak to a clinician's reality, there should be better reporting on the "noncompleters" who were taken off research protocol. This problem usually is addressed in a footnote that simply indicates the percentage of the research sample that had to be discontinued. Unlike researchers, practicing clinicians cannot simply dismiss those who deteriorate precipitously or who are noncompliant with treatment methods. It is somewhat surprising that such problems are not given a more salient place in reports of "efficacy." If, for example, the research protocol reports a 75% improvement rate using a given approach, clinicians should not be expected to replicate that rate. Clinicians have to count the (sometimes substantial) percentage of their clients who are not compliant with any approach, or who need additional interventions to respond to emergencies or other unexpected circumstances.

THEORY IS ESSENTIAL TO THE PROPER
INTERPRETATION OF SYMPTOM CHANGE

In their review of therapy research and practice, Goldfried and Wolfe (1996) fully developed the idea that research contexts often diverge importantly from situations faced by practicing clinicians. Reiteration of their points is not needed here. One of their examples documented the gap between research protocol and clinical practice by reporting that a well-known psychotherapy researcher exclaimed, when asked what to do about noncompliance with the treatment, "Well, I just tell them they can't be in the study!" Because the practicing clinician cannot threaten the patient with expulsion from the study, the critics implied that the investigator's procedure for eliciting compliance would not apply outside of the research context.

A theoretical approach elaborated below would suggest that the researcher might have unwittingly described an interpersonal process that is indeed available to the practicing clinician. Of course, the published research did not make that possible link explicit. For purposes of the present discussion, it could be useful to consider whether the research-based therapy invoked an ordinary treatment principle without including it in the manual. Suppose that the subjects in that study cared about receiving the researcher's approval? Suppose they did want to stay in the study to please their therapist and or to maintain the privilege of participating in the research environment that may have involved interesting groups? In that case, the practicing clinician could consider making use of the therapy relationship in a similar paradoxical way. Attachments between patients and therapists and therapy groups are probably vital to therapy change. To some extent, clinicians can make themselves more or less available, depending on patient compliance with the therapy agenda.

To illustrate, I sometimes tell my personality-disordered patients, who seem invested in escalating symptomatology, that our approach does not seem to be working. "Maybe this means we should meet less frequently," I say. "If we can't turn this worrisome trend around, I'll have to work with you to help find another approach." Such a threat to withdraw treatment can help the patient mobilize his or her strengths and get serious about growth rather than regression. The comparison to the researcher who, likewise, threatens expulsion would reframe the research study's description of its procedure in important ways.

Such suggestions that research studies attend to context, sequencing, alternative interpretations and mechanisms underscore the need for better articulated, more testable theories of therapy. Once a valid, overarching theory about the mechanisms of action is formulated, there is no limit to the predictions that can be made about etiology, treatment, and prevention. Such a theory can inform outcome measures in vital ways. For example, the EVT protocol unquestioningly calls for improvement. Symptoms should decrease more for the experimental than for the control group. However, in the clinic where longer term therapy is conducted, it is widely recognized that "things can get worse before they get better." This complicates assessment for the researcher and the clinician.

In some cases, the EVT assumption is probably correct: Increases in symptoms such as depression or anxiety might reflect true deterioration. Such findings would mark ineffective or even destructive therapies. In other cases or therapies, rather than signifying deterioration, increases in symptomatology might represent significant progress. However, if the argument is that things might get worse before they get better, a testable and refutable hypothesis that accounts for the worsening is called for. On the one hand are individuals mentioned above, who like to escalate symptoms in service of satisfying fantasies of infinitely available nurturance. On the other are patients confronting the waste that has resulted from their old habits and beliefs. They may be deciding to give up cherished but impossible wishes and fantasies, and the like. When this is happening, they are understandably likely to be upset and highly symptomatic. Such discomfort in these cases may represent a vital developmental stage on the road to constructive change. Here, simple "bean counting" of symptoms is going to miss the mark. For one group, increases in symptoms means the therapy has gone awry. For the other, increases in symptoms means that the therapy is doing its work. Integrative theory that accounts for symptom change can help guide the clinician and the researcher through such complicated realities of everyday practice.

Consideration of Alternative Perspectives

The state of the art is more likely to advance if alternative perspectives generated by testable theory are routinely considered in research studies. For example, systematic measurement of subjects' perception of themselves and their situations might help clarify whether the effective aspect of the intervention was pharmacological, cognitive–behavioral, interpersonal, or something else. This may be particularly useful in studies of depression because there is some evidence to suggest that perceptions of being overwhelmed or helpless are likely to accompany depression. Whether perceived helplessness is causal of or secondary to the depressive condition is not clear. The question merits further exploration. One interpretation would suggest that helping the patient cope with an overwhelming situation could be helpful, while the other requires no particular attention to environment. Simply showing a decrease in symptoms with a given therapeutic approach (e.g., pharmacology) may not be enough. Already substantial evidence (Frank, Kupfer, Wagner, McEachran, & Cornes, 1991) exists to show that enhancing interpersonal skills as well as prescribing antidepressants can substantially reduce the risk of relapse in depression. A better understanding of how and why this is so might lead to even better treatments.

I have occasionally created an informal and attractive version of "hospitalization" in my private practice. This intervention highlights the need to consider alternative interpretations of the results of interventions (e.g., hospitalization), preferably by using testable theory. This pseudohospitalization involves recommending that a patient in crisis take a long-needed vacation instead of going to the hospital (taking care to ensure that the therapy relationship is strong enough to suggest this is a physically safe alternative). Such an intervention includes some, but not all, of the elements of hospitalization. There should be an understanding of which factors do most of the therapeutic work in and out of the hospital. This line of thought leads to the somewhat uncomfortable realization that, in addition to controlling for safekeeping and rest and rehabilitation, a placebo for psychotherapy itself should routinely control for the effects of kindly listening. The bottom line is that high fees for psychotherapists and hospitals surely should be justified by demonstrations that they do *more* than these less costly and less elaborate functions of providing safekeeping giving a stressed individual a break, and an explanation for his or her condition, and a kindly listening ear.

Hope for an Integrated Theory of Research and Practice

"All well and good," the experienced reader might say. But where are we to get a theory that can interpret symptom change, generate and properly interpret effective interventions, and satisfactorily address clinicians' everyday concerns? How can we find a theory that is testable and refutable and that still covers complexities and subtleties? Is it impossible to develop a theory that both follows the rules of science and encompasses such vital subtleties in clinical process? Perhaps it is better not to pretend we can do so. By analogy, should we stop having orchestras if we cannot operationalize making beautiful music? The same may be true for the art of psychotherapy. Science may not encompass all that is good and even all that is useful. Let psychotherapy flourish as an art and stop contaminating it with rules that interfere!

Ultimately, that perspective may prevail. Those of us who believe that the therapy process is subtle, delicate, and elusive while it also is powerful and intense will make our choices. Will we be artists or scientists? Can we be both? My personal choice is to pursue the application of scientific methods, but not the atheoretical, purely empirical versions. Perhaps I make this choice because I have long been organized by the theme of the childhood story entitled *The Little Engine That Could*. The story touts the merits of relentless effort and good faith, no matter how hard a task becomes. The little engine modeled the process—keep on trying.

The Goal: Encompass Clinical Complexities With Testable Theory

The goal is set by the benefits gained from attempts to apply scientific methods to other elusive and complex problems. For example, applications of scientific methods in physics, mathematics, biochemistry, and genetics are truly awesome. We are fortunate that these scientists did not declare their challenges to be impossibly difficult. If they had, we would have missed all that we now know about the structure of matter, the nature of the human genome, or the orgin of the universe. Even more exciting is the fact that present knowledge about those profoundly complicated matters evolves rapidly. Revisions of theory do not show how hopeless it is to try to explain; rather, they mark the never-ending growth in our ability to understand. Nor does the scientific quest interfere with work in other domains, such as metaphysics, art, or religion. In fact, it is possible for the artists, poets, philosophers, and theologians to find ever-deepening inspiration in these products of good science.

Out of this faith in the value of trying, I am presently writing about my version of a generic theory of therapy (Benjamin, in press). The theory draws heavily on interpersonal psychiatry, developmental psychology, attachment theory, and learning theory. I am attempting to provide a descriptive system that, after continued revision, would have the capacity to more closely codify the elements in the longer term therapies that are truly effective. The theory attempts to address subtleties recognized by clinicians but not usually included in research protocols, and to mark and codify variables such as context, nonverbal factors, unconscious and conscious forces, and the need to stage interventions and assessments. The rules for on-line assessment of the effect of interventions and the contextual interpretation of outcomes are specified. It would be worse than excessive to claim all this has been achieved. But it is being attempted and described in terms that can be tested, refuted, and communicated to others. Young therapists who have been trained in this approach, called reconstructive learning therapy (RLT), consistently report that they have been told by their subsequent supervisors that their clinical wisdom is well beyond their years of practice. These young therapists are more willing than others to accept difficult referrals, and say that their patients like them and feel their work together under RLT is both different and better. That is promising preliminary feedback.

The task of explaining RLT is not simple, even in space afforded by a book-length project. Let it be clear at the outset that this is not a new therapy; rather, it is a set of ideas that organize and codify under one generic schema much of the clinical wisdom that has abounded for generations. Users of RLT simply have guidelines that help them pick and choose on a moment-by-moment basis from the wide array of already available therapy approaches and techniques.

A CASE EXAMPLE PROVIDES THE CHALLENGE

For purposes of this chapter, I will sketch the theory very broadly and apply it to a single hospitalized psychiatric inpatient. At the time of the request for consultation, the case had been diagnosed and was being treated by "state-of-the-art" formulations. Symptoms were targeted and addressed by focal approaches shown by EVT protocol to be effective (pharmacologic and cognitive–behavioral). Because the case involved alleged sexual abuse, the patient also had been approached with the popular practice of admitting the "facts" and confronting the abuser. This case provides a real-world illustration of both sides of the dilemma under consideration. EVT-based interventions were applied. Clinician "favorites" were applied, although the data for efficacy of confronting alleged sexual abusers are controversial at best. Finally, the theory behind RLT was applied to help understand the whole person and her symptoms and to then suggest a sharply focused and organized plan for treatment. The example is offered to underscore the need for organizing theory if therapy research is to provide useful suggestions to the practicing clinician.

As a consultant specializing in personality disorders, and therefore, highly likely to see "intractable" cases, I have frequent opportunities to meet the "state of the art" in its most frustrated condition. Here is but one of many possible examples of how symptom-focused therapy is working in these complex situations. The material and interpretation that follow are from a single consultative inpatient interview conducted during a very brief hospitalization.

Presenting Problems

This 46-year-old married mother of five comes to the hospital for evaluation following the loss of her marriage and her job. Suicide was "an option," and she exhibited additional signs of depression including weight gain, loss of sleep, lowered energy, anhedonia, lack of motivation, as well as considerable anxiety. The precipitating event was the discovery by her husband of a logbook detailing her many seemingly casual affairs with co-workers. This calendar was supplemented by volumes of detailed accounts of the affairs. Here was material for many novels, but that did not seem to be the purpose of the journals. Instead, the patient stated that the notebooks were the result of "compulsive writing." She simply could not stop having the encounters and writing in obsessive detail about them. In addition to compulsive sexual activity and compulsive writing, she also was a compulsive shopper for highly specific items. She bought and kept hundreds of elaborate dolls and also had a collection of shoes that might be coveted by Imelda Marcos. The patient showed little remorse about her infidelity or spending; there was no evidence of grief about the loss of her husband and children. She appeared to assume she would be able to get another job and new friends without much difficulty. She stated that after a while, she would "find herself" and then be ready to resume parenting duties.

Previously, the patient had recognized that her compulsions were out of control and had entered psychotherapy; however, she terminated treatment when the therapist asked her to confront her father with charges of child abuse and to give up her sexual activities. Together, they had reasoned that she must have been sexually abused, and that the affairs were a residual of this early injury. Confronting the perpetrator might help her stop acting out this ancient hurt. However, she was unwilling to stop the affairs, and she could not see any constructive purpose in charging her father. The evidence was fairly indirect and could be seen as normative (e.g., father looking at her at age 4 when she was in the bathtub). The therapist had observed "there must be more." The patient did recall that her mother would lie down with her in her bed every night until she fell asleep. Perhaps this was to protect her from her father, the patient reasoned. Moreover, one time the mother and father had a big fight about the patient, but she cannot remember the details.

The DSM-IV Diagnosis

In addition to her major depression and anxiety, the patient qualified for the label histrionic personality disorder, according to the fourth edition of the *DSM* (*DSM–IV*; category 301.5; American Psychiatric Association, 1994). She met the following criteria:

1. She enjoyed being the center of attention, although she said she was not compelled to be.
2. She acknowledged that she often interacted in a sexual manner, even if not appropriate to the context. For example, she said she "uses sexual innuendo at work."
3. Although she described herself as the calm and steady one within the family and said she wished she could have broader swings of mood, she nonetheless seemed very bright in mood during this interview which focused on rather depressing circumstances. Her expression of emotions could be characterized as "shallow." She did add that, underneath, she was "scared to death."
4. She stated that she greatly emphasized physical appearance to draw attention to herself. The patient explained that her mother taught her "appearance is everything," and she said she faithfully implements that teaching in every possible way.
5. She did not emphasize detail and did not consider herself a perfectionist. For example, her boss would complain that she would forget to include important details in her reports.
6. Although she did not show dramatic mood swings, her daily episodes were somewhat theatrical, and she did appear to be the centerpiece. Perhaps not coincidentally, she said she often participates in local theatrical productions.

I believe that the Axis II disorders in the *DSM–IV* capture useful clinical wisdom, and that the widely lamented overlap among categories can be reduced by invoking necessary and sufficient conditions (Benjamin, 1996a). This patient met the "necessary" conditions for histrionic personality disorder in that her identity centered on her ability to entertain and delight others with her dramatic productions (and sexual prowess). By contrast, she did not meet the necessary condition for the label narcissistic personality disorder. Most notably, she did not feel entitled to service and privilege. In fact, she said she "had a thing about imposing on others."

The patient worked hard to be noticed and treated well. Unlike a person with a narcissistic disorder, she did not expect attention and praise to come without effort. Nor was she focused on a plan of becoming famous or otherwise fantastic.

Treatment Approach to Date

The inpatient staffing plan placed her with various specialists who focused on her specific symptoms. Because of the presence of sexual problems and an alleged history of sexual abuse, she was sent to a special group for treatment of victims of sexual abuse. For her various compulsions (sexual, writing, shopping), she was given medications and rehearsal treatment. For her depression, she was given medications and cognitive–behavioral therapy to help her change her self-talk. Finally, to help restore her marriage, she and her husband were referred to couples therapy to see if there could be reconciliation over her compulsion to have affairs.

Any HMO administrator might be pleased with the adherence to the EVT standard of excellence. Except perhaps for the referral to a sexual abuse group, every intervention is well established as effective for the class of symptoms addressed. However, as my preceding plea for total system assessment would suggest, I doubt the longer term efficacy of this piecemeal approach. Being biased as I am in favor of the need for and merits of a longer term reconstructive psychotherapy, I would predict that this woman would be discharged fairly rapidly and go home on medication, with a possible referral for continued couples therapy, if the husband is willing. However, the patient's "addictions" would not stop with the lessons in self-talk, and the depression would recur. I would predict that the fate of the marriage would likely depend more on her family and social system's response than on any character change as a result of a brief hospitalization. The chance that she would go on to find a new marital partner and then repeat this pattern seems high. Formal research studies of follow-up after discharge would be helpful in assessing efficacy within this broader framework. No follow-up is presently available for this case.

A TESTABLE THEORY OF ETIOLOGY AND TREATMENT OF PERSONALITY DISORDER

The following is a telescopic summary of the assumptions used to explain this woman's chief complaints: the compulsions, the depression, the anxiety, and the marital troubles. The proposed model attempts to follow the rules of science in being specific enough to make predictions that can be tested by observation and proven wrong. Moreover, the therapy process itself is "scientific." Together, patient and clinician develop hypotheses about patterns, ways to change them, and their goals. The patient's narrative, dreams, associations, opinions, feelings, and so forth provide the raw data. The data may cause the hypotheses to change, and the hypotheses may help unearth more data. Each informs the other, and the patient is the ultimate judge of whether the process is useful and makes sense.

Basic Assumptions of the Theory

The primate's adjustment centers on attachment, which is manifest at birth by the reflexes of startle, cling, grasp, root, place, nurse, and more. Literal clinging is accompanied in the human by visual clinging. This attachment reflex evolves as the central nervous system develops, and it has major impact on both physical and mental development. For example, studies show that poor attachment in the early years affects biochemistry (Eisenberg, 1995; Kraemer, 1992) and social behavior. These effects interact with inherited traits. The principle of behavioral complementarity (Benjamin, 1974) makes it likely that social patterns that emerge early will draw for "matching" behaviors in subsequent years. The reciprocity between the developing child and the environment then sets habits that become deeply ingrained traits. Although the patterns that evolved in the earliest years "made sense" originally, they may or may not be appropriate in later, different situations. In that case, adherence to the early ways can be severely maladaptive.

Connections Between Problem Patterns and Early Learning

The easiest way to see the impact of early attachment on adult traits in personality disordered individuals is to

1. Identify the problem patterns in relation to self and others. Preferably these patterns are described in terms of the dimensions named by Structural Analysis of Social Behavior (SASB; Benjamin, 1974, 1984, 1996a). These dimensions are as follows: focus (you on me; me on you; me on me); love–hate; and enmeshment–differentiation. Patterns stripped down to these three underlying dimensions are clear and can be easily traced across seemingly different contexts.

2. Note that the present problems correspond directly to relations with important early persons (parents, siblings, or extended family with whom there was intense contact). The link is through one of three *copy processes* (Benjamin, 1993, 1995, 1996b). Comparisons are in terms of the three SASB dimensions: (a) Be like him or her (e.g., blame everyone in

sight); (b) act as if he or she is still there (e.g., be resentfully complaint); or (c) treat yourself as he or she did (e.g., blame and put yourself down).

The connections are amazingly direct. These childhood patterns are sustained in adulthood, despite the fact that they may have become inappropriate and maladaptive in the objective sense. The rewards for behaving according to the old rules are not in the present; rather, the payoff is in (unconscious) fantasies that support wishes for reconciliation with or restitution from those early figures. It seems as if returning to patterns that brought proximity to these early figures provides psychic security. This reenactment of old rules functions as a "psychic hug." Such regressive behaviors, therefore, comfort people, much as a toddler is reassured by a hug from his or her caregiver. For example, the person with an important blaming parent may constantly display compliance and defer resentfully to others, put him- or herself down mercilessly, and occasionally become judgmental and condemning of others. The hypothesis is that she is imitating her parent, acting as if the parent is still present, and treating herself as did the parent. The "reason" is that these patterns are familiar and apparently what the parent "wanted." Maybe maintaining those positions will finally bring the desired affection from the internalized representation of that parent. I have summarized this idea that there is a deep connection between maladaptive behaviors of adulthood and early attachments under the heading "Every Psychopathology is a Gift of Love" (Benjamin, 1993; see also 1996a).

Treatment Implications That Stem From Recognizing Links

An initial treatment implication is that the problem patterns must be acknowledged by the patient. Following this must be a reckoning with the possibility that the problem patterns are organized and sustained by the wish for better intimacy with the person or persons who helped shape them. Accordingly, the sustaining wishes must be given up if there is to be change. This means that no amount of instruction in different cognitive styles or communication skills will alter patterns that the patient does not want to give up. Usually the underlying wishes for proximity to the early attachment persons are not consciously recognized. Patients are regularly astonished by the consultative interview that helps them see how this process has worked. They will say, "I thought I hated him. I thought she didn't matter any more. But I see that I HAVE been acting JUST like him or her and I guess I DO love him, her. After all, he IS my father [mother, brother]."

Using This Theory to Explain Treatment Failures

It follows that therapies that fail to bring the patient to a point of choice in relation to such underlying motivators will be less likely to result in lasting change. It is also true that therapies that do follow this model are by no means assured of success. There are many ways to fail. Two common causes of failure of this approach are (a) patients refuse to collaborate with the therapist to work on their problem patterns because they seek respite primarily through changes in others and (b) patients understand the connections but choose not to give up the old wishes. Change is too frightening or costly. Not infrequently, these patients have eroticized the basic dimensions of the underlying patterns (e.g., dominance, punishment, loneliness, rejection, submission, humiliation). In this case, they simply don't want to give up the addiction. For them, known benefits outweigh the risks.

The Five Basic Treatment Steps

The overall model of RLT therapy holds that there are five correct levels of intervention, no matter what the school of therapy from which the intervention is drawn (Benjamin, 1996a, 1996b). The steps, or levels, are, very generally speaking, sequential.

1. Collaborate against the problem patterns.
2. Learn to identify patterns, where they came from, what they are for.
3. Block maladaptive patterns.
4. Enable the will to change.
5. Learn new patterns.

Therapies that begin at Level 5 without fully engaging with Level 4 will not be successful. Each therapy intervention should successfully address one or more of the five steps. Detail about how to implement each of these steps is presented in Benjamin (in press).

The theory of psychopathology that directs treatment planning for RLT draws on a vast number of studies in literatures focused on various topics, including attachment processes, learning processes, developmental principles, and temperamental variance. Methods are detailed for discovering patterns and their links during individual, group, and other therapies. The patterns and links emerge spontaneously from the patient's narratives when the interviewing style helps them develop the "white heat of relevance" (Benjamin, 1996a). There is constant iteration between hypotheses about patterns and the data that emerge in the narratives. Integrative logic prevails. If a story is told that contradicts a working hypothesis, the hypothesis has to be reexamined.

Although the theory about etiology and treatment optimization is refutable and testable, the element of will cannot be operationalized. The loop between data and hypothesis as well as other known features of scientific method are used in helping the patient recognize his or her patterns and to *make the decision to change by giving up old hopes (and fears)*. Unfortunately, mobilization of the will to change seems beyond science. Determinism stops at the threshold of free will. Yet, as B. F. Skinner is alleged to have said, "the more you know about what determines you, the freer you can be." This means that the therapist who chooses to function as a scientist using the RLT model can, at best, maximize the chances that the patient will choose to move beyond old wishes and fears and their associated maladaptive patterns. This choice point provides a clear limit to the application of scientific method to the process of psychotherapy conducted according to the RLT model.

APPLICATION OF THE THEORY TO THE ILLUSTRATIVE CASE

Connections Between Problem Patterns and an Important Early Relationship

What were this woman's gifts of love? What unconscious attachments organized her symptoms of compulsive sexuality, compulsive spending, compulsive writing? The working hypothesis, affirmed at the end of the assessment interview by the patient, was centered on her attachment to the mother. Her detailed description of her relationship with her mother showed rather direct connections to her presenting problems. All the interviewer had to do was repeatedly ask for very specific examples of the patient's descriptions of herself and others, and reflect them back with relentless accuracy. This process is intensified by using the SASB model to sharpen clinician perception and the articulation of key aspects of patterns.

What follows is the case formulation that emerged. The analysis depends on the validity of Sullivan's (1953) "beta press." In other words, people's behavior is determined by how they see their world, not necessarily by "reality." Like all cases, there is more than one central theme. Nonetheless, the following analysis focuses only on one specific early attachment that seems to parallel many of the patient's current problem patterns. That only one relationship accounts for so many patterns is unusual. Usually there are two or three key figures. In this case, however, the patient is deeply identified with her mother. The patient says that her mother adored her and that she was her mother's "doll." There was little discipline and much attention. From a very early age until the patient left home for college, the mother would lie down with the patient in her bed until she fell asleep. They would talk at length. Each detail of the day was reviewed. The mother would tell the patient stories that made her cry. The mother told about difficulties with the father, including his affairs. The mother described herself as "a hot number" and explained that she could have had every man in the city. The patient learned that her mother got fired from her job, and now thinks perhaps the firing was because of an affair.

Those years of intimate disclosures as they lay talking together in bed shaped many of the patient's present beliefs, values, and behavioral patterns. During college, the patient was disappointed that she herself had not been courted by hoards of men. It was only after she got married and had children that she became "a hot number." She was, her mother observed, "a late bloomer." The patient was living out the script she learned during bedtime story times with her mother. The detailed writing in logbooks was very like the lengthy review of every detail of each day with mother. As the patient writes in her logbook, she achieves psychic proximity to the pattern set during those thousands of nights lying in bed with mother.

The identification goes far beyond the concept of being a "hot number" who lost her job because of sexual indiscretion. For example, both mother and daughter accepted the value of preserving good appearances above substance. "You must always look nice, and try not to let people see you in the same thing twice." Both the mother and the patient "settled for second best" in choosing a husband. Both do their sexual duty at home and overlook sexual infidelities and generic incompetency from their husbands. Both equate money with love. Both have husbands who are financial failures. Both were able to hold jobs and act as the calm and steady member in the face of family crisis. They both think of buying things as a way to restore happiness. Both believe that "rich is happy and good."

The students observing this interview were astonished to note that during the medical presentation, the patient's compulsion to shop was reported in terms of inordinate purchasing of dolls and shoes. Later, when discussing childhood under the RLT model, the patient said, "I was supposed to be happy. If I was not, mother would say, 'Lets go buy shoes. A new doll will make you feel better.'" The compulsion to shop for dolls and shoes may, therefore, be seen as a rather exact recapitulation of lessons with mother to feel better by shopping. "Psychic proximity" replays early programs in exacting detail.

Treatment Implications That Stem From the Case Formulation

This RLT analysis would hold that any therapy intervention that failed to address the underlying need to stay close to mother by being so much like her would not be accompanied by lasting change, thus the reason for the prediction that a good outcome for this case would probably require a longer term psychotherapy. If the (histrionic) symptoms of self-definition through dramatic episodes involving sexual acting out and betrayal are to stop, the patient must understand, at a deep level, her compliance with mother's "rules." She needs to decide to give up the wishes that lead her to follow those rules so faithfully. Unfortunately, at present, if she gives up the patterns, the patient will feel she does not "exist." This would be terrifying and unlikely to happen unless an alternative vision of herself is in place. The therapist can draw on every school of therapy, every known intervention in every known mode to assist the patient in this developmental change. Optimally, each intervention will successfully address one or more of the five steps. Success is measured by patient response, not by therapist intention.

Comparing Theoretical- With Research-Based Treatment Plans

Under the RLT perspective, the hospital treatment planning would have been excellent if the patient had worked through her attachment to and identification with her mother. If she were ready to separate from her internalizations of her mother and go her own way, the lessons in rehearsal techniques and changes in self-talk and couples therapy could help her navigate Step 5, learning new patterns. The hospital treatment plan could put the patient on a dramatically different and very helpful new course. However, if the patient was not helped first to negotiate Step 4, enabling the will to change, those interventions are likely to be ineffective. Step 4 is the most important and most difficult part of therapy with personality disordered individuals. Steps 1–3 may be skipped, but Step 4 may not. A person need not have "insight" into patterns and their early links to show character change. Insight can help a person mobilize the will to change, but it is not an end in itself. For example, an antisocial soldier could be socialized without ever learning to recognize his patterns and connect them to the reckless violence in his childhood. The "cure" could be implemented instead by his learning to trust a tough but beloved sergeant under battle conditions. In effect, the sergeant becomes a new internalization.

Rapid development of new internalizations that can prevail over the older ones is rare in adulthood, and likely requires life-threatening conditions or a sexual connection—two conditions that cannot and should not be a part of talking psychotherapy. Still, it is possible. And to a much lesser degree, in longer term talking therapy, the therapist becomes a new internalization and facilitates the development of benign new internalizations from current figures in the patient's life. That process takes time.

CHALLENGES TO THE THEORETICAL
RESEARCHABLE APPROACH

This generic description of psychopathology and psychotherapy does promise to address some of the key questions listed by Goldfried and Wolfe (1996) in their review of the gap between research and practice. They issued a challenge for a perspective that can (a) treat patients who suffer from more than one Axis I disorder, (b) address mechanisms and processes in generic terms, (c) treat underlying "personality issues," and (d) accommodate variations within a given disorder (e.g., depression that is achievement based vs. depression that is abandonment based).

The illustrative case raised each of these challenges. For example, the patient qualified for diagnoses of major depression and generalized anxiety disorder. Her depression can be understood as a natural result of having been blocked in her plan to live out the maternal pattern of affairs, carefully chronicled. Her parents had been very rejecting of her when her marriage broke up. Divorce did not look good and was not supposed to happen. When her sexual activities were exposed, she was kicked out of her house and rejected by her parents. She experienced both helplessness and significant object loss. Given that data show depression follows being trapped (Seligman, 1975) or follows object loss (Bowlby, 1969, 1977), it is easy to see why the patient might be depressed.

Anxiety is frequently comorbid with depression, and I believe it is encouraged by the same conditions as depression. It differs from depression only in that the patient is anxious when there is a will to cope with the situation (trap or loss). Depression follows when the person gives up. People with different temperaments are more or less likely to attempt to cope and, therefore, more or less vulnerable to becoming anxious rather than depressed. As the will to cope waxes and wanes, so do anxiety and depression. Zinbarg, Barlow, Brown, and Hertz (1992) reviewed animal studies in support of this view of the relation between anxiety and depression. The RLT analysis suggests that any psychotherapy that helps the patient identify and successfully cope with feelings of being trapped, helpless or of loss would help with both anxiety and depression.

The RLT formulation also addresses other points raised by Goldfried and Wolfe (1996) in that mechanisms and processes are described in generic terms and that the approach treats underlying "personality issues." The formulation can accommodate variations within a given disorder.

The proposed theoretical approach has not yet been scientifically validated. As is the case with any hypothetical construct (MacCorqoudale & Meehl, 1948), there is an infinitude of implications. Many studies at the diagnostic and treatment levels come to mind. Obviously there would be a lengthy trial period between the present formulation and acceptance of RLT as a scientific effort that successfully addresses key concerns about how to maximize efficacy in longer term psychotherapy. In its present stage, there are only described applications to *DSM* personality disorders (Benjamin, 1996a, 1996b), various research studies of selected aspects of the theory (e.g., Benjamin, 1996c), and a palpable amount of clinician acceptance. Despite its nascent condition, this version of a scientist–clinician approach to longer term psychotherapy is sketched here in order to remind the reader of differences between the "brief" symptom-based approach (present view of science within mental health) and a more integrated formulation (a possible future view of science within mental health).

It is important that some approach, if not the proposed one, attempt to reach the same goals. If somebody does not keep the whole person and natural developmental processes in sight while invoking scientific procedures, the integrated vision may slip from view. Then the wisdom of so many profoundly helpful clinicians (Meyer, Sullivan, Fromm-Reichmann, Freud, Sandler, Fairbairn, and dozens of others) will drift too far from the mainstream. That would not be cost effective.

SUMMARY AND CONCLUSION

The problem of the relation between psychotherapy research and practice was approached from the perspective of longer term psychotherapy. An admittedly complex version of psychotherapy, longer term psychotherapy does not easily meet present-day requirements for "clinical trials protocol." It does not show success in terms of symptom reduction over a brief, say 6-week, interval. Moreover, it encompasses elusive (nonmanualized) variables such as unconscious wishes and the importance of context and sequencing, the human relationship, and existential choices.

Nonetheless, those of us who believe in the efficacy of longer term psychotherapy are understandably wary of current requirements that psychotherapy be purified, codified, and applied to specific populations demonstrating specific symptoms. The use of short-term protocols to establish symptom change in "validated" therapies probably is penny-wise and pound-foolish when it comes to severe mental disorders (e.g., personality disorders). Longer term psychotherapies may be more cost-effective when assessed systemwide over a greater period of time.

The case analysis illustrated these points. The patient had been approached with the presently popular, symptom-based "empirically validated therapies." Carved up into unrelated pieces, her treatment was turfed out to specialists for (continued) medications, cognitive–behavioral treatments for her various compulsions, a sexual abuse treatment group for her sexual acting out, and marital therapy for her failing relationship. An analysis was offered that accounted for her disparate symptoms (depression, compulsions, sexual acting out) with one integrated perspective. A sketch of a recommended (five-stepped) treatment approach was given that would guide the clinician in decisions about which psychotherapies to apply and when and how to apply them. The hypothesis is this: Without transformation of her underlying devotion to patterns set in relation to her mother, none of the brief interventions would be likely to be effective. During this brief hospitalization, it was not possible to implement and test the recommendations. Previous cases have suggested that they would be more effective than the brief interventions that were under way.

There are many challenges. One is how to implement any of the longer term therapies in ways that ensure they are effective. Another is to establish that longer term therapies in general, and the recommended therapy in particular, are effective. Longer term psychotherapy admittedly has a long way to go before it is articulated well enough to qualify as a science. A corollary of this observation is that research directly addressing most relevant aspects of longer term psychotherapy will be difficult to implement. However, I argue here that it is possible to use the rules of science to greatly improve the sharpness of clinician focus and interventions— even when the therapy approach includes elusive "unscientific" concepts such as unconscious wishes and existential choices. Although I have had considerable clinical success applying the recommended approach (RLT) to patient's cases that had conspicuously failed in previous therapeutic attempts—both pharmacologic and psychologic—it does not always work. That may be due to limitations of the approach or to errors in implementation. Articulation of the reasons for failure will be as important as better understanding of the reasons for success.

REFERENCES

American Psychiatric Association. (1994). *Diagnostic and statistical manual of mental disorders* (4th ed.). Washington, DC: Author.

Benjamin, L. S. (1974). Structural Analysis of Social Behavior. *Psychological Review, 81,* 392–425.

Benjamin, L. S. (1984). Principles of prediction using Structural Analysis of Social Behavior. In R. A. Zucker, J. Aronoff, & A. J. Rabin (Eds.), *Personality and the prediction of behavior* (pp. 121–173). New York: Academic Press.

Benjamin, L. S. (1993). Every psychopathology is a gift of love. *Psychotherapy Research, 3,* 1–24.

Benjamin, L. S. (1995). Good defenses make good neighbors. In H. R. Conte & R. Plutchik (Eds.), *Ego defenses: Theory and measurement* (pp. 53–78). New York: Wiley.

Benjamin, L. S. (1996a). *Interpersonal diagnosis and treatment of personality disorders* (2nd ed.). New York: Guilford Press.

Benjamin, L. S. (1996b). An interpersonal theory of personality disorders. In J. F. Clarkin (Ed.), *Major theories of personality disorder* (pp. 141–220). New York: Guilford Press.

Benjamin, L. S. (1996c). Introduction to the special section on Structural Analysis of Social Behavior (SASB). *Journal of Consulting and Clinical Psychology, 64,* 1203–1212.

Benjamin, L. S. (1997). Special features: Personality disorders—Models for treatment and strategies for treatment development. *Journal of Personality Disorders, 11,* 307–324.

Benjamin, L. S. (in press). *Reconstructive learning therapy: An approach to treating the untreatable.* New York: Guilford Press.

Bowlby, J. (1969). *Attachment and loss: Vol. 1., Attachment.* London: Tavistock Institute of Human Relations.

Bowlby, J. (1977). The making and breaking of affectional bonds. *British Journal of Psychiatry, 130,* 201–210, 421–431.

Eisenberg, L. (1995). The social construction of the human brain. *American Journal of Psychiatry, 152,* 1563–1575.

Frank, E., Kupfer, D. J., Wagner, E. F., McEachran, A., & Cornes, C. (1991). Efficacy of interpersonal psychotherapy as maintenance treatment for recurrent depression: Contributing factors. *Archives of General Psychiatry, 48,* 1053–1059.

Gabbard, G. O., Lazar, S. G., Hornberger, J., & Spiegel, D. (1997). The economic impact of psychotherapy: A review. *American Journal of Psychiatry, 154,* 147–155.

Gaston, L., Marmar, C. R., Gallagher, D., & Thompson, L. W. (1991). Alliance prediction of outcome beyond in treatment change as psychotherapy progresses. *Psychotherapy Research, 1,* 104–112.

Goldfried, M. R., & Wolfe, B. E. (1996). Psychotherapy practice and research: Repairing a strained alliance. *American Psychologist, 51,* 1007–1016.

Guntrip, H. (1973). *Psychoanalytic theory, therapy and self.* New York: Basic Books.

Henry, W. P., Schacht, T. E., & Strupp, H. H. (1990). Patient and therapist introject, interpersonal process, and differential therapy outcome. *Journal of Consulting and Clinical Psychology, 58,* 768–774.

Kraemer, G. W. (1992). A psychobiological theory of attachment. *Behavioral and Brain Sciences, 14,* 1–28.

MacCorqoudale, K., & Meehl, P. E. (1948). On a distinction between hypothetical constructs and intervening variables. *Psychological Review, 55,* 95–107.

Matthews, S. M., Roper, M. T., Mosher, L. R., & Menn, A. Z. (1979). A nonneuroleptic treatment for schizophrenia: Analysis of the two year postdischarge risk of relapse. *Schizophrenia Bulletin, 5,* 322–333.

Pilkonis, P. A., & Frank, E. (1988). Personality pathology in recurrent depression: Nature, prevalence, and relationship to treatment response. *American Journal of Psychiatry, 145,* 435–441.

Piper, W. E., Rosie, J. S., Joyce, A. S., & Azim, H. F. A. (1996). *Time-limited day treatment for personality disorders: Integration of research and practice in a group program*. Washington, DC: American Psychological Association.

Raimy, V. (Ed.). (1950). *Training in clinical psychology*. New York: Prentice Hall.

Seligman, M. (1975). *Helplessness: On depression, development and death*. San Francisco: W. H. Freeman.

Sullivan, H. S. (1953). *The interpersonal theory of psychiatry*. New York: Norton.

Task Force on Promotion and Dissemination of Psychological Procedures, Division of Clinical Psychology, American Psychological Association. (1995). Training in and dissemination of empirically-validated psychological treatments: Report and recommendations. *The Clinical Psychologist, 48*, 3–23.

VandenBos, G. R. (1996). Outcome assessment of psychotherapy. *American Psychologist, 51*, 1005–1006.

Zinbarg, R. E., Barlow, D. H., Brown, T. A., & Hertz, R. M. (1992). Cognitive-behavioral approaches to the nature and treatment of anxiety disorders. *Annual Review of Psychology, 43*, 235–267.

III

BENEFITS OF A RESEARCHER–PRACTITIONER ALLIANCE

11

BUILDING THE RESEARCHER–PRACTITIONER ALLIANCE: A PERSONAL JOURNEY

STEPHEN SOLDZ

Like so many others, I was drawn to psychotherapy as a profession out of my personal experiences with suffering and the help I experienced from therapy. Adolescence and early adulthood had been extremely diffi-cult for me. Progress out of the quagmire in which I was stuck appeared to derive from my extensive experiences as a therapy patient. My explo-ration of my internal life in therapy converged with an intellectual interest in psychoanalytic theory arising, initially, from my readings in the Freudian left. Social thought and depth psychology converged in psychoanalysis. When the opportunity arose for psychoanalytic training, I grabbed it, even

I thank Peter Kreiner and Nina Kammerer for comments on drafts of this chapter. The evaluation of Project Second Beginning described herein was supported by a grant from the Substance Abuse and Mental Health Administration's Center for Substance Abuse Prevention to Associates for Human Potential. The research at the Boston Institute for Psychotherapy was generously supported by the institute out of very limited funds. These sources of support are gratefully acknowledged. The view expressed here are solely the views of the author and are not necessarily those of any organization.

as I obtained the more traditional credentials: a master's in counseling and a doctorate in clinical psychology.

Unlike many who are drawn to psychoanalytic theory and practice, I had an extensive background in the "hard sciences," having studied advanced mathematics and related fields for many years. In addition, I am temperamentally a skeptic. Taking anything on faith is contrary to my nature. I therefore quickly wondered about the evidential bases for various therapeutic propositions.

My skepticism received a boost from the experience of case conferences in clinics where I worked. Traditionally, a case conference involved a patient being presented to, and frequently interviewed by, a prominent therapist from outside the agency. What I quickly noticed was that the guest expert never seemed to have trouble determining in half an hour exactly what ailed the patient and what should be done about it. For those of us in the audience, however, there was frequently a problem. Our local in-house expert usually also had determined the nature of the patient's problems, and his—it always was a he in those days—prescription often differed radically from that of the outside expert. What were we to do? Here we had two distinct assessments and treatment prescriptions, each asserted with great confidence by experts we respected, but the prescriptions differed from each other. In many cases, if one was right, the other would clearly have to be wrong. If so, what happened to the hapless patients who went to the "wrong" therapist? How could they possibly get better? Furthermore, I knew that many patients didn't go to therapists trained in the intricacies of psychoanalysis. In fact, in those days, many patients went to Gestalt therapists, encounter groups, client-centered therapists, and so forth. Although none of my personal acquaintances went to behaviorists, I knew that many patients did go in that direction. What happened to all these patients? Did they get better despite the limitations (as perceived by me) of the theoretical orientations of their therapists?

As a neophyte therapist, how was I to choose between the numerous rival claimants to my attention? Having a scientific background, my natural inclination was toward research. "Surely," I thought, "the data will tell us which treatment approaches work." Unfortunately, the available evidence is confusing at best. Luborsky, Singer, and Luborsky (1975) had summarized the available outcome data and came to the conclusion that "everyone has won and all must have prizes," as the Dodo bird expressed it in *Alice in Wonderland*. All therapies appeared to work essentially equivalently well. Smith, Glass, and Miller (1980) came to much the same conclusion. More recently, Project Match, a $28 million attempt to match types of patients to alcoholism treatment, experienced a spectacular failure: No differences were found.

What differences that have been found between treatments have tended to favor behavioral treatments. To some degree, these studies could be disturbing to a psychodynamically oriented therapist. But in these studies, researchers have tended to compare brief therapies for very circumscribed conditions, using outcome measures tailored to the particular targeted behavior problems. It took no great leap to see these studies as largely irrelevant to much of psychodynamic therapy as practiced with patients with multiple, often rather amorphous problems, such as being chronically unhappy and dissatisfied with one's life, having difficulties experiencing intimacy with others, and so forth. Many of the patients I saw had already completed one or more courses of focused brief therapy but often felt that their core problems had not even been identified, much less addressed, in the process.

For example, one patient I am currently seeing, Mr. King,[1] came into treatment because of a depression that was interfering with his work functioning. He refused to even consider medication, which was just as well, because his depression remitted fairly quickly. He then was left with the feeling that he hadn't been very happy, at least since his mother died in adolescence. He had never had a satisfying relationship with a woman, and people in general were experienced as more of a bother and a threat to his stability than as pleasurable. Eventually he came to identify his central dilemma as having to decide whether he would want relationships with others. Perhaps life as a loner would be good enough for him and better than the suffering that involved attempting to interact with others. What could the clinical trials literature tell me about the best way to treat this patient? Nothing, as far as I could see.

One approach to this perceived irrelevance of outcome research to many psychodynamic practitioners involves the development of outcome measures that more faithfully measure the problems experienced by these types of patients. Such efforts are ongoing, but have proven difficult. The development of valid, useful psychological measurement techniques is normally hard, and measurement of fairly obscure constructs regarding aspects of psychological life that are not directly observable is extremely difficult. Psychotherapy researchers have, in general, found that patients' perceptions of their changes owing to therapy bear only a limited relationship to the changes perceived by the patients' therapists, even when the same construct is being assessed. If other observers or interviewers are brought in, yet more perspectives are generated. Thus, sophisticated psychotherapy research projects have taken to using multiple measures from multiple perspectives. The result is somewhat greater fidelity to clinical reality accompanied by much greater complexity of interpretation. In any case, studies using elaborate outcome packages haven't led to clearer guidelines for clinicians.

Although I have not given Mr. King a packet of standardized outcome

---

[1]Patient names cited here have been fictionalized.

measures, I suspect that he would exhibit moderate depression on a symptom questionnaire and might even exhibit difficulties with intimacy on one of my favorite self-report questionnaires, the Inventory of Interpersonal Problems (Horowitz, Rosenberg, Bauer, Ureno, & Villasenor, 1988; Soldz, Budman, Demby, & Merry, 1995b). However, no questionnaire or standardized interview that I am aware of would elucidate the problem he came to identify: whether to want relationships with others. The standardized questionnaires and interviews traditionally used in psychotherapy research, although providing much useful information about this man, would fail to inform the user of the nature of his problem from *his* perspective and whether that problem had improved.

One solution to the outcome problem is to develop methods of measuring individualized problems. Such methods have been regularly pursued. In fact, the one instrument I did administer to Mr. King was a form of George Kelly's (1955) repertory grid. The grid was enlightening to me. It showed that Mr. King bifurcated people into two classes, those who were "rational" but "boring," and those who were "irrational," "emotional," and incomprehensible to him. The use of the grid allowed us to refine our goals for treatment, but such subtleties would be missed in most psychotherapy research programs. And even if Mr. King's problems could be measured adequately, I'm still faced with deciding how to treat him in the absence of much guidance from the treatment literature.

GUIDANCE FROM PROCESS RESEARCH

The solution to this lack of clear guidance for clinical practice from much of psychotherapy outcome research that I believed in a decade ago, and still do believe in to some extent, involves the need to develop a clearer understanding of the curative mechanisms of psychotherapies. One way of elucidating these mechanisms is to study the process of therapy. Over the decades, much research has taken this tack (Soldz, 1990). The most notable results from this work so far have involved the therapeutic or working alliance between patients and therapists (Horvath & Greenberg, 1994). Many studies have found that the quality of the alliance predicts outcomes, as traditionally measured, in many therapies, including psychodynamic, cognitive, and group (Budman, Soldz, Demby, Feldstein, & Springer, 1989). The alliance literature is important in indicating, as psychodynamic therapists have long believed, that the relationship between the patient and therapist is important to the patient's outcome.

An implication of this work on the alliance is that a therapist should strive to maximize the alliance with a patient. Or is it? Unfortunately, so far we have no studies examining whether deliberate attempts to improve the alliance lead to improved outcomes. In particular, we need to know whether there are techniques that can be applied that will lead to improved alliances—and, possibly, outcomes—for the more severely disturbed personality-disordered patients who are extremely difficult to treat and who frequently drop out prematurely or have poor outcomes (Strupp, 1980).

Another general conclusion from the psychotherapy process literature is that patients who are more disturbed with poor histories of relationships with others are not successfully treated by most therapists. This conclusion was driven home to me when I was writing a survey article on psychodynamic process research for a clinical audience (Soldz, 1990). I started out summarizing a number of classic studies in the area. However, I did not start out with a conclusion in mind. When I got to the section of the paper where I needed to write about the implications of the research, I was struck by the consistency of findings: "Difficult" patients with poor histories of relationships were rarely successfully treated. Strupp (1980) expressed the results of detailed analyses of successful and unsuccessful cases in one of his classic psychotherapy research studies: "In our study we failed to encounter a single instance in which a difficult patient's hostility and negativism were successfully confronted or resolved" (p. 954). Because these patients typically form poor alliances with their therapists, we need to know whether these alliances can be improved, and whether improving the alliances will lead to better retention and outcome. Unfortunately, the process research literature so far provides little guidance regarding these types of questions. This research didn't help me decide which, if any, of the impressive "experts" I heard at case conferences I should trust.

In general, my impression of the process literature is that it provides an exciting first step in helping us understand the change processes in psychotherapy, but that most of this work is far from providing concrete clinical guidance. I have hopes that this research will evolve in a more applicable direction, but I am far from convinced. If this work is to be applied, one of two things will have to happen. Either research should focus on the ability to deliberately change therapeutic processes, as in the example of alliance research where investigation would focus on the ability to improve alliances and determine whether improved alliances lead to improved outcomes, or researchers could explicate in fine detail processes that lead to patient improvement. This direction was strongly promoted about a decade ago when Rice and Greenberg (1984) published an important book titled *Patterns of Change*. Many of us expected this book and its strong reception among psychotherapy researchers to spur process research in this direction. If researchers could describe change processes in detail, there would be a reasonable chance that such knowledge could be incorporated into therapists' techniques. Just as therapists now learn from hearing how a respected colleague would treat a case, they could learn from research that indicated that which styles on responding, in what particular circumstances, with what types of patients, would be most helpful.

For whatever reasons, however, the expected surge in research on change processes did not occur. I expect that the reasons this research has not surged are twofold. One set of reasons has to do with the extreme difficulty of getting such research funded. In the past decade, the federal funding sources that provide almost all funding for large-scale psychosocial treatment research have focused most of their resources on randomized clinical trials that compare treatments, based on the pharmacological model for comparing two drugs. Process research is virtually unfundable at this point. Thus, only small-scale studies, based on volunteer or graduate student labor can be completed. Although every year yields quite a number of interesting studies of this type, they often remain too small to lead to cumulative knowledge that could be usefully applied by clinicians.

A second set of reasons that this type of process research hasn't flourished involves the lack of good, precise, theories of human change processes that can serve as the basis for this type of fine-grained analysis. In the absence of these detailed theories, researchers are left adrift when confronting the mass of material generated by even a brief therapeutic interaction.

As I treat Mr. King, I am aware of little process research that can aid me. Knowing that he has a history of very poor relationships with others, beginning in childhood, the process research would alert me to the dangers that he would terminate prematurely. I did not need research to raise my awareness in this area, however. Mr. King was referred to me by a colleague whom he had seen for a few sessions and promptly discarded. Our sessions were full of intense interactions in which I would say something that would lead to him feeling misunderstood and thinking of terminating. A large part of our interactions were spent repairing these ruptures in our alliance. Although it is nice to know that research supports the importance of repairing ruptured alliances (Safron, Muran, & Samstag, 1994), I cannot honestly say that my attempts in this area were improved through my knowledge of this research.

GROUP THERAPY RESEARCH

My own experiences with process research primarily took place at the Mental Health Research Department of Harvard Community Health Plan (HCHP), where I was affiliated for the first 8 years of my research career. At HCHP, we investigated interactional group therapy. The first study, which I entered as the project was in progress, involved assessing the cohesiveness of brief (15-session) therapy groups. Our main finding was that the cohesiveness of groups, as rated by clinical observers of videotapes, was strongly related to the outcomes of the patients in the groups. As our group cohesiveness measure was developed to be a group analog of the therapeutic alliance, we thus extended the work on the alliance in individual therapy to the group setting. I well remember the excitement when we ran our first data analyses and realized that the results were going to come out as predicted (Budman et al., 1989).

Yet, were there clinical implications of this finding? We weren't sure. As we examined videotapes of low- and high-cohesiveness groups, it was clear that the groups differed in their functioning. It was also clear that the low-cohesiveness groups differed in composition of the patients, as well. The patients in them seemed to be less psychologically minded, among other things; they didn't seem to have a particularly rich set of constructs for thinking and talking about the internal lives of themselves and the other group members. So, was low cohesiveness a cause of patient change, or simply a result of patient characteristics that prevented the patients from creating a group that could lead to positive change? We studied cohesiveness for a number of years (Budman, Soldz, Demby, Davis, & Merry, 1993), but never really answered this question.

Similar issues bedeviled our research into the behaviors of individual patients in the groups (Soldz, Budman, Davis, & Demby, 1993; Soldz, Budman, & Demby, 1992; Soldz, Budman, Demby, & Feldstein, 1990; Soldz, Budman, Demby, & Merry, 1995a). We found out a number of interesting things. For example, the patients who spoke the most in our groups were the most disturbed, and what they spoke about so much was themselves, rather than the other group members. Although this finding may not seem surprising when stated, many clinicians to whom I have described the study predict that the opposite will be the case until hearing the results; then they find these results obvious. We also found that personality-disordered group therapy patients could agree with each other and their therapists regarding the personalities of their fellow patients, but had little agreement with the others regarding their own personalities. We found, further, that the patients with the greatest agreement with fellow patients about their own personalities were those with the greatest degree of personality disturbance: This latter finding is never predicted by people to whom I describe the study.

As we studied group process and patient change in these groups, we gradually realized that we were hoping that patient personality could be changed by way of group therapy. Many of the patients who enter psychotherapy come not to have particular symptoms relieved, but because their personality patterns lead to problematic and unsatisfying interactions with the important other people in their lives. Could group therapy change these patterns? We created a set of 18-month groups for patients with personality disorders, based on interpersonal principles and informed by our research experiences (Budman, Cooley, et al., 1996). These groups were modestly successful: Those patients who stayed in them tended to get better, but many of the patients, especially those with borderline personality diagnoses, did not complete the groups (Budman, Demby, Soldz, & Merry, 1996). This latter result is reminiscent of Strupp's (1980) comments above about the failures of the therapists in his study to successfully treat hostile patients with poor histories of relationships.

In our years studying therapy groups, we made many discoveries, but their meaning was never unambiguous enough for me—the inveterate skeptic—to feel that we knew enough to issue treatment recommendations. In my opinion, it would have taken several research careers and an amount of grant money that was unimaginable even in less fiscally conservative times to have advanced our knowledge enough to have given us a shot at making definitive recommendations. Other members of the research group were less reticent about making recommendations based on limited data. In either case, there did not appear to be any large audience of clinicians or policy makers interested in listening to any recommendations we would have made.

EVALUATION

If randomized clinical trials and process research lead to little knowledge of use to practicing clinicians, does this mean that research cannot usefully aid practice? Many have come to this conclusion. By accident, I was exposed to an area where research and practice intersect that provides a useful model for future efforts.

A colleague who had to leave town due to death in the family called me and asked if I would write an evaluation plan for a substance abuse prevention grant. I am now embarrassed to admit that my first question to him was "What is an evaluation?" In my training and experience in research, I had learned much about statistics, research design, and the relationship of theory and research, but the existence of program evaluation was never mentioned. What I discovered as I helped this colleague was that evaluation was an established domain where research skills were used to provide data-based guidance to program administrators and policy makers.

A couple of years later, after a few rewrites and resubmissions, the project for which I wrote that first evaluation plan was funded by the Federal Center for Substance Abuse Prevention (CSAP). This project, named Project Second Beginning (PSB), involved the provision of case management to substance abusing women who were either parents or pregnant. As the project evolved, a treatment model was formed that was based on the relational model of women's development that had been developed by theorists and researchers at the Stone Center at Wellesley College. This model involved a clinically trained staff (psychologists, social workers, and nurses) providing what came to be called *relational case management* to the women (Markoff & Cawley, 1996). Relational case management involved the clinician forming a supportive relationship with the client that provided a model of healthy gratifying relationships while simultaneously helping her navigate through the morass of social service agencies in order to meet her life needs for food, shelter, day care, vocational training, and the like.

When I started out as project evaluator, I naively assumed that my job was simply to assess whether the program was successful in helping the women. I quickly realized that I was expected to play many roles. While I was to report on the clients' outcomes, I was also expected to provide both qualitative and quantitative information on the functioning of the project. This information, referred to in the evaluation literature as *process evaluation data* (not to be confused with psychotherapy process research), was expected to be used both for documentation purposes and to improve the project. The model for the relationship between the project and its evaluation that was frequently referred to by the CSAP staff and their consultants involved the creation of a self-correcting system. The idea was that evaluation data would be fed back to the project folks, who would then use it to improve the project, in a never-ending cycle, at least until our funding ran out.

Shortly after PSB was funded, I met with the newly hired program staff to modify the evaluation plan I had quickly drawn up for the grant in order to reflect the evolving program model. Without knowing how controversial it was (Patton, 1986; Shadish, Cook, & Leviton, 1991), I naturally developed a collaborative model whereby the evaluation of the project was the creation and responsibility of all of us—administrators, clinicians, and myself as the evaluator. We held numerous discussions regarding the staff's conceptualizations of the project, focusing on the changes they expected to occur in their clients. We then jointly discussed various instruments for measuring these changes, with several staff members and I sharing responsibility for trips to the library to find relevant research literature, and for phone calls to other projects that had faced similar evaluation issues so that we could learn from their experiences. Although I contributed my research expertise as we selected instruments and designed an evaluation protocol, there was no assumption that I was the only one whose expertise was important.

What I did contribute was based on my years of experience in psychotherapy research. As we selected outcome measures, I was aware of the complexities of the measurement of change, including such issues as the desirability of measuring change from multiple perspectives (such as self, clinician, others); the value of including multiple measures to compensate for the peculiarities of particular instruments; the importance of including more than two time points when measuring change; and the danger of assuming that an instrument necessarily measures what it purports to measure without clear validity evidence.

Nonetheless, our evaluation design was less than optimal due to the extremely limited resources at our disposal, as well as to our collective naiveté. We assumed, for example, that our first experiences with clients who tended to stay a long time would generalize, leading us to schedule our follow-up measurements at too long an interval, which we gradually discovered was after many clients already had left. We were also well aware that we would ultimately not be able to definitively attribute to PSB any changes in the women since we were unable to include any control or comparison group. Nonetheless, we hoped that the evaluation data would provide at least some useful information regarding what happened to the women in the project.

After the project and evaluation had been going for a while, we had the pleasant experience of being called to task by our CSAP project officer for basing our project on the Relational Model of Women's Development and not measuring the relationship between the woman client and the case manager. In response, we decided to introduce into our evaluation materials the Working Alliance Inventory (Horvath, 1994), a measure of the alliance developed for psychotherapy research.

As the data were collected and analyzed, we developed preliminary findings. In addition to the bureaucratic requirement that results be communicated to CSAP periodically, we held meetings of all staff to discuss the emerging findings. I presented aspects of the data that I found either intriguing or confusing, leading to long discussions regarding possible meanings. Among the results we discussed collaboratively were those directly relevant to assessing how well the program was doing as well as those confusing relations between variables that I didn't understand.

One set of results we often discussed concerned client retention. Overall, clients stayed a median of 7 months. This length of stay was less than we had originally planned, but was quite respectable when compared with other substance abuse projects. However, we also found that clients with more serious psychiatric symptomatology stayed significantly less long.[2] The clinical staff had not been aware of this latter fact until I presented the data. A number of discussions ensued over the succeeding months regarding the reasons for this finding and ways of trying to identify and improve the treatment of these women. The working alliance appeared to predict length of stay, but, alas, the women with more psychiatric symptomatology had worse alliances. Despite these repeated discussions and the attempts of staff to be more attuned to the needs of these women, it appeared that we never successfully improved the treatment of this more disturbed group to the extent that they stayed as long as others.

---

[2]Note the similarity to the findings from psychotherapy research discussed above.

In conducting the process evaluation, we were interested in innovative ways to document the treatment model developed by the PSB case managers. From our perspective, the primary function of this documentation was to communicate the cumulative knowledge being developed by the project. We were especially interested in finding ways to capture some of the implicit knowledge gained by clinicians in the course of their work. We experimented with two techniques for capturing this knowledge. One technique, concept mapping (Trochim, 1989; Trochim, Cook, & Setze, 1994), involves a structured brainstorming session, followed by computer manipulations, leading to a group interpretation of the resulting graphical output. Our general feeling was that this process did not lead to any deeper understanding.

We then decided to explore CareMaps,[3] a way of systematically recording, in a matrix format, the procedures involved in a treatment process, based on the best practices known to a given group of clinicians. After the CareMap matrix is created, it can be used to document the treatment course of a given client. An essential aspect of the use of CareMaps is that variation from the expected course of treatment is systematically recorded and analyzed by way of variance analysis, either leading to improved protocols or to the development of separate CareMaps for identified subgroups. Second Beginning staff spent many long hours developing and refining our CareMap. The resulting product contained, in my opinion, an enormous amount of information about the steps and processes that could aid the substance abusing mothers targeted by the project. The clinical staff were less convinced of the value of their product. It seemed to me that their skepticism was due to the fact that the resultant CareMap represented knowledge that had become second nature to them through years of hard work, but that could be extremely valuable to others beginning such a project. Furthermore, it is possible that if the CareMap had been used systematically variance analysis would have helped improve treatment for certain clients, including, perhaps, those with psychiatric impairment.

As I was involved in evaluating PSB and a number of other demonstration projects, I witnessed a marked change in the relationship between research and practice among many substance abuse programs. The federal requirement for an evaluation of each project forced researchers, program administrators, and direct service staff to work closely together. Rather than familiarity breeding contempt, in many instances it bred increased respect for the perspectives and expertise of the others. Clinical staff and administrators were exposed to the processes and the insights of research and researchers at close range, leading to greater appreciation. At the same time, researchers got to know and respect the difficulties faced

[3]The CareMap name and concept are copyrighted by the Center for Case Management in South Nattick, MA. I thank Kathleen Andolina of the center for her wonderful assistance during the development of the CareMap.

by treatment programs and the dedication of their staff. In the best instances, the creation of exemplary programs, and of excellent evaluations became a shared responsibility.

Furthermore, as programs sought this federal money, there was an increasing demand that any proposal be based in the existing "knowledge base" in the area, making it routine for those writing grants to examine existing research and evaluation literature as they designed a program. Initially, this examination was solely for the purpose of justifying a preexisting idea, but gradually, the literature review became a source of information on what was known to work or not work. The grant writers and program administrators also became aware that the existence of data suggesting that their program was effective materially increased the odds of getting funded. As the director of one program in the retardation area to whom I had consulted on the design of information systems put it: "When we apply for funding, we have the data to show them exactly what their money will buy. As a result, we always get the money" (Joan Beadsley, personal communication, 1994). The tie between knowledge of relevant research and the existence of program data and the awarding of funding increased program administrators' respect for the research process. My sense was that these processes radically changed the relationship between research and practice in the substance abuse area, making them, in many cases, natural allies rather than wary adversaries. The federal demonstration grant program was thus, perhaps inadvertently, a demonstration to the field that research and practice can cooperate productively. Similar experiences are currently being forced on the mental health field by the cry for outcomes data from managed care companies and public funders.

BOSTON INSTITUTE FOR PSYCHOTHERAPY

Other important experiences that helped develop my thinking about the research–practice interface came out of my efforts in the past decade to develop a psychotherapy research program in an institute committed to training and practice in psychodynamic psychotherapy, the Boston Institute for Psychotherapy (BIP). Through a fortuitous accident, I connected with the BIP just as a couple of Institute graduates were completing their doctorates and were attempting to set up postdoctoral fellowships with a significant research component. They, along with myself and a BIP staff member who had a long history of social psychological research, decided to establish a program of research into the treatment provided in the BIP's Treatment Center. After a period of preparation, we decided to conduct regular outcome measurements on willing patients, while recording some therapies for future analysis of the patient–therapist interaction. Despite the expressed support of both the BIP board and program directors (the senior management of the Institute), we encountered fierce resistance from a number of staff (Mordecai, Soldz, & Gumpert, 1993). Many clinicians appeared afraid that the research would be used to judge the quality of their work, while others were worried about its intrusive effects on the therapy they provided. There was also a small but vocal group who argued that traditional research into dynamic psychotherapy was useless at best, as the essence of this type of therapy involves subtle processes that can never be measured.

In order to confront these resistances, we sought to involve the BIP clinicians in the design of our research through conducting focus groups with them regarding the nature of outcomes in dynamic psychotherapy and through regular presentations to the treatment center's Case Conference. We were also instrumental in the establishment of a monthly Grand Rounds series that combined clinical and clinically relevant research presentations. For a number of years, I also taught the course on Freud and classical psychoanalysis to the second-year trainees in which I insisted on integrating research on psychoanalytic concepts with the historical and clinical material. The result of these efforts was a greater appreciation among many BIP staff of the value of research and attitudes ranging from tolerance to excitement about our efforts.

After several years of functioning, the research group became familiar with the CareMap concept and decided to experiment with its application to open-ended dynamic psychotherapy. In order to create a CareMap for a given group of patients, it is necessary to identify a relatively homogeneous subgroup of patients who can normally be expected to have a similar course of treatment. We decided to concentrate on young adults in their twenties who had identity and relationship difficulties because this type of patient was common in the BIP treatment center. Although we were impressed with our ability to identify expectable events for this population—such as "She will become concerned about dependency on the therapist within the first 6 months of treatment"—we also became aware that we did not know enough about the normative course of treatment to construct a CareMap. For example, our clinical experience led us to believe that some patients changed in a slow, continuous manner; some changed rapidly for short periods with long plateau periods of no clear change in between; and yet others got worse at certain points in the treatment, only to improve later. But were our clinical intuitions consonant with reality? We modified our goal of constructing a CareMap to one of exploring the nature of change over the course of treatment, at least as that change is viewed by the therapist.

We thus undertook the construction of an instrument to be completed by therapists on a monthly basis that would assess patient change on a broad range of dimensions relevant to psychodynamic therapy. Over a year later, our product, the Boston Institute for Psychotherapy Change

Assessment Tool (BIP-CAT) emerged. The BIP-CAT contains scales measuring patient functioning and change in four broad areas: problems and symptom, external life, internal life, and the therapeutic relationship.

The Problems and Symptoms section captures information about the problems and symptoms that are identified by either the patient or therapist. Given our orientation toward using the BIP-CAT to record the therapist's perceptions of changes in the patient, the therapist is allowed to identify a problem or symptom that has not been explicitly identified by the patient.

The subsections of the other three sections, with sample items are as follows:

1. External Life
   Romantic relationships (Sample item: "Quality of sex life"); Friendships (Sample item: "Ability to see other's point of view"); Family of origin relationships; Self-care (Sample item: "Pleasurable activities [Fun]"); Work (Sample item: "Presence of stable career goals")
2. Internal Life
   Self (Sample item: "Sense of well-being"); Object relations (Sample item: "Significant distortion of others"); Defenses; Thought (Sample item: "Awareness of wishes/longings"); Affect
3. Therapeutic Relationship
   Content of sessions (Sample item: "Pt notes patterns in feelings, thoughts, and actions"); Frame (Sample item: "Therapist finds it difficult to negotiate frame"); Transference (Sample item: "Pt idealizes therapist"); Countertransference (Sample item: "Therapist experiences boredom"); Intervention types

Each item on the BIP-CAT is rated at intake and every 6 months thereafter on its severity as a problem for the patient. In addition—and this is the heart of the instrument—it is rated every month in terms of whether the patient changed (either improved or got worse) on the item. If completed systematically, the BIP-CAT would provide an "X ray" of the therapy, allowing us to view its vicissitudes over time.

One of the unique features of the BIP-CAT is that therapists are asked to rate both patient level of functioning and change over the past month for the scales in the first three areas. It is our hope that the direct ratings of change will allow us to detect small changes that would need to accumulate over many months before being assessable as change of even one point on a direct rating of patient functioning.

As we completed the BIP-CAT and wrote a detailed manual, we started presenting it to the BIP administrators and clinicians. Many of them responded to it with intense excitement, because they could see the direct links between the clinical constructs important to them and the dimensions of the instrument. Thus, they did not feel that we were trying to fit the square peg of psychodynamic therapy into the round hole solely of symptom relief. They could see that through the BIP-CAT, we were attempting to measure such subtle clinical constructs as object relations or defense use. As the therapists found that they could relate to the BIP-CAT, they also became more interested in our other research projects. Meanwhile, the BIP directors group, of which I was a member as the director of research, became more interested in using data on our patients in order to manage the Institute. Where did the patients come from? Did certain types of patients drop out "prematurely"?[4] Would certain modifications of intake procedures lead to greater patient retention? The answers to these questions clearly require the development of data systems. The BIP is thus moving toward the development of evaluation systems, with the assistance of the research group. These modifications are leading the BIP toward including research and evaluation in the routine functioning of the Institute, thus breaking down barriers between research and clinical practice.

CONCLUSION

The experiences I have described, as well as many others, have led me to rethink the relationship of research to practice. Initially, I was hopeful that research could provide a guide to practice with individual patients, that it could help me decide between the advice of the various case conference presenters. I no longer think that the primary impact of research is likely to be at this level. However, there are a number of other ways in which research can affect practice more directly. Such efforts will involve collaborative efforts between clinicians and researchers, with neither side having primacy. To successfully impact practice, these collaborative efforts will require the creation of a strong, vibrant, researcher–practitioner alliance.

The primary lesson derived from my experiences over the years is that bridges are built between research and practice primarily when researchers and practitioners work together. This working together may be driven by internal forces, as has occurred at the BIP, or by external forces, as with the Demonstration Project programs. But, as in so many other areas of life, mutual understanding and respect occur when people of different backgrounds find themselves working together on common projects of mutual interest.

Thus, I and my fellow clinicians may not treat Mr. K. and other patients with a treatment directly based on research. Yet, if a collaborative

---

[4]This issue had already been investigated by Boston Institute for Psychotherapy staff and reported in a journal article (Pollack, Mordecai, & Gumpert, 1992).

researcher–practitioner alliance can be built, the treatment of future Mr. King may be improved through the feedback and research-based input that can be glimpsed in some of the experiences I have described. Psychotherapy may never be purely an applied science, as some researchers dream. With luck, however, it may become more suffused with the insights and knowledge of science than is now the case. If that future should develop, it is my belief and desire that researchers, therapists, and their patients will all find psychotherapy to be a richer, more valuable experience.

REFERENCES

Budman, S. H., Cooley, S., Demby, A., Koppenaal, G., Koslof, J., & Powers, T. (1996). A model of time-effective group therapy for patients with personality disorders: The clinical model. *International Journal of Group Psychotherapy, 46,* 329–355.

Budman, S. H., Demby, A., Soldz, S., & Merry, J. (1996). Group therapy for patients with personality disorders: Outcomes and dropouts. *International Journal of Group Psychotherapy, 46,* 357–377.

Budman, S. H., Soldz, S., Demby, A., Feldstein, M., & Springer, T. (1989). Cohesion, alliance and outcome in group psychotherapy: An empirical examination. *Psychiatry, 52,* 339–350.

Budman, S. H., Soldz, S., Demby, A., Davis, M., & Merry, J. (1993). What is cohesiveness? An empirical examination. *Small Group Behavior, 24,* 199–216.

Horowitz, L. M., Rosenberg, S. E., Bauer, B. A., Ureno, G., & Villasenor, V. S. (1988). Inventory of Interpersonal Problems: Psychometric properties and clinical applications. *Journal of Consulting and Clinical Psychology, 56,* 885–892.

Horvath, A. O. (1994). Empirical validation of Bordin's pantheoretical model of the alliance: The Working Alliance Inventory perspective. In A. O. Horvath & L. S. Greenberg (Eds.), *The working alliance: Theory, research, and practice* (pp. 109–128). New York: Wiley.

Horvath, A. O., & Greenberg, L. S. (Eds.). (1994). *The working alliance: Theory, research, and practice.* New York: Wiley.

Kelly, G. (1955). *The psychology of personal constructs.* New York: Norton.

Luborsky, L., Singer, B., & Luborsky, L. (1975). Comparative studies of psychotherapy: Is it true that "Everyone has won and all must have prizes?" *Archives of General Psychiatry, 32,* 995–1008.

Markoff, L., & Cawley, P. (1996). Retaining your clients and your sanity: Using a relational model of multi-systems case management. *Journal of Chemical Dependency Treatment, 6,* 45–65.

Mordecai, E., Soldz, S., & Gumpert, P. (1993, June). *Resistances to research: The Boston Institute for Psychotherapy experience.* Paper presented at the annual meeting of the Society for Psychotherapy Research, Pittsburgh, PA.

Patton, M. Q. (1986). *Utilization-focused evaluation*. Newbury Park, CA: Sage.

Pollack, J., Mordecai, E., & Gumpert, P. (1992). Discontinuation from long-term individual psychodynamic psychotherapy. *Psychotherapy Research, 2*, 224–234.

Rice, L. W., & Greenberg, L. S. (1984). Pattern of change: *Intensive analyses of psychotherapeutic change*. New York: Guilford Press.

Safron, J. D., Muran, J. C., & Samstag, L. W. (1994). Resolving therapeutic alliance ruptures: A task analytic investigation. In A. O. Horvath & L. S. Greenberg (Eds.), *The working alliance: Theory, research, and practice* (pp. 225–255). New York: Wiley.

Shadish, W. R., Cook, T. D., & Leviton, L. C. (1991). *Foundations of program evaluation: Theories of practice*. Newbury Park, CA: Sage.

Smith, M. L., Glass, G. V., & Miller, T. I. (1980). *The benefits of psychotherapy*. Baltimore: Johns Hopkins University Press.

Soldz, S. (1990). The therapeutic interaction: Research perspectives. In R. A. Wells & V. J. Giannetti (Eds.), *Handbook of the brief psychotherapies* (pp. 22–53). New York: Plenum.

Soldz, S., Budman, H., Davis, M., & Demby, A. (1993). Beyond the interpersonal circumplex in group psychotherapy: The structure and relationship to outcome of the individual group Member Interpersonal Process Scale. *Journal of Clinical Psychology, 49*, 551–563.

Soldz, S., Budman, S., & Demby, A. (1992). The relationship between Main Actor behaviors and treatment outcome in group psychotherapy. *Psychotherapy Research, 2*, 52–62.

Soldz, S., Budman, S., Demby, A., & Feldstein, M. (1990). Patient activity and outcome in group psychotherapy: New findings. *International Journal of Group Psychotherapy, 40*, 53–62.

Soldz, S., Budman, S. H., Demby, A., & Merry, J. (1995a). Personality traits as seen by patients, therapists and other group members: The Big Five in personality disorder groups. *Psychotherapy, 32*, 678–687.

Soldz, S., Budman, S. H., Demby, A., & Merry, J. (1995b). A short form of the Inventory of Interpersonal Problems Circumplex Scales. *Assessment, 2*, 53–63.

Strupp, H. H. (1980). Success and failure in time-limited psychotherapy: A systematic comparison of two cases (comparison 4). *Archives of General Psychiatry, 37*, 947–954.

Trochim, W. M. K. (1989). An introduction to concept mapping for planning and evaluation. *Evaluation and Program Planning, 12*, 1–16.

Trochim, W. M. K., Cook, J. A., & Setze, R. J. (1994). Using concept mapping to develop a conceptual framework of staff's views of a supported employment program for individuals with severe mental illness. *Journal of Consulting and Clinical Psychology, 62*, 766–775.

12

WITH SCIENCE AND SERVICE WE CAN SURVIVE AND THRIVE

JAMES O. PROCHASKA

Psychotherapy science and service are remarkably similar. They both involve human problem solving, one under more controlled conditions, the other under more chaotic conditions. But unless we appreciate that all of human behavior and experience is conditional, we can make major mistakes when we seek to transfer research directly from laboratory to clinic conditions.

Let me explain what I mean by *conditional* with a story. My first major venture occurred in 1971, 2 years after beginning my career as a scientist–practitioner. Consulting with the Rhode Island Department of Health, I received a modest federal grant to establish an anxiety disorders clinic and lab. This was to be a state-of-the-art science setting that would not only provide best practices for clients but also could serve to train practitioners and generate additional knowledge.

Robert Marzille, a psychology intern, and I developed therapy protocols for a range of anxiety-based disorders, including phobias, obsessive–compulsive disorders, and sexual dysfunctions. After applying these research-based protocols to practice cases, we were ready to offer our science and service to a broader population.

A reporter from the *Providence Journal* wrote a wonderful story describing our science and service across the range of problems with which we were practicing. But the headline writer for the front page of the Sunday newspaper titled the story "*State Opens Sex Clinic!*"

The governor was on vacation in Maine but when he saw the first page of the paper, he immediately called the director of mental health: "What the hell do you mean the state opens a sex clinic. This is a Catholic state and I'm up for reelection!" he shouted.

The next day the director called me on the carpet. By that time, however, there were already an unprecedented number of patients calling for our services, especially sex therapy. There were also numerous calls to radio talk shows, the majority praising Rhode Island for being the first to create a state supported sex clinic. The support and the demand generated by that headline writer transformed my early career into specializing in sex therapy.

At first I felt confident. I reassured myself that the therapy research generated by Masters and Johnson (1970) had been published in a book that could serve as a virtual manual for each of the major sexual dysfunctions. Working late evenings and long weekends, we scheduled couple after couple for sensual holidays in Newport and Narragansett, Rhode Island. In the privacy of their ocean view rooms, they would practice the sex therapy steps they learned each day.

Our initial enthusiasm rather quickly became anxiety from having too many clients. We were seeing many more complications than Masters and Johnson ever reported in their research: couples dropping out rather than proceeding to the sensual holidays; couples fighting rather than working on the "pleasuring" in their oceanfront rooms; and couples failing to progress through sex therapy at the rapid rate reported by Masters and Johnson.

We experienced a paradox between the assumed etiology of the sexual dysfunctions and sex therapy expectations. The most important cause across sexual dysfunctions was supposed to be performance anxiety: Individuals who are highly goal-oriented observe their performance in bed and negatively evaluate their own or their partner's performance. The number one cause of dysfunctions was people feeling pressure to perform and pressure to reach their goals.

But here we were, practicing goal-oriented sex therapy in which people were expected to perform satisfactorily in the first 4 days of treatment. Ready or not here they come! But many didn't, many more than Masters and Johnson reported in their research. And we could not figure out why.

The pressure we were placing on ourselves and on our clients was deeply distressing. Here we were supposed to be reducing performance anxiety and goal-oriented sex. Yet faithfully following the science from St.

Louis meant that we were pressuring our patients to perform in order to reach the goal of successful sexual encounters within 4 days.

For too long I questioned my competency rather than questioning the conclusions from highly controlled clinical science. It was not until 6 years later when we were doing addictions research that I discovered the likely reasons why Masters and Johnson were having so much more scientific success than were we. Implicitly or explicitly, they had screened out particular patients who were not ready for their action-oriented therapy. Who would be prepared to spend $3,000 in the early 1970s for sex therapy? Who would take off 2 weeks to travel to St. Louis to focus entirely on sex therapy? Who would be recommended by a therapist for participation in such a program? Clearly couples who were ready and deeply committed to change would be much more likely to clear such hurdles and make such commitments than would patients plagued by defensiveness, ignorance, or ambivalence. Add in the early requirement of having to complete at least 6 months of psychotherapy before being eligible for the trip to St. Louis, and we can see what a select sample Masters and Johnson had screened for their study.

DISCOVERING THE STAGES OF CHANGE

Once we discovered the stages of change, it became crystal clear that Masters and Johnson had screened out patients who were not ready for their action-oriented therapy. This discovery began with my search for an integration of the major systems of psychotherapy, a search that emerged from both personal and intellectual crises.

Personally I was depressed that my research and scholarly career were going nowhere. I was successful as a teacher of undergraduates and as a trainer of clinical PhD students. I had a thriving part-time private practice. I was a tenured professor with security, status, and a happy home. Still, I was depressed.

I was reminded of my depression as a graduate student. I had chosen to go to Clark rather than Harvard for my PhD in clinical psychology. Clark didn't work out for me in part because my wife-to-be was back home. So I transferred to Wayne State where I had completed my undergraduate degree.

As part of my training therapy, I remember sharing with my psychodynamic therapist my depression over not having gone to Harvard: "I'll never be able ever to do anything great!" I complained. His only response was, "Why not?"

When I was depressed as a faculty member at the University of Rhode Island, I said to myself, "I should have taken a position at Penn State or the University of Colorado. I'll never be able to do anything great." Then I remember hearing that internalized voice say, "Why not?"

I broke out of my depression by following my passions. I felt that my research and scholarly work were not original. I was testing other people's theories and methods. What I cared most about were two related questions: The first was the Dodo bird question: "Is it true that all have won and all must be given prizes?" Is it true that very diverse theories of therapy produce very common outcomes? Were there common pathways to change that cut across diverse psychotherapies, behavior therapies, cognitive therapies, and chemotherapies?

These questions were related to my second core concern: How could we integrate the field of psychotherapy, which, at that time, was fragmenting into 150 therapies and later into 300 therapies?

I decided that to fulfill my dream of contributing some special science and scholarship I should follow a strategy used by Picasso. This approach was to master some of the masters. Once I could view the therapeutic world from inside alternative systems of therapy, I assumed I would have a more solid foundation for integration and creation.

So I spent a seminar with some special students seeking to abstract the processes of change from major systems of psychotherapy. This search led to my first book, *Systems of Psychotherapy: A Transtheoretical Analysis* (Prochaska, 1979).

Next, Carlo DiClemente, a graduate student at the time, and I decided to assess how frequently people used different processes of change to overcome an addiction. We studied smokers who had participated in professional therapies and compared them with others who had tried to quit on their own. We applied the eclectic set of 10 change processes abstracted from major systems of psychotherapy (Prochaska, 1979). This set included consciousness raising from Freudian therapies, dramatic relief from Gestalt therapy, self-reevaluation from cognitive therapy, self-liberation from existential therapy, helping relationships from Rogerian therapy, contingency management from Skinnerian therapy, counterconditioning from Wolpe's desensitization, and stimulus control.

During interviews, our research participants told us that they used some of the processes such as consciousness raising, dramatic relief, and self-reevaluation much more before they quit. Then they used other processes such as contingency management, counterconditioning, and stimulus control much more after they quit.

Listening with the third ear of trained clinicians, we had the insight that their experiences with struggling to overcome addictions had unfolded through a series of stages of change. We interpreted their experiences to mean that behavior change of chronic conditions involves progress through a series of 6 stages that we labeled as follows:

1. Precontemplation (I'm not sure I have a problem.)
2. Contemplation (I'm not sure I'm ready to give up my problem.)
3. Preparation (I'm not sure what to do.)
4. Action (I'm not sure I can keep doing it.)
5. Maintenance (I'm getting it.)
6. Termination (I am home free; Prochaska & DiClemente, 1982, 1984; Prochaska, Norcross, & DiClemente, 1994)

This discovery of the stages of change reveals that not only can we rely on research to enhance our clinical practice, but we can also rely on our clinical expertise to enrich our research.

The stages of change were not delivered to us as a set of data neatly packaged with their labels on them. The stages emerged from confusing communications of individuals who were sharing their struggles to overcome a powerful addiction. As clinicians we appreciated their struggles and recognized how much they matched what we had often experienced in our struggles to help clients overcome addictions and other chronic conditions.

Precontemplation

We recognized *precontemplation* as the stage in which individuals were not intending to take action on their dangerous or dysfunctional patterns. Individuals could be stuck in this stage because of defensiveness, such as the common clinical view of alcoholism as a disease of denial. Or they could be in this stage out of ignorance, such as the millions of Americans who have no awareness that being a "couch potato" can kill them. Or they could be here because of demoralization, like many obese Americans who have tried too many times and too many treatments to lose weight and have given up on their abilities to change.

With individuals stuck in this stage, we can better understand why they are not ready to take immediate action. But that does not mean they are not ready to change. Applying a process such as consciousness raising can help them become more aware of how they defend their dysfunctional patterns and resist efforts of others to get them to take action. Or they can learn about the multiple risks of their current lifestyle and the benefits that could come from a more active lifestyle. Then there are those who could overcome some of their demoralization by becoming aware of new therapies that offer new hope for chronic conditions like obesity, depression, or schizophrenia.

Contemplation

Once individuals progress to the contemplation stage, they are more aware of the benefits of changing, but often they also become more aware of the costs of changing. The losses, the time, the inertia, the risk of failure, and their changing sense of self can be major costs of change. So while individuals in the contemplation stage are intending to take action in the foreseeable future (usually the next 6 months), they can stay stuck in this stage because of the profound ambivalence they experience. They contemplate the negatives. Should I risk further failure? Am I ready to let go of my favorite substance that has been like a friend during times of stress and emotional distress? Will I feel controlled by others who have been pressuring me and coercing me to change? What will fill the void left by the former pattern of passivity, dependency, or impulsiveness?

In the face of such ambivalence, the desire to leap into immediate action is likely to fail. On the other hand, matching clients stuck in chronic contemplation with clinicians who love to contemplate can be a prescription for interminable therapy. Actually, many of these clients are ready to take the smaller steps involved in progressing toward preparation, so a series of stepwise changes can be made. They can gradually begin to let go of the past, while experiencing some of the benefits of a healthier or happier future. While experimenting with a new way of being or behaving, they can also have a fresh opportunity to resolve their profound ambivalence.

Preparation

People in the preparation stage are ready to take more immediate action. They are convinced that the benefits of changing outweigh the costs. This includes the benefits of therapy outweighing the costs of therapy. They can enter immediately into a therapeutic relationship. They are not experienced by the therapist as defensive or resistant, but rather are seen as highly motivated to move. The risk here is that therapists who cannot be action-oriented and need a lot of time to contemplate can give clients reason to conclude that they are not receiving the help they need.

Looking back to our earlier experiences with Masters and Johnson's approach to sex therapy, it is now clear why most clients were not yet in the preparation stage. In contrast to the extremely motivated Masters and Johnson patients, clinicians in the community take all kinds of clients at all different stages of change. Look at the chaos we can create when we move to action with clients who are not even convinced that there is a problem. Are they likely to have a successful sensual holiday when at least one of them is plagued by profound ambivalence toward the other? What kind of defensiveness or resistance can we create in clients who find they are being pressured or coerced into action without adequate preparation?

How can research help with such potential clinical chaos? We now know we can predict who signs up for therapy, who shows up for therapy, who finishes up therapy, and who ends up better off after therapy (Prochaska, 1996). We can use this scientific knowledge to create therapeutic programs that dramatically increase participation, continuation, progress, and impacts even in relatively brief encounters. Building service on such science can create a future in which behavioral health care can thrive and not only survive.

We will use smoking as a case study in part because there is so much science about smoking and in part because our professional services have failed the vast majority of smokers. Beginning with participation rates, we know that if HMOs offer free action-oriented cessation clinics, only about 1% of eligible smokers participate. We simply cannot make much impact on the number one killer of our time if we only reach 1% of the at-risk population.

So here are two principles for more successful practice: First, if we offer programs geared to or developed for smokers at each stage of change, we can increase participation dramatically. Second, we need to proactively reach out to eligible participants rather than passively wait for them to reach us. When we first proposed to proactively offer stage matched programs to 5,000 smokers, we estimated that 80% would join the program. Our peer reviewers were skeptical, to say the least. We were relieved and pleased when we surpassed our expectations and recruited 82.5% of this population. Since then we have replicated such results with 85% and 90% in two other large clinical trials with over 4,000 smokers in each trial. This is a quantum increase in our ability to help entire populations with behavioral health problems.

Some clinicians will automatically say, "Well that's smoking. What about more traditional mental health problems?" Consider depression, the second-most expensive disorder of our day. Research reveals that the majority of people with clinical depression go undiagnosed, untreated, or mistreated. The same thing is true with alcohol abuse, another costly condition for individuals, families, and health care systems. The fact is, less than 25% of people with diagnosable mental health disorders and less than 10% of people with health behavior disorders ever participate in professional therapies (Veroff, Douvon, & Kulka, 1981).

Consider these figures: Health care costs in the United States are $1 trillion per year and growing. Of that, total pharmaceuticals account for 7%. Behavior accounts for 50% to 60% (Prochaska, 1996).

All of the "top 10" killers of our time are behaviors, such as smoking, alcohol abuse, sedentary life styles, unhealthy diets, obesity, and stress. These are the most common causes of chronic diseases. But the way our health care services are structured, biological medicine treats the symptoms rather than the causes of these conditions. Behavioral health care currently impacts on less than 5% of the total behavioral costs. If we only reach 1% of smokers with professional programs, for example, there is no way we can adequately treat this common killer and reduce the considerable health care costs that accompany this addiction. These figures mean that there are huge unmet needs. That means there are great opportunities for growth. Those who will thrive and not only survive are those who are prepared to meet these needs and respond to the growing opportunities for behavior health.

How did I come to this conclusion? I was told it by leaders of global corporations and national organizations who are paid big bucks to envision the future. They are working to transform their organizations, including pharmaceutical companies, health care product manufacturers, and health care systems, so that behavior change becomes their primary business.

Action

Because we therapists are experts on behavior change, are we leaders in behavior health care? Leaders are those who help create the future. Too many clinicians were socialized to be passive–reactive as professionals— to sit back and wait for patients in acute distress to seek therapeutic services, and then resist. Too many of those clinicians are now acutely distressed because their futures are being created (or destroyed) by others, such as managed-care leaders. Unless we experts also become leaders, we will see the needs and the opportunities met by others.

Below is an example of the impacts we can have by being proactive with our therapeutic programs: Last year the therapeutic programs we created for smokers from our research reached several thousand smokers. This year these programs can reach 100,000 smokers. Next year if our current initiatives progress as planned, we will start to reach 10 million smokers. Such growing impacts are the result of partnering with governments, businesses, and health care systems in North America, Europe, and Asia to help provide some of the best services our behavior change science can support. Health care systems are going to need comparable programs for other costly conditions such as depression and addictions.

Either we create the future for behavior health care through the best that our science and service have to offer, or the future will be created for us. Based on recent experiences, most of us will not be pleased with the future created for us. We can complain and we can resist. We can insist that we are the leaders in mental health and behavior change. But the reality is that the leaders in an industry and in any practice are those who create the future. I cannot imagine how psychotherapy service can create a better future without an intimate partnership with behavior change science.

Once we reach many more people, will we retain them in our therapeutic programs? Dropout from treatment is one of the skeletons in our therapeutic closets. Across 125 studies, the average dropout rate was about 50% (Wierzbicki & Pekarik, 1993). This meta-analysis found few variables to predict dropouts, other than minority status and addictions. In contrast, a series of recent studies by different researchers found that stage-related measures were the best predictors of dropout for alcohol abuse, obesity, smoking, heroin and cocaine abuse, and a diverse set of mental health disorders (Prochaska, 1996). In our study on psychotherapy dropouts across diverse disorders, we were able to predict 93% of premature terminations as judged by therapists (Medeiros & Prochaska, in press). The profile of the 40% of the clients who terminated quickly and prematurely was a profile of patients in the precontemplation stage. The group that finished quickly but appropriately as judged by their therapists had a profile of people in the action stage.

How do I apply such research in practice? If a client entering therapy for help with an addiction is in the action stage, then what therapeutic strategy would I consider? From the literature one promising approach with someone who has recently stopped abusing a substance would be relapse prevention, à la Marlatt and Gordon (1985).

But would relapse prevention make any sense with the 40% of patients entering therapy in the precontemplation stage? Of course not. What strategy might make sense? My approach is to practice dropout prevention. I help clients to become conscious of being in the precontemplation stage. I share with them my concern that they are at risk for dropping out before therapy can make a difference in their lives. I ask them to let me know if they feel pressured or coerced into moving faster than they wish. I encourage them to express what they experience when others are trying to pressure or coerce them into taking action, when they may not even be convinced there is a problem. How do they resist such unreasonable requests from others? How do they defend against such demands?

Here is a dilemma for contemporary clinicians struggling to be sensitive and effective in today's managed care context: We are expected to help the majority of our patients overcome chronic conditions in a relatively small number of sessions. Do we experience ourselves as being pressured or coerced into taking action when we or our clients are not ready?

One way we can demoralize our clients and ourselves is to try to move to action with a population of patients who are not prepared for it. The best data we have suggests that in an HMO population of 20,000 patients across 12 health behaviors (e.g., smoking, diet, and exercise), 40% are in precontemplation, 40% in contemplation, and 20% in preparation. What happens when physicians try to get all their smokers to set a quit date, to take immediate action? The data indicate that they can double the quitting over the next year from 3% to 6%. But can the physicians see the difference between 3% and 6%, or will they still see 94% failure rates?

What is the first reason physicians do not want to do counseling? Some will guess time, and others will guess money, which are the second and third reasons. The number-one reason is that two thirds of physicians believe that their patients either cannot or will not change their behavior (Orleans, 1993). When change equals action we can become demoralized by the action paradigm, because only a minority of members at-risk populations are prepared to take action. So why should physicians waste their valuable time if 94% of patients will fail?

If change equals progress through the stages, then we can assess and see success for the majority of our patient population. Over 4,000 health professionals in the National Health Service in England have been trained in the stage model for proactively counseling all of their patients with alcohol, drug, diet, exercise, and smoking problems. The first feedback from England is a marked increase in morale, since the professionals can see success with most of their clients. Furthermore, they have skills to match the needs of clients at every stage and not just of those who are ready to take action.

In time-effective therapy, we need to set realistic goals for each session. Our goal is to try to help each client get unstuck and start to progress toward the next stage. Our data suggest that if we help people progress one stage in 1 month, we double the chances that they will take effective action in the next 6 months. If they progress two stages, we quadruple the chances.

If clients are progressing, they can take a break from therapy. We can encourage them to progress on their own using bibliotherapy, such as our book *Changing for Good* (Prochaska et al., 1994), or using individualized computer feedback reports. If they progress all the way to action, maintenance, and termination on their own, that's terrific. They have become much better experts at change and can have the awareness and skills to apply these principles to other problems that may emerge.

On the other hand, if they get stuck in a stage, they know they can call on us for further assistance. In some of our programs we encourage them to think of us as the American Automobile Association of behavior change. Call on us if you get stuck. Or come by for consultation and guides for more proven pathways to change.

CONCLUSION

Here is how I would summarize what I see for the future based on the science and service I have experienced. Current organizations will be transformed from illness services to health services. They will shift from an almost exclusive reliance on cutting costs to a large investment in preventing costs. This can only happen if we have behavioral health services that can impact on the chronic lifestyle conditions that are the most common causes of chronic disease, premature death, and high-cost health care for the symptoms of these diseases. These chronic lifestyle conditions include behaviors that have been the domain of mental health, such as alcohol abuse, addictions, depression, obesity, stress, and social isolation. But they also include behaviors from the rest of health, such as healthy diets, regular exercise, and smoking cessation.

Our health care systems, including the National Institutes of Health, will be driven first and foremost by behavior science and secondarily by biological science. Behavior change will become the primary business not only for health care systems but also for most organizations that threaten to be overwhelmed by stress and distress lest we help the majority of people learn how to master the complexities of change more effectively, efficiently, and humanely.

There will be huge opportunities for expert change agents who break out of the box and recognize that their expertise is needed for all of health and not just mental health. Their change expertise is needed for entire populations and not just for individual clients. One consulting company is currently recruiting 15,000 additional change management experts with starting salaries of $115,000 for recent MAs.

Those change agents who are prepared to create the future will be those trained to be proactive, to be preventative, to be population based, to apply interactive technologies as well as interpersonal skills, and to be at the cutting edge of science and services that respond to the huge current needs of our time. Every major science has ultimately succeeded by creating at least one major industry. Psychotherapy is best positioned to be the science and the service that can best understand and solve the dynamics and complexities of change.

Let me close with a story about the process of writing this chapter. One of the reviewers kept writing, "Tell Prochaska to preach less and share more about himself." Here is something else I should share about myself. When I first started college, I was on a Presbyterian scholarship to become a preacher. I struggled with my major, believing that if I stayed with a more subjective discipline like English I would be more likely to hold on to my religion than if I majored in a more objective science like psychology.

What I have come to learn is that scientists at their best, like clinicians at their best, care passionately about the problems with which they are confronted. Scientists need not be objective; only science needs to be objective. So if I preach in this chapter about how my science influenced my service, it is because I am passionate about our search for a better future for our clients, our communities, and ourselves.

REFERENCES

Marlatt, G. A., & Gordon, J. R. (Eds.). (1985). *Relapse prevention: Maintenance strategies in addictive behavior change*. New York: Guilford Press.

Masters, W., & Johnson, V. (1970). *Human sexual inadequacy*. Boston: Little, Brown.

Medeiros, M. E., & Prochaska, J. M. (in press). Predicting termination and continuation status in psychotherapy using the Transtheoretical Model. *Journal of Integrative Psychotherapy*.

Orleans, C. T. (1993). Treating nicotine dependence. In C. T. Orleans & J. Slade (Eds.), *Nicotine addictive: Principles and management* (pp. 145–161). New York: Oxford University Press.

Prochaska, J. O. (1979). *Systems of psychotherapy: A transtheoretical analysis* (2nd ed.). Pacific Grove, CA: Brooks/Cole.

Prochaska, J. O. (1996). A revolution in health promotion. In R. S. Resnick & R. H. Rozensky (Eds.), *Health psychology through the life span* (pp. 361–376). Washington, DC: American Psychological Association.

Prochaska, J. O., & DiClemente, C. C. (1982). Transtheoretical therapy: Toward a more integrative model of change. *Psychotherapy, 19*, 276–288.

Prochaska, J. O., & DiClemente, C. C. (1984). *The transtheoretical approach: Crossing the traditional boundaries of therapy*. Melbourne, FL: Krieger.

Prochaska, J. O., Norcross, J. C., & DiClemente, C. C. (1994). *Changing for good*. New York: Morrow.

Veroff, J. E., Douvon, R., & Kulka, A. (1981). *Mental health in America*. New York: Basic Books.

Wierzbicki, M., & Pekarik, G. (1993). A meta-analysis of psychotherapy dropout. *Professional Psychology: Research and Practice, 29*, 190–195.

13

INTEGRATING RESEARCH AND PRACTICE: WHAT HAVE WE LEARNED?

LEIGH McCULLOUGH AND STEPHEN SOLDZ

As we read and reread the contributions to this book, we were struck by both the value of their unique contributions and the commonalities among chapters. Here we draw out some of the themes that we found common to several contributions. The elaboration of these themes allows us to assess the state of the research–practice relationship, as seen through the eyes of these scientist–practitioners. In several places we have taken the liberty to go beyond the individual contributions to draw conclusions and make policy recommendations that may not be endorsed by all the authors. In so doing, we hope to encourage discussion regarding ways to improve mutual understanding and collaboration between practitioners and researchers.

Many of the authors in this book gave us feedback on earlier versions of this chapter. We thank them for their help. We, of course, maintain responsibility for all opinions expressed.

253

RECOMMENDATIONS FOR COLLABORATION BETWEEN PRACTICE AND RESEARCH

In reviewing the many and diverse chapters of this book, the contributing authors have offered many excellent suggestions. In the conclusion of this chapter, we wish to compile the main recommendations for improving relations between research and practice. These recommendations include the following:

1. There is a need for improvement in training.
2. Collaboration and communication between researchers and practitioners need to improve.
3. Researchers and practitioners need to collaborate in assessing outcomes.
4. There is a need for improved process research and single-case design.
5. Theory, qualitative analysis, and transtheoretical macroprocesses can play a bridging role in integrating research and practice.
6. Scientist–practitioners need to recognize the important role that passion plays in both the best research and the best practice.

IMPROVEMENT IN TRAINING: THE VIABILITY OF THE SCIENTIST–PRACTITIONER MODEL

The professional contributions of the scientist–practitioners who authored this book demonstrate vividly the value of having professionals equally at home in the worlds of research and practice. The work of each remains clinically relevant while making significant contributions to the scientific understanding of the nature of psychotherapy. Whatever the final decisions on the balance of practical and research training in various graduate programs, we are convinced that there is great value to having a group of professionals who are at home in both worlds. To better develop these professionals, modifications in graduate training programs to increase respect for the conflicting demands of practice and research are called for.

However, as noted in the Addis and Anderson accounts of their graduate training, many "scientifically oriented" programs implicitly devalue clinical experience as a distraction from the research training that constitutes their raison d'etre. As dramatically depicted by Anderson, many programs are beset by a contradiction: On one hand, the vast majority of graduate students become practitioners. On the other, their mentors often have intense disdain for practice, and all too often the graduate school dictum is "go into research or go to hell."

One of the strongest proponents in this volume for improved training is Addis. He advocates an approach to the student process that is not from an "idealized ultimate scientist–practitioner" stance, but rather a realistic appraisal of the difficulty of integrating research and practice. He discusses the value of providing role models that successfully bridge both worlds, such as the authors represented here. Addis feels that access to such models will help students become aware of attainable integration and also help deter dichotomization. Perhaps role models can even help deter the split between clinicicans and researchers all too common among the faculty in graduate programs.

Both McCullough and Goldfried point out the potential of research-based tools contributing to a deepening of clinical training. Psychotherapy transcripts, audiotapes, and videotapes, systematically examined, can be invaluable tools for training therapists in clinical skills while simultaneously fostering a deepening of the critical thinking more commonly associated with research training. Furthermore, greater attention to process research, which often has greater immediate clinical relevance than do other types of clinical research, could build bridges between practice and research even for the majority of students ultimately aiming at a clinical career. Such systematic process examination, combined with more careful attention to the measurement of outcomes, could increase practitioners' understanding of, and respect for, clinical research.

In developing new training models, it is important to remember that not all students will become active researchers, and a training system built on that assumption will lead to frequent disappointment. What we should strive for in graduate training is mutual understanding and respect, while accepting that the scientist–practitioner's career path is not for everyone.

Although this discussion has perhaps its greatest immediate salience in professional psychology graduate programs, it is also relevant to related fields struggling with the research–practice relationship. Both social work and nursing, for example, are increasingly emphasizing research training in their graduate programs. These fields may thus derive the lesson from the experience of psychology that systematic attention needs to be given to ways of building mutual understanding and respect between research and practice if the painful splits occurring in psychology are to be avoided.

BETTER COLLABORATION BETWEEN RESEARCHERS AND PRACTITIONERS

Goldfried points out that there are times when both practitioners and researchers are deluding themselves in thinking that they alone will advance the field. But, as he emphasizes, both groups very much need each other. Either we will view ourselves as collaborators, or we will wind up adversaries. Which of those two relationships is going to be the most constructive and lead to the most productive activity? "If one views the split between clinicians and researchers from outside the entire system, it becomes more evident that both groups are deluding themselves in thinking that they alone will advance the field" (Goldfried & Padawer, 1982, p. 33).

However, as we discussed in the introduction, there are serious cognitive and stylistic differences between research and clinical practice that interfere with collaboration. Nonetheless, the primary message of this work is that these differences can be reduced, both within individuals and among researchers and therapists as groups. The chapters in this book demonstrate many ways in which these obstacles can be overcome. Anderson, for example, stresses the need for communication, humility, patience, and respect for the differing traditions, preoccupations, modes of thought, and communication styles characteristic of these two endeavors. He emphasizes that researchers need practitioners, who are greatly underused in the research process. Soldz supplements this message by emphasizing the importance of the patience and respect that arises from joint work on mutually important projects. It is through collaboration, they argue, that improved relations between these two groups will be developed.

Collaboration between researchers and practitioners can further be facilitated by the National Institutes of Health (NIH) and other major funding agencies. For example, many of the substance abuse treatment studies in which Soldz has been involved in recent years have included service provider advisory groups to help researchers design the studies, develop research instruments, interpret the findings, and give information back to the practitioner communities that were so generous in facilitating the research. Funding sources, such as NIH, could encourage such collaborative processes by including them in requests for proposals or by giving points for their inclusion in grant reviews. Notable is the fact that the federal Substance Abuse and Mental Health Services Administration already does this for many of the studies they fund. Researchers might also be encouraged to have active clinicians involved in their research projects from conceptualization through publication. Similarly, practicing clinicians might be included on grant committees.

BETTER COMMUNICATION BETWEEN RESEARCHERS AND PRACTITIONERS

Neimeyer (chapter 7, this volume) laments the difficulties of communication exemplified by the very different "languages" used in research and clinical endeavors. "Like a speaker of both Spanish and English, I am prone to take up one or the other in different conversational contexts, drawing on the somewhat different resources of each 'language' to envision and navigate the world of psychotherapy a bit differently. . . . Neither represents a complete language, . . . neither can claim superiority to the other, and . . . both are evolving" (p. 144).

Anderson and others note that researchers do not often read practitioner journals or attend practitioner conferences, nor are clinicians likely to read research journals. He recommends, therefore, that researchers should proceed from journal publication to clinical publication. Practitioners, after all, have often complained of the impenetrability and lack of utility of research publications.

In the development of improved vehicles for communication, attention should be paid to the different needs and traditions of writings aimed at researchers versus practitioners. For example, if researchers expect therapists to pay attention to what they have to say, it would behoove the researchers to pay respectful attention to the issues, modes of thinking, and concerns of clinicians. In addition to helping researchers better to understand clinical practice, it is further necessary that the research community become more aware of practical issues that surround the practice of psychotherapy, such as concerns about the impact of managed care and the declining length of treatment.

The new mechanisms of communication between practitioners and researchers that are needed may include "clinically oriented publications" such as the new journals described by Goldfried, books of well-studied transcripts such as those described by McCullough, clinical manuals as developed by Elliott, research newsletters for clinicians, clinical briefings for researchers, new forms of collaborative conferences and case conferences, and so forth. Experimentation is needed—starting with the development of multiple channels of communication—to determine which mechanisms are most appropriate for communicating what information to particular audiences. Research from the domains of communication studies and adult development may prove useful here. Perhaps, also, the creation of sophisticated psychological "science writers" could also help bridge the communication gap.

NEED FOR COLLABORATION IN TREATMENT EVALUATION AND ASSESSING OUTCOMES

The assessment of the outcomes of clinical interventions is important, both to respond to the demands for accountability characteristic of the current health care climate and to guide attempts to provide improved services (e.g., the development of improved therapies). The measurement of outcomes provides numerous opportunities for collaboration between researchers and practitioners. Members of the two groups can cooperate in the development of new outcome measures, leading to more user-friendly measures, as advocated by Anderson, for example. Such collaborations are simultaneously likely to have the positive effects discussed by Soldz, and to help ensure that the resultant measures are clinically relevant as well as psychometrically sound.

The field could benefit from the development of a widely used omnibus instrument such as described in chapter 6. But in lieu of a single instrument, many specific measures currently exist. Goldfried recommends that clinicians be encouraged to use existing tools that they are familiar and comfortable with. Such tools include the Beck Depression Inventory, the Role Construct Repertory Grid, the Minnesota Multiphasic Personality Inventory, the Structural Analysis of Social Behavior, or target complaint ratings. The Inventory of Interpersonal Problems, which assesses a range of interpersonal presenting problems of psychotherapy patients, is another good example here (Horowitz, Rosenberg, Bauer, Ureno, & Villasenor, 1988). These measures, obtained at intervals during treatment, can be a great way to provide feedback about the effectiveness of treatment.

The Policy Makers

There is a whole constituency or group of stakeholders that has not been addressed in this discussion: the policy makers. They range from federal and state bureaucrats to payers (including managed care companies, employers, insurance officials, etc.). These groups are having a profound influence on practice in the field of psychotherapy, and yet they are often ignored by the research world and in the discussions of the relationship of research and practice. These forces are moving rapidly and strongly. Already the nature of psychotherapy and other psychosocial treatments has been transformed through their influence. The calls for accountability and periodic outcome measurements are radically changing the terms of the debate in a way that is almost invisible to a reader of any of the major research journals in the field.

For example, in Massachusetts, the main trade association for the large mental health clinics has adopted an outcome measurements initiative, whereby all patients at their participating clinics (numbering in many thousands a year) will be receiving a standardized intake and periodic outcome measurement, partly as a response to the influence of Medicaid managed care in this state. As another example, federal initiatives are under way to encourage all states to develop outcomes monitoring systems for publicly funded substance abuse treatment. These types of initiatives are growing rapidly, much more rapidly than the influence of traditional researchers. Thus research is being forced into the clinical realm in a way that often is carried out by people—such as program evaluators, health services researchers, economists, and for-profit companies selling outcomes instruments—who are different from traditional psychotherapy researchers and triggered by different issues and arising out of different traditions.

Note that only a few of the authors have devoted much attention to these issues. The image of therapy and practice that most of us have, is that of the traditional private practice clinician, a model that is rapidly diminishing, either through the transformation of therapists becoming salaried employees, or the new model of quasi-employment of people on managed care panels where significant decision making is being done by officials of managed care companies, transforming what are nominal private practitioners into virtual employees. Although there is considerable uncertainty regarding the future of managed care in particular, it seems likely that in the future we will continue to see an evolution toward organized systems of care of one type or another. Very few of our contributors, including ourselves, seem to acknowledge the public sector practice of therapy or the trends just described that may herald the decline of the private practitioner as the primary provider of psychotherapy. As pointed out by Benjamin, however, much of the managed care provision of "treatment" amounts to nothing more than a 6-session assessment and has little to do with therapy at all. Despite whatever transformations occur in the way psychotherapy is delivered, there does remain and will remain the need to find effective ways to heal human suffering. Private practice, at least for some, may remain because it may be that the only way patients can obtain a significant period of treatment is to pay directly for the service.

In any case, as demonstrated by the contributors to this book, psychotherapy research, through elucidating the nature and processes of change, has great potential to contribute to the development of more effective treatments. Greater efforts are needed, however, to figure out how it can be incorporated into the evolving structures of health care delivery. The research on short-term psychotherapy, for example, has been translated into procedures and methods that can be used in a managed care setting, but research sometimes ends up accomplishing far less than anticipated.

Prochaska's chapter suggests a model for using research knowledge in a forceful and far-reaching way to guide new forms of practice. To make a strong impact on large numbers of people, he is in favor of implementing research-based systems through programs involving government, business, and health care. Prochaska says clinicians and researchers together need to be proactive to create the future of behavioral health care, or the future will be created for us. He sees the future (based on science and service) in which organizations will be transformed from illness services to health services, shifting from an almost exclusive reliance on cutting costs to a large investment in preventing costs. He even envisions "change management experts"—proactive, preventative, and population-based—applying interactive technologies as well as interpersonal skills to continue to be at the cutting edge.

Empirically Supported Treatments

Despite their potential benefits, an emphasis on the potential limitations of empirically supported treatments (ESTs) is apparent in most of the chapters in this book. Most of the authors, researchers all, appear to be at least as troubled about the dangers of ESTs as straitjackets for the field as they are pleased by their potential benefits. Benjamin, for example, argues strongly that the EST approach may be "penny-wise and pound-foolish" and may result in depriving us of long-term therapies so needed for the more severe (notably personality) disorders. Goldfried emphasizes that clinical work varies greatly, while research protocols do not. Anderson raises the point that a focus on ESTs often distracts from the primarily interpersonal nature of psychotherapy. Dahlbender and Kaechele complement Anderson's arguments with a focus on what they see as some of the political aspects of the EST movement. Addis, who, among our authors is most sympathetic to the intent toward identifying and training in ESTs, still has reservations regarding the degree to which the research leading to identification of ESTs is applicable to the majority of patients seen in real-world clinical settings.

There are several additional issues only tangentially raised in the chapters in this book but that are crucial nonetheless. Underlying much of the critique of ESTs is that few of these "empirically supported treatments" have actually been shown to be more effective than more common alternative treatments. At the current state of knowledge, that a treatment is not on the approved list is far from evidence that the approach is ineffective.

A further concern with ESTs as practice standards is how new, more effective therapies will be developed if therapists are restricted in their experimentation. Unlike pharmacology, where the enormous profits that accrue to the developers of new drugs motivate drug companies to spend hundreds of millions of dollars in research and development, in psychotherapy, as with food supplements, there is no funding source that will underwrite any such large-scale development efforts. Mandatory practice standards thus threaten the development of new treatments. Such issues will have to be resolved prior to wide-scale adaptation of ESTs or other forms of binding practice guidelines. Nonetheless, as noted, there are increasing trends toward accountability and evidence-based or science-based practice. Where the proper balance lies between accountability and clinical intuition and experimentation is far from clear. As the struggles of our authors suggest, this issue will remain with us for quite a while.

David Winter points to what may be the best solution given the current extent of our knowledge. He notes that although the British National Health Service is interested in identifying therapeutic approaches for which there is clear evidence of efficacy, they caution against an "overprescriptive, cookbook approach," which might "stifle innovations" in therapy. The solution of the National Health Service was not to limit reimbursement to therapies that have empirical validation, but rather to insist that those therapies provided must be willing to subject themselves to research evaluation (Roth, Fonagy, & Parry, 1996). In other words, if proponents of a therapy model are not willing to cooperate in evaluation, the model should be out of the game.

IMPROVED PROCESS RESEARCH AND SINGLE-CASE DESIGNS

Abundant clinical trials have demonstrated *that* psychotherapy works, but we are only beginning to understand *how* it works, as well as for whom and under what conditions. One of the most promising ways we have of answering the pressing questions of patient-specific treatment is through controlled, intensively recorded and studied, single-case experimental designs. Optimally we might envision in the coming decades a worldwide accumulation of hundreds or even thousands of well-executed, single-case studies (following a standardized format) to begin to discern specific mechanisms of change.

A number of authors, including Goldfried, McCullough, and Elliott (see chapters 1, 2, and 6, this volume, respectively), advocate that therapists and clients explore the value of audio, video, or transcribed recording of treatment. Video recording is now frequently done in surgery and in athletic coaching. Close scrutiny of the session allows the therapist, like a football coach, to understand how important events were actually sequenced. Furthermore, this allows the therapist as well as researchers to assimilate therapy content that is often too complex, too fast-paced, and too emotion laden to grasp fully while it is ongoing.

Recording of the therapy process can provide the necessary behavioral grounding so that comparisons among treatments can be made even decades from now. Inevitably, methods will change, and treatments will change, but the frequency, intensity, and duration of maladaptive behavior and treatment interventions (if carefully documented) can be compared across time.

For many psychotherapy researchers, the ultimate goal of research is to improve actual therapeutic practice. Our authors provide illustrations of several ways such goals can be achieved. Many, for example, modified their own therapy practices as a result of their research findings. Some went so far as to develop treatment manuals in order to communicate their deepened understanding of the clinical process. Others view the research–

practice relationship as a necessary, yet never quite harmonious and always difficult, attempt at cross-fertilization between those with different tastes, styles, and agendas.

Both Goldfried and McCullough tell stories of trying to conduct a live demonstration to colleagues of a pure therapy technique and finding they could not adequately address the needs of the patients they were treating by rigidly adhering to one model. Goldfried describes how his colleagues encouraged him to "come out" from behind his one-way mirror demonstration, and follow his clinical intuition rather than a treatment manual. Both Goldfried and McCullough went on to develop new forms of therapy to encompass their clinical impasses.

Many of the contributors are implicitly adopting a craft model in which psychotherapy is seen as a skilled endeavor, based on slowly acquired knowledge and understanding and requiring adaptation to the unique characteristics of the material—in this case—the patient and the relationship, that perhaps may never flow on a one-to-one basis from scientific findings, but nevertheless, would be enriched and improved through scientific understanding. Research can inform through providing a skeptical framework for challenging cherished beliefs, examining the actual outcomes of therapeutic activity, and suggesting new perspectives on change processes. At the same time, researchers need to remain ever mindful that, in the minds of numerous clinicians, many common research strategies appear to simplify the complexity of artful interaction almost to the point of absurdity.

The authors of this book drive home the point that the relationship of research to practice is not one way. They emphasize that research on psychotherapy has a tremendous amount to learn from those who practice it. The consensus of most is that clinical work serves, at a minimum, as an arena for a discovery process—and research as a refinement, if not a radical revision—of that discovery. Practice is "search." Ultimately, most of the authors come down on the side of a collaborative model, whereby a greater whole can be forged from the cooperation of researchers and practitioners, and from the researcher and practitioner within each of us.

Many of the authors address the theme of the human relationship as at the core of good therapy of whatever persuasion. They thus argue that clinicians should remain free to follow their intuition, and that researchers should follow, humbly and respectfully, behind those on the front lines who are interacting under fluid circumstances with ever-changing patients.

THE BRIDGING ROLE OF QUALITATIVE ANALYSIS, TRANSTHEORETICAL CHANGE PROCESSES, AND THEORY BUILDING

One of the dilemmas of psychotherapy research is whether to investigate a particular model of therapy when the conclusions may only be relevant to practitioners of that particular model (and we have, of course, hundreds of different models). An alternative is to try to identify generic change processes that are transtheoretical.

There is far less research out there than clinical decisions to be made. It takes decades to do clinical trials, and it takes years to do process studies. Therefore, we have thousands of clinical decisions, for which there exists only a handful of research findings. So it is at the macrolevel that research is likely to have a broader impact. From a wide-range perspective, the more encompassing or inclusive our research hypotheses, the more useful they are going to be for clinical work. So, perhaps to make research more conversant or more helpful to clinical work, we need to find the common factors that all can recognize.

Although many of our authors have developed their own models of therapy, they also have used qualitative analysis to describe many generic processes within these models. We briefly summarize the processes they have identified here. Goldfried studied the clinical process at a level of abstraction somewhere between that of theory and technique to find common principles that promote change, such as (a) client expectations, (b) therapeutic alliance, (c) alternate ways of understanding, which sets the stage for (d) corrective experience. Goldfried uses these common principles as starting points and then returns to clinical observation to study them further.

In her generic theory, Benjamin identified five processes: (a) agree to fight problem, (b) learn to recognize problem and reasons for it, (c) block maladaptive patterns, (d) enable will to change, and (e) learn new patterns. Neimeyer and Winter used the overarching conceptual scaffolding of personal construct theory and its emphasis on personal–meaning–making as the essential component of therapy to guide their research. McCullough applies the well-studied behavioral principles of exposure and response prevention to "desensitize" conflicted feelings in psychodynamic treatment. In her model, the responses to be prevented are the maladaptive defensive behaviors. Exposure is to feared inner experience such as grief or anger, and later to appropriate expression of those feelings interpersonally.

Shiang adapted Beutler and Clarkin's Systematic Treatment Selection by incorporating cultural considerations to guide her clinical work because these principles help order the overwhelming amount of information from the client and help guide her clinical thinking. Her modifications of these processes include the following four areas: (a) client variables, including culture; (b) client–therapist relationship and cultural match; (c) treatment contexts; and (d) psychotherapeutic strategies and procedures.

Prochaska has six identified stages of changes that indicate readiness for psychotherapy: (1) precontemplation (it's not my problem); (2) contemplation (I'm not sure I'm ready to give up my problem); (3) preparation

(I'm not sure what to do); (4) action (I'm not sure I can keep doing it); (5) maintenance (I'm getting it), and (6) termination (I'm home free).

Elliott's research-derived principles include the following six elements: (a) connect with and respect the client, (b) offer a warm empathic relationship, (c) facilitate client collaboration, (d) facilitate optimal client processing or experiencing, (e) foster client growth and self-determination, and (f) facilitate completion of specific therapeutic tasks.

We can see much overlap in these generic processes. More than one author has noted the importance of attention to the following elements: (a) client and therapist factors, (b) therapeutic connection or alliance, (c) the blocking or preventing of maladaptive processes, (d) corrective experience, and (e) maintenance of gains. Furthermore, these common factors are easy to understand and to teach to clinicians.

Studying these broad-reaching transtheoretical processes appears to be a way to get the most mileage out of research efforts that will have the greatest relevance to practicing clinicians. The identification of major change processes also is of utility for theory building, which is addressed below.

Theory Building in Research–Practice Collaboration

Scientific research always has a strong relationship with theories and theory building. Theories are, to varying degrees, formalizations of the current understanding of the causal mechanisms involved in a domain. Theories are thus one of the main mechanisms whereby understanding can be communicated between researchers and practitioners.

Clinicians are often fond of theories because they communicate ideas about what phenomena a therapist should pay attention to and contain ideas about what processes are likely to facilitate change. Thus, behavioral theories attract the clinician's attention to the client's repetitive behavioral patterns and to the possible reinforcers in the environment, while cognitive theories focus attention on the thinking processes of the client. Many schools of therapy are based on a particular theoretical system, and clinical changes are often expressed in theoretical terms.

Given that both researchers and clinicians are interested in theories and theory development, theory construction and elaboration constitutes a potential important common ground between practitioners and researchers. In many instances, clinicians will find research results more comprehensible if those results are expressed in theoretical terms rather than as isolated empirical findings. Similarly, as clinical intuitions become codified in theories, the theories become more amenable to comprehension, resulting in testing and refinement by way of research practice. Thus, at a minimum, theories constitute a possible common language between therapists and researchers. The testing and refinement of theories may also constitute a fertile area for creative and mutually beneficial collaboration between researchers and practitioners.

The field is, in the language of Kuhn (1977), in a *preparadigmatic* state in which there are many competing theories, with no consensus in the field as to the most fertile approach to pursue. Each of these competing theories attempts to express part of the truth about human problematic functioning and ways of changing that functioning. Strong collaboration between researchers and clinicians in developing and refining theories may help the field to move to the next stage.

Improved theories can be used by therapists to guide therapeutic practices. Theories may also offer a more flexible way to communicate research-based conceptualizations of desirable practice than do more rigid manual-based approaches.

Several of our authors illustrate this process. Elliott, for example, changed his theoretical orientation at least partially based on his research findings, moving to a more experiential conceptualization of the therapeutic change process. Prochaska created a new theory of change processes and of stages of readiness for change; the resulting theory has been applied by numerous clinicians and program developers in a wide range of domains. Similarly, Benjamin has combined her extensive clinical experience with her understanding of many contemporary strands of research to try to develop a "generic theory" that not only might encompass both research and practice but also guide and possibly improve therapeutic practice for personality disorders. McCullough took the traditional Freudian conflict model and reinterpreted it in learning theory and affect theory terms.

Thus, our recommendation, implicit in several of the chapters, is that more explicit attention be given to theory development and propagation as an area for fertile collaboration between therapists and researchers. The development of better, more clinically rich and empirically supported theories is likely to contribute to improved clinical practice.

Uniformity Myth of Research–Practice Integration

In working on this volume, we glimpsed indications of a "uniformity myth" that many of our authors appear to be challenging: that clinical practice should be based in some uniform or general way on research. Such a myth obscures the nature of the research–practice relationship in that not all research is the same. There is much variability in psychotherapy research, including traditional randomized clinical trials (RCTs) of outcomes, efficacy studies of treatments in real-world settings, development of assessment instruments, many varieties of process research, from idiosyncratic microprocesses to common factors or macroprocesses, as well as program evaluation and health services research. Thus, there cannot be any single research–practice relationship. Although this conclusion may seem obvious, much of the discussion of the topic seems to assume that all research is of one sort, often randomized clinical trials. The authors discuss the research–practice relationship, as if an argument for the lack of utility of RCTs is an argument for the lack of utility of research in general. Although many of our authors have engaged in RCTs at various stages of their research programs, none have conceived of research as remotely synonymous with this particular research design. By the accidents of selection (many of the contributors we solicited for the book declined due to other commitments), the book does not contain contributions by any of the foremost proponents of RCTs, who have recently become involved with the movement to identify and promote empirically supported treatments (Beutler, 1998; Chambless, 1996; Chambless & Hollon, 1998; Kendall & Chambless, 1998).[1]

It is therefore essential to keep in mind what type of research we are referring to. When considering integration of research and practice, we might specify, for example, type of research, conditions, and patients. And, how well the research matches or replicates the actual process of therapy and if the process generalizes to other treatments.

ACCEPTANCE OF PASSION IN SCIENCE AND PRACTICE

One of the recurring themes among our authors was the passion, for both science and clinical practice, that drives researchers and therapists. This passion is an essential component of both high-quality science and excellent clinical practice. In each domain, the passion taps rational and intuitive cognitive processes. Prochaska, for example, concluded his chapter with a spirited account of the passion driving him. McCullough quoted Liam Hudson, who argued that *bias* (his term for passion) is an essential component of the research process. Goldfried told of Neal Miller, who confessed to being "quite free wheeling and intuitive" in following hunches, varying procedures, trying out wild ideas, and taking shortcuts in designing a study. Miller first convinced himself and then tried to convince his colleagues. Goldfried himself addressed the "artistry" and intuition that is necessary in the development of hypotheses.

In Benjamin's chapter, passion shines through in her striving to maintain the highest standards for her clinical practice. Soldz, in turn, expresses passion about the need for researchers and practitioners to collaborate.

Passion, by its nature, is never entirely rational. Thus, someone else's passion very well may be perceived by those who disagree as wrong-headed bias. Nonetheless, passion will never disappear from either research or practice. In fact, its presence in both domains is another common element. If

---

[1] See the special section by Kendall and Chambless (1998).

researchers and therapists acknowledge and learn to value each other's passion, greater mutual respect might result, respect that could only further the collaborations we seek to foster. Thus, our final recommendation in assisting collaboration between research and practice is for the recognition that others' passions are probably not that different from one's own.

REFERENCES

Beutler, L. E. (1998). Identifying empirically supported treatments: What if we didn't? *Journal of Consulting and Clinical Psychology, 66,* 113–120.

Chambless, D. L. (1996). In defense of dissemination of empirically validated psychological interventions. *Clinical Psychology: Science and Practice, 3,* 230–235.

Chambless, D. L., & Hollon, S. D. (1998). Defining empirically supported therapies. *Journal of Consulting and Clinical Psychology, 66,* 7–18.

Goldfried, M. R., & Padawer, W. (1982). Current status and future directions in psychotherapy. In M. R. Goldfried (Ed.), *Converging themes in psychotherapy: Trends in psychodynamic, humanistic, and behavioral practice* (pp. 3–49). New York: Springer.

Horowitz, L. M., Rosenberg, S. E., Bauer, B. A., Ureno, G., & Villasenor, V. S. (1988). Inventory of Interpersonal Problems: Psychometric properties and clinical applications. *Journal of Consulting and Clinical Psychology, 56,* 885–892.

Kendall, P. C., & Chambless, D. L. (Eds.). (1998). Empirically supported psychology therapies [Special section]. *Journal of Consulting and Clinical Psychology, 66,* 3–167.

Kuhn, T. (1977). *The structure of scientific revolutions* (rev. ed.). Chicago: University of Chicago Press.

Roth, A., Fonagy, P., & Parry, G. (1996). Psychotherapy research, funding, and evidence-based practice. In A. Roth & P. Fonagy (Eds.), *What works for whom? A critical review of psychotherapy research,* (pp. 37–56). New York: Guilford Press.

AUTHOR INDEX

SUBJECT INDEX

relevance of outcome research, 27–29

reliance on empirical support, 58–60

research knowledge as support for therapist, 56–57, 162

research practice in historical development of, 153

sensitivity of research to client–therapist interaction, 140–141

shaping of student attitudes toward, 53–55

significance of client personal style, 69–71

significance of clinician personal style, 69, 78

significance of relational qualities, 87

as source of research questions, 21, 24

status of, in psychology training, 62, 90

testable implementation of change theory, 23–24

theory as support for therapist, 128

transtheoretical commonalities, 23, 263–264

as unique research setting, 158–159

use of coding systems for analysis of clinical material, 26–27, 103–104

use of research procedures in, 42

use of silence, 115

use of video recordings for analysis of clinical material, 102–104

wasted therapy time, 113, 114

Clinical significance, concept of, 161–162

Clinician factors

confidence, 58–60

cultural considerations, 189–192

as obstacle to integration, 85, 89–90, 197–198, 235

in success of therapy, 20

treatment attitudes, 69

Coding system of therapeutic focus (CSTF), 26–27

Cognitive–behavioral intervention

facilitating change in client awareness, 24–25

limitations of research knowledge, 19–20

research knowledge as support for therapist, 56–57

therapeutic alliance in, 25

Cognitive style

compartmentalization of clinical-research perspectives, 128–129

research vs. practice, 95, 125–126, 170–171

systemic thinking, 170

Cognitive therapy, 18

brief adaptive psychotherapy, 106–107

conceptual basis, 135–136

emergence of, 129

outcome studies, 130–137

personal construct therapy with, 132

repertory grid measures, 132

therapeutic alliance in, 25–26

therapeutic change mechanisms in, 25–26

vs. short-term dynamic psychotherapy, 106–107, 111–112

Collaboration, researcher–practitioner, 6, 29, 237–238, 255–256, 266–267

treatment evaluation, 257–258

Collectivism, as cultural value, 175

Communication between researchers and practitioners

differences in style, 7, 8

media for, 89, 257

opportunities for improving, 256–257

session transcripts and, 118

Comprehensive process analysis, 36

Conditioned avoidance, 19

Confrontive therapy approach, 106–109

Constructivist thinking

cognitive therapy and, 135

construction of meaning in therapy, 142

epistemology, 124, 135

sexual abuse treatment, 137–141

Content analysis, 36

categorization of patient–therapist interaction, 103–104

facilitating awareness in therapy, 25–26

therapeutic alliance, 26

therapeutic change mechanisms, 26–27

Contextual factors, 92, 127–128

implications for assessment, 177, 178

Contingency management, 57

Corrective experience, 23

Creativity, 20

Crisis intervention, 57, 124–127

CSTF. *See* Coding system of therapeutic focus
Cultural beliefs and adaptation profile, 177–178
Cultural factors
 adaptation, 171
 assessment of, 176, 177–181
 case example, 179–181, 184–186
 in childhood education, 169
 Chinese culture, 187–188
 in client's problem presentation, 168
 in clinical conceptualizations, 172–173
 definition, 173
 in diagnosis, 185–186
 implications for clinical practice, 168
 implications for research, 168
 implications for therapeutic alliance, 168, 178–179
 individualistic–collectivistic values, 175
 in instrumental action, 173–175
 psychological significance, 171–172, 173
 in self concept, 175–176
 in suicidal behavior, 171
 symptom manifestation, 187–188
 therapeutic alliance with Chinese clients, 188–189
 therapist cultural background, 189–192
 treatment planning, 181–185
Cultural issues, 12

Day treatment, 200
Defensive processes
 categorization of therapist–patient interaction, 103–104
 client awareness of, 36
 outcome predictors, 104–106, 110
 responding in confrontive therapy, 109
 response to interpretation, 105
Denial, 245
Depression
 anxiety and, 215
 client perception of therapeutic change, 203
 cultural considerations in diagnosing, 186
 outcome studies, 129–130, 132–133, 136–137

process–experiential therapy with, 39
psychotherapy effectiveness, 136–137
stages of change, 247
Desensitization techniques, 22
Diagnostic and Statistical Manual-IV (DSM–IV), 185
 Axis II disorders, 207
 cultural considerations in, 186
Dialectical behavior therapy, 57
Dropouts
 accounting for, in research outcomes, 201–202
 from therapeutic program, 248–249
 from therapy research project, 107–108

Eclectic practice, 198
Effect size, 161–162
Empathic attunement, 40
Empathic conjecture, 40
Empirically supported treatments (EVTs)
 benefits of, 155
 effects on new treatment research, 260
 efficacy measurement, 199–200, 260
 interpretation of symptom change, 202–203
 limitations of, 155, 199–200, 260
 potential benefits, 6–7
 as practice guidelines, 6
 pressure for use of, 6, 28, 78–79, 198–199
 quality of research base, 28–29
 threats to longer–term therapy, 199
Ethical issues
 dropouts from therapy research project, 107–108
 therapeutic efficacy, 58
Evaluation of program performance, 230–234
EVTs. *See* Empirically supported treatments
Expectations, clients
 as change mechanism, 23
 clinical significance, 69–70
 construing in clients with schizophrenia, 73–74
Experiential–humanist approach
 in process–experiential therapy, 39
 training for, 34–35
Experiential theory, 87–88

Experimentation, 20, 68
  threats to, 260
Experimenter effects, 93–94
Extinction burst, 57

Free–association, 158–159
Funding, 234, 256, 260

Generalizations, conceptual differences
    in, 8
Gestalt therapy, 38, 39
Goals conflict, 176–177
Government role, 78–79
Graduate education
  admission and acceptance process, 54
  evolution of theoretical orientation,
      34–35
  implementation of Boulder model, 5
  obstacles to research–practice integra-
      tion, 60–63, 90
  opportunities for research–practice in-
      tegration, 63–65
  sources of conceptual tension in, 51–
      52, 54, 55
  student perceptions of research career,
      62–63, 90, 253–255
  time pressures in, 60–61
  valuation of research and practice in,
      62, 90, 254, 255
  See also Training and education of cli-
      nicians
Graduate training
  implementation of Boulder model, 11,
      17–18
Group therapies, 129–130
  for agoraphobia, 72–73
  client feelings of universality in, 70–71
  clinical significance of individual be-
      haviors, 229–230
  cognitive approach, 132
  cohesiveness, 228–229
  See also Interpersonal transaction group

Handbook of Psychotherapy and Behavior
    Change, 152, 155–156
Health care system, future of, 250–251,
    258–260

Heisenberg's uncertainty principle, 93
Histrionic personality disorder, 207–209
Homework, 133
Hospitalization/rehospitalization, 200, 203
Humanist approach, 34
  in process–experiential therapy, 39
Hypothesis generation in clinical setting,
    21, 24
Hypothesis invalidation, 76–77

Immigrant populations, 171
  assessment, 176–178
Individualism, as cultural value, 175
Insight
  in behavior therapy, 21
  in reconstructive learning theory, 214
Insurance, mental health coverage, 153–
    155
Integration of practice and research, 10–
    13, 95–96
  activities/topics for, 29, 44, 96, 264–
      265
  attitudes for, 96, 162–163
  in Boulder model, 51–52
  as collaboration, 6, 237–238, 255–256
  communication style as obstacle to, 7,
      8, 256–258
  constructivist approach, 137–140
  within individual, 8–9, 11, 21, 223–
      226
  influence of training experience, 53
  involvement of clinicians in research
      design, 235
  mutual benefits, 11, 30
  objections to, 9–10
  obstacles to. See Obstacles to integra-
      tion
  in personal construct theory, 68
  in process–experiential therapy, 42–43,
      44
  in program evaluation, 230–234
  prospects, 144–145
  public policy pressures for, 5–6
  rationale, 7–8, 29–30, 119, 204, 254
  recommendations for education process
      to foster, 63–65
  reconstructive learning theory for,
      204–205, 214–216
  role of funding agencies, 256

difficult patients with relationship problems, 227
early psychoanalytic therapy, 152–153
EVTs efficacy, 199
for health care policy design, 154–155
hospitalization/rehospitalization measures, 200, 203
interpreting results of, 133–135
intrafamilial sexual abuse, 137–141
longer–term measures, 199–200
measures of efficacy, 199, 204–205, 225–226
meta-analysis, 136–137, 157
multidimensional view, 91–92
need for researcher-practitioner collaboration, 257–258
no difference between therapies, 130–131, 224–225, 244
process–experiential therapy, 39, 41
program funding and, 234
psychotherapy program evaluation, 230–234
relaxation training, 21–22
researcher bias, 136
response to transference interpretations as outcome predictor, 110
short–term dynamic psychotherapy, 111–112
systems for analysis of clinical material, 26–27, 36
technical implementation of change theory, 24–26
therapeutic alliance in, 86, 226–227
treatment manual adherence, 198
validity, 28–29, 78–79

Passion, 266–267
Personal construct therapy, 68, 128, 129, 141–142
agoraphobia treatment, 71–73
in cognitive therapy, 132
outcome predictors, 70–71
research practice, 77–78
schizophrenia treatment, 73–76
Personality disordered clients
attachment experience in etiology of, 209–210
group therapy, 229

reconstructive learning therapy case example, 205–208, 212–214
Phenomenological research approach, 35–36, 37–38
Practice guidelines, 6
limitations of, 19–20, 26
policymaking context, 153–154
Prevention, 249–250
Process disclosure, 40
Process–experiential therapy
conceptual basis, 35–36
current practice directions, 41
integration of practice and research in, 42–43, 44
principles of treatment, 40
rationale, 36–48
research support, 40–41
technical and theoretical evolution, 38–40
Project Second Beginning, 230–234
Projective techniques, 18
Psychoanalytic theory-practice, 223–224
early outcomes research, 152–153, 224–225
obstacles to integration of research, 85–86
Psychodynamic–interpersonal therapy
facilitating change in client awareness, 24–25
therapeutic alliance in, 25
Psychotherapy assessment checklist forms, 117–118
Psychotherapy interaction coding system, 104
Public policy
insurance coverage for psychotherapy, 154–155
political contexts, 161
pressures for practice-research integration, 5–6
role of clinical expertise in, 153–156
significance of, for psychotherapy, 153–154
sources of practice-research conflict, 91
stakeholders, 258

Randomized controlled trials, 156–157, 159–160, 265–266
Reality testing, 23

Reconstructive learning theory
assessment and diagnosis, 206–208
case example, 205–208, 212–214, 216
of change, 210, 211–212, 214
conceptual basis, 209–210
future developments, 215
goals for, 204–205
as integrative theory, 214–216
scientific method in, 208–209, 212
of treatment failures, 210–211
treatment planning, 211–212, 213–214
Reimbursement system, 6, 198–199
Relational case management, 231
Relaxation training, 21–22
Repertory grid, 71–72, 73, 75, 132, 226
group therapy dynamics and, 139
Research knowledge
absence of support for clinical practice, 58–60, 68
appropriate use of, 59
basis for empirically supported treatments, 28–29
on clinical change processes, 22–23, 227–228
communicating findings to practitioners, 89
contributions of practice to, 24, 91–94, 162, 262
contributions to practice, 18–19, 22, 42–43, 86–89, 104, 106, 110, 117–118, 162, 237–238, 261–262
distinctive nature of, 4
in evolution of clinician's theoretical orientation, 34–35
future of health care and, 259–260
goals, 116–117
as gradual process of accumulation, 7
limitations of, in clinical practice, 19–20, 21–22
as support for therapist, 56–57, 162
therapist resistance to implementation, 78, 235
under–researched therapies, 78–79
vs. clinical knowledge, 3–4, 7
Research process
accounting for noncompliance-noncompletion, 201–202
benefits of clinical approach to, 24
cognitive style for, 95, 170–171

confirming merit of research question, 24
consideration of client perspective, 203
creativity in, 20
cultural considerations, 168
development of clinical tools from, 117–118
experimenter effects in observing therapy, 93–94
hypothesis generation, 21, 24
implication of ESTs, 260
involvement of clinicians in, 235
nature of, 4
participant–observer paradigm, 94
personal construct theory, 77–78
phenomenological approach, 35–36, 37–38
researcher characteristics in success of, 20
role of clinician in, 156–157
role relationships in therapy and, 94
sensitivity to client-therapist interaction, 140–141
shaping of student attitudes toward, 53–55
significance of hypothesis invalidation, 76–77
significance of setting, 77
single–case experiment, 118–119, 160
systems for analysis of clinical material, 26–27, 36
use of confrontive techniques, 107–108
validity issues, 157
Research questions, 21
confirming merit of, 24
to foster integration of practice and research, 29, 96
significance of hypothesis invalidation, 76–77
Research values, 42
Role models, for psychology students, 62–63, 64, 255
Rorschach, 18

SASB *See* Structural analysis of social behavior
Schizophrenia, 73–76
outcome measures, 200

ABOUT THE EDITORS

Stephen Soldz, PhD, is the director of research at Health and Addictions Research, Inc. He is on the faculties of Harvard University Medical School and the Boston Graduate School of Psychoanalysis and its Institute for the Study of Violence. He is also codirector of research at the Boston Institute for Psychotherapy and has been director of research and evaluation for advocates for human potential and senior research associate in the Mental Health Research Program of Harvard Community Health Center. He is on the editorial boards of *Psychotherapy Research* and the *International Journal of Constructivist Psychology.* He is especially interested in the successful collaboration of researchers, practitioners, and policymakers to improve human services. He maintains a psychotherapy practice in Brookline, Massachusetts. He lives in Roslindale, Massachusetts, with his wife, Vivienne, and son, Isaac.

Leigh McCullough, PhD, is an associate clinical professor and director of the psychotherapy research program at Harvard University Medical School. She was the 1996 Voorhees Distinguished Professor at the Menninger Clinic and received the 1996 Michael Franz Basch Award from the Silvan Tomkins Institute for her contributions toward the exploration of affect in psychotherapy. She is on the editorial board of the journal *Psychotherapy Research,* conducts training seminars in short-term psychotherapy around the world, and maintains an independent clinical practice in Dedham, Massachusetts. She is also the author of the book *Changing Character: Short-Term Anxiety-Regulating Psychotherapy for Restructuring Defenses, Affects and Attachments* (Basic Books, 1997).

Dr. McCullough has held positions as director of research at the Beth Israel Medical Center's Short-Term Psychotherapy Research Program in

New York City and director of assessment at the Center for Psychotherapy Research at the University of Pennsylvania. For the past 7 years, she has been a visiting research associate and clinical supervisor for the Norwegian Short-Term Psychotherapy Research Program at the University of Trondheim, where researchers are conducting a clinical trial comparing her short-term dynamic treatment model with a cognitive therapy model.